HESS
THE BRITISH CONSPIRACY

HESS
THE BRITISH CONSPIRACY

John Harris and M.J. Trow

André Deutsch

First published in 1999
This paperback edition published in 2000 by
André Deutsch Limited
An imprint of the
Carlton Publishing Group
20 Mortimer Street
London W1T 3JW

Reprinted in 2009

A catalogue record for this title is available from the British Library

ISBN 978 0 233 99433 8

Typeset by
Derek Doyle & Associates, Liverpool.
Printed and bound in the UK by CPI Mackays, Chatham ME5 8TD

Crown copyright material in the Public Record Office
is reproduced by permission of the
Controller of Her Majesty's Stationery Office.

Contents

'His flight was madness: when our actions do not,
Our fears do make us traitors.'

Macbeth

The Story of Flying Rudolf

When the heads came tumbling down
At the Führer's angry frown,
All good little Nazi boys
Stayed at home to mind their toys.
Rudolf thought 'No place is surer
Than to stand behind the Führer.'
So he did and for a bit
He was IT,
All the Führer's joy and pride.
Here you see them side by side.

But there eyed him still askance
Himmler's cold and fishy glance
And the Führer screamed 'Don't dare
Take a plane into the air!'
Rudolf thought – 'To leave by stealth
Will be better for my health.'
So he flies
To the skies,
Never heeding Adolf's cries
Till appears a tiny dot
O'er the land of Burns and Scott.

It is Rudolf's parachute!!
Can a rift be in the lute?
Has he come to seek for solace
On the soil of Bruce and Wallace?
Down he bumps on Scottish ground
And they've put him in the pound.
Now, it isn't very clear
What he's wanting over here.
Only, this one thing is plain,
Rudolf won't go back again.

StruwwelHitler
A Parody of Struwwelpeter,
Cautionary Tales for Children

ACKNOWLEDGEMENTS

In the seven years' research culminating in this book, many people have helped me and I would like to take this opportunity to thank them all for their support and guidance: R. Allason, G. A. Armatage, Mark Bachelar, Miss U. Bevir, Mr Borenius, J. Costello, James Douglas-Hamilton, Alexander Hamilton, M. R. D. Foot, E. Greville-Heygate, R. Griffiths, W. R. Hess, W. J. Kean, Lennoxlove Estate Office, Tony Noble, Ordnance Survey, Peter Padfield, A. Page, E. Playfair, the late Donald McCormick, Rowe & Pitman/Warburgs, Mark Sanders, Frau Schroder-Haushofer, Sikorski Institute, London, A. Stewart-Roberts, Royal Ordnance, Pierre Verkeye, R. Wilbourn; my agent, Andrew Lownie; my indexer, Carol Trow; M. J. Trow; but most of all, my wife, for her patience whilst sharing her life with Rudolf Hess.

INTRODUCTION

The Old Lady

An extraordinary thing happened on 10 May 1941. In some ways it was the most bizarre event of the Second World War. And it has never been fully explained. On that spring day, Rudolf Hess, the Stellvertreter or Deputy to Adolf Hitler, took off from Augsburg airfield in a Messerschmitt Bf 110. His target was somewhere in Scotland and over the purple-heathered lowlands, alone and in the dark, Rudolf Hess baled out of his aircraft and floated into eternal imprisonment.

My own interest in the case of Rudolf Hess was kindled as a result of reading Nicholas Mosley's biography of his father Oswald, the maverick Labour politician-turned-Fascist whose blackshirts marched the streets of London's East End in the 1930s. Researching further, I became fascinated by the aristocratic links between Britain and Germany which in some ways could have formed the bedrock of an international rapport between the two countries before 1939. This in turn led me to the notion, commonly held since 1941, that Hess's flight was an attempt to broker a peace deal between Britain and Germany at what was a critical time for both protagonists. The first full book on the case I read was Hugh Thomas's *The Murder of Rudolf Hess* and, finding the arguments there unsatisfactory, I began to research further.[1]

The accepted conventional view of this flight and the reasons behind it form the first chapter of this book. Hess was acting, conventional wisdom and dozens of books contend, entirely alone, to cease hostilities with the British, in order to give Hitler the breathing space he needed to unleash Operation Barbarossa, the invasion of Soviet Russia. Such a deal would also have restored Hess's reputation, dwindling by the early Forties in Hitler's eyes.

Contemporaries commented on Hess's slavish devotion to his Führer and on his lack of intellect. Some said he was plain mad and the official Berlin communiqué was that party member Hess had been suffering from a worsening mental condition which had forced Hitler to ban him from flying. The official note that Hess left – 'And if my Führer, this project . . . ends in failure . . . simply say I was mad'[2] – gave the authorized version all the ammunition it needed. So too did Hess's behaviour for the rest of his life. From his imprisonment in 'Camp Z' – Mytchett Place in Surrey – to the long, lonely days of Spandau, Hess groaned in his sleep, claimed he was being poisoned, talked to the walls and attempted suicide. This was perfect fodder for the 'lone flyer' enthusiasts. Hess was clearly deranged, even by the time of his trial for war crimes at Nuremberg in 1946. Why not before? Why not on 10 May 1941? No sane, rational man would have made that flight.

But there were two men – two rather important men in the scheme of things – who didn't believe a word of it. The 'lone flyer' theorists should have listened to them. In October 1944, Winston Churchill, then enjoying his cigars, his brandy and his finest hour, was visiting his ally 'Uncle Joe' Stalin at the Kremlin in Moscow. In the ancient triangular citadel, already a symbol of the stern, uncompromising Communism that Churchill would warn the world against two years later, the Russian leader raised his glass in a toast to the British Intelligence Service. Churchill had been quizzed by Stalin over the Hess flight and

2

the Prime Minister had said that Hess was clearly mad – despite the fact that every doctor and psychiatrist who ever interviewed the man essentially disagreed. They certainly found Hess unstable and liable to mood swings, but he was not insane in the technical or legal sense.* Churchill also attested at this meeting that Hess and Hitler had been lovers.

Stalin's toast continued: 'To the British secret service which inveigled Hess into coming to England. He could not have landed without being given signals. The Intelligence Service must have been behind it all.'[3] Churchill's strenuous protests were a little too ebullient for Stalin who merely smiled in that enigmatic way of his and said: 'There are many things my Intelligence Service does not tell me about.'[4]

Churchill was clearly rattled by this – not the fact that his secret service was dealing behind his back but that his own position had been divined by Stalin. In short, in the street language of post-war Britain, Churchill had been rumbled.

And it wasn't only the cynical and quietly murderous Stalin who doubted the 'lone flyer' theory and Churchill's ignorance of it. Some ten days after Hess landed, American President Franklin D. Roosevelt – whom Churchill had informed of the incident by letter – sat down to dinner with his aides Robert Sherwood, Harry Hopkins and Sumner Welles, the diplomats who knew Germany and Hess quite well. Welles painted the now familiar picture of Hess's character for Roosevelt – the rather dim, fanatical Nazi with a dog-like devotion to Hitler. Roosevelt didn't believe it either, any more than Stalin had. 'I wonder,' he said, 'what is really behind this story?'[5]

This book sets out to answer Roosevelt's rhetorical question. It attempts to tie up the loose ends that dangle like parachute cords in the case of Rudolf Hess. The behaviour of the central

---

* The state of Hess's mind clearly varied during his long years in captivity. Psychiatric reports are discussed in Chapter 8.

figures in the story can only be explained if they *knew* that Hess was coming. Take Jack Colville for instance. He was Churchill's private secretary at the time, a position in which a man learns a great many secrets and is often required to stuff skeletons in cupboards and keep them there. In one of the many apparent coincidences, that are really nothing of the sort in the Hess case, the night of 10–11 May saw the heaviest bombing of the Blitz and Colville – unlike Churchill himself or his Foreign Secretary, Anthony Eden, or his Minister of Economic Warfare, Hugh Dalton – spent it trying to sleep at 10 Downing Street. A few hundred yards from him the palace of Westminster suffered several direct hits from Goering's Luftwaffe and was still smouldering throughout the next day.

Colville claimed to have had a vivid dream that night that revolved around a novel he had read months before – *Flying Visit* by Peter Fleming, brother of the creator of James Bond. The plot of this book, written in 1940, was that a leading Nazi (specifically Hitler) had parachuted into Britain to negotiate peace. On 11 May, when the Duke of Hamilton*, commanding officer at Turnhouse RAF base in Scotland, rang to speak to Churchill urgently, he told Colville that something extraordinary had happened. He would only say that it was like something out of an E. Phillips Oppenheim novel. Colville asked, 'Has somebody arrived?' and Hamilton said, 'Yes.'[6]

The private secretary's explanation for his extraordinary question – that he had just had a relevant dream about a novel he had read months before – defies belief. It is likely that Colville knew exactly who had arrived and was not at all surprised to hear Hamilton's voice at the other end of the line. And if Colville knew it, Churchill knew it. He knew it because he had been in on the plan almost from its inception. Why else would the Prime Minister, on hearing that the strange, polite, heel-clicking airman

---

* Formerly Lord Clydesdale.

who had landed in the lowland heather was Rudolf Hess, the third most powerful man in Nazi Germany, have smiled wryly and gone to a private showing of a Marx Brothers film?

At the Berghof, Hitler's beautiful mountain retreat at Berchtesgaden in the Bavarian Alps, a similarly odd reaction came from the Führer. The accepted version of events is that 'he received an explanatory letter from Hess via the Stellvertreter's adjutant, Karl-Heinz Pintsch, early on the morning of Sunday, 11 May. How odd that Hitler, who notoriously lay in bed late (to the extent that no one dared wake him even on 6 June 1944 to tell him that the D-Day landings were under way in Normandy) should be up and fully dressed by 7.30 that morning. Like Jack Colville, he was waiting for something – news that Hess had landed, had been welcomed by the peace party he was told to expect and was on his way to negotiations with Halifax or Lloyd George or Lords Brocket or Buccleuch* – *anyone* other than the warmongering Churchill, who was clearly beyond all hope.

Instead, he woke to find no news. There is strong evidence that Hitler already knew that Hess had flown.[7] In fact, as this book will explain, it now seems certain that Hitler knew exactly when Hess intended to fly and why. The Stellvertreter went with his Führer's blessing and his Führer's peace proposals – not the first he had proffered – tucked into his flying suit. Peace proposals which have never been published; peace proposals which have still not seen the light of day.

In Cambridge, at the start of the Second World War, lived an old lady called Mary Violet Roberts. She was the widow of an academic, comfortably off and coping with recent bereavements. Her husband had died seven years earlier and tragically, her son, a diplomat with a promising career ahead of him, had been

---

* The actual involvement of these men in the Hess case is at best tangential. The point is that Hess may well have believed that such a peace party existed and could be used to obtain some sort of truce.

killed in Greece in a road accident five years after that. In letters to her friends, she talked of summer days in her garden and the problems of keeping warm in the winter that lay ahead. She talked of bottling fruit, of her black Scottie dog and of her memories, fond and tragic.

Mary Violet Roberts is not the Miss Froy of Hitchcock's film *The Lady Vanishes*. Delightful though it would be to conjure her, in rough tweeds and stout brogues, outspying the deadliest agents in Europe with a razor mind and a smoking Webley, Violet Roberts is nothing of the sort. But it was Violet and the harmless letters she wrote to her old friends, the Haushofers, that lie at the heart of the riddle of Rudolf Hess. Because Mary Violet Roberts had a nephew involved in one of the most secret and unfathomable organizations of the British secret service – the department known in 1941 as Special Operations 1. So arcane is this group that the official secret service history of the war devotes to it only two single-line references in hundreds of pages.[8]

The world since 1945 has become hardened to conspiracies great and small. From the disappearance of Lionel 'Buster' Crabb in Portsmouth harbour[9] through the assassination of President Kennedy to the death of Diana, Princess of Wales,[10] a tangled web of secrecy, contradiction and confusion obscures the core of fact. And there are far more theorists of conspiracies than there are conspiracies. One of them, historian John Costello, who helped in the early stages of this book, was found dead on a transatlantic flight home to Miami in August 1995. This was rich food for the conspiracy theorists, for John Costello was then writing *A Feast of Scorpions* which threatened to take the lid off Soviet spying in Britain by using newly opened KGB files in Moscow. And it was food that probably killed him – a rotten shellfish in a London restaurant rather than the poisoned umbrella of a Soviet agent.*

* The method used to kill Bulgarian defector Georgi Markov in September 1978 as he waited at a bus stop near Waterloo Bridge.

Costello was described by one of his many critics – the British were always less impressed by him than the Americans – as 'an unmitigated menace'.

Some professional historians, including one who read this book at proof stage, throw up their hands in disdain at conspiracy theories. Writer Jeffrey M. Bale sums up the situation expertly:

> Very few notions generate as much intellectual resistance, hostility and derision within academic circles as a belief in the historical importance or efficacy of political conspiracies. Even when this belief is expressed in a very cautious manner, limited to specific and restricted contexts, supported by reliable evidence, and hedged about with all sorts of qualifications, it still manages to transcend the boundaries of acceptable discourse and violate unspoken academic taboos.
>
> The idea that particular groups of people meet together secretly or in private to plan various courses of action, and that some of these plans actually exert a significant influence on particular historical developments, is typically rejected out of hand and assumed to be the figment of a paranoid imagination.
>
> The mere mention of the word 'conspiracy' seems to set off an internal alarm bell which causes scholars to close their minds to avoid cognitive dissonance and possible unpleasantness, since the popular image of conspiracy both fundamentally challenges the conception most educated, sophisticated people have about how the world operates . . .[11]

The irony of the particular conspiracy theory central to this book is that it concerns British intelligence acting for the nation's greater good, at a time of national emergency. The fact that the plot succeeded is even more reason to rejoice, yet the traditionalists still cling to their narrow view of events.

The menace of the conspiracy theorists will never go away as long as there are locked files, top secret classifications and official obfuscation. Some archive material has been scattered to the winds. The Haushofers, who provide the all-important link between Violet Roberts and Rudolf Hess, lived at Hartschimmelhof near Munich. Karl Haushofer was Hess's tutor (who, it will be seen, probably suggested to Hitler the concept of *lebensraum* ('living space') which features in *Mein Kampf* and was such a vital part of his foreign policy). Albrecht Haushofer, his son, was Hess's friend and Hitler's expert on all things British. Neither man would survive the war and its aftermath. Albrecht was shot through the back of the head on wasteland outside the grim walls of Moabit prison in Berlin, unpublished poems still in his hand . . .

> I should have sooner seen my duty,
> I should have sharper condemned evil,
> I have too long delayed my judgement,
> I now accuse myself.[12]

On 11 March 1946, Professor-General Karl Haushofer and his wife Martha went for a walk in the woods near their home. In the blustery winds of that night, they took poison together. Some of the papers father and son left are still at Hartschimmelhof, but they were rifled by the American military at the end of the war and some documentation was taken to Alexandria, of all places, for microfilming. Today those papers, originally from Berlin and Munich, are stored in Washington and Koblenz – plenty of scope for all sorts of vital evidence to be 'mislaid'.

To add to the problems of research, a family dispute about access to the papers has arisen. Albrecht's niece, Andrea Haushofer-Schroder, told me in an interview that she believes the Americans effectively stole the papers and, not unnaturally, wants them back. In this welter of confusion, involving five cities, three countries and two sections of a family, who knows what has disappeared which could shed light on the complexities of the Hess flight? Speculation on exactly what *is* missing is largely fruitless. The Haushofer archives, however, are vast and do contain such minutiae as Karl Haushofer's gun licence. It seems decidedly odd that among all this documentation there should be no correspondence at all from the Roberts family. As we shall see in Chapter 6, the Roberts and Haushofers would have been in regular contact.

Then, there is the curious case of the papers of the Duke of Bedford. The Duke himself is tangential to the Hess case, although his pacifist views may have made him an ideal pawn in the very dangerous game played by Special Operations 1, who used the Duke's Woburn Abbey stables in 1941 to plan their propaganda. When I requested permission to consult the family papers, I was told that they had not been sorted properly since the Duke's death in 1953. The application form for access contained no embargoes or caveats, yet the present Duke instructed his archivist to tell me that the 100-year closure rule applied to the wartime documents.

Most firmly closed of all are Foreign Office files held in the misnamed *Public* Record Office. Under reference number FO 898 there are 553 files available for scrutiny: for instance, the hierarchical chain of command in Special Operations 1 as it was three months before Hess's flight. These were not released until 1995 although all the men whose names are involved are long dead. The file dealing with Swiss matters, FO 898/257, is on permanent loan to the Foreign Office and is unlikely to be released in the foreseeable future. This is, to say the least, a pity. Revelations about the pro-Nazi activities of many Swiss, especially in relation to Jewish gold, have recently come to light via a different route. For reasons that will become apparent, I personally believe that the Swiss file contains vital evidence on the wartime record of the head of the Red Cross in Geneva, Carl Burkhardt, who undoubtedly had a hand in bringing Hess to Britain.

As early as 6 September 1944, orders were issued concerning the storage of papers belonging to Special Operations 1. They fell into four categories:

A. Those which you consider should be retained permanently.

B. Those about which you are doubtful as to whether they should be destroyed.

C. Those which you consider should be eventually destroyed.

D. Those which you consider might be destroyed now.[13]

No more specific guidelines were laid down for the criteria of salvage or destruction. Category A papers were the only ones which definitely survived, but who decided which they were and whether 'permanent' is to be interpreted literally? Issues and matters which were ultra-sensitive in 1944 are merely quaint history now. Yet the doors are closed and the tabs remain in place. 'As could be expected,' writes Ellic Howe in *The Black Game*, 'no files containing material which was regarded as sensitive eventually reached the [Public Record Office].' Somewhere in those files, I believe, were copies of letters written by British Intelligence to Karl Haushofer suggesting a 'flying visit' for the sake of peace.

In July 1998, as this book was in its draft form, the government released (precisely why is unknown) a number of papers from the Special Operations Executive, including Operation Foxley, a 120-page dossier on an assassination plot against Hitler. This operation was the brainchild of Major-General Colin Gubbins, head of SOE in 1944 and involved three possible plans. There was even a designated 'hitman' – Captain E.H. Bennett, a military attaché at the British Embassy in Washington.

The details of Foxley are irrelevant to Hess, but the can of worms the revelation has opened is more pertinent. It points to a series of covert operations acknowledged by no one until now and not therefore discussed by orthodox historians. The telegram which sparked the whole Foxley idea off, from SOE's undercover office in Algiers on 19 June 1944, speaks volumes for the whole *raison d'être*, not only of SOE, but of its role in the Hess case too – 'We are not, repeat not, mad nor is this a joke.' It could be printed as a reminder to sceptical readers on every page of this book. On the weekend of 23–25 January 1999 the government announced the release of further files (KV2/3, 35, 36, 37, 38) which, according to the *Daily Telegraph*, represented an 'opportunity finally to dispel the conspiracy theories attached to Hess.' In fact the release of this documentation was a storm in a teacup, mainly concerning the treatment of Hess after his arrival in Britain and MI5's indignation over the initial Glasgow interrogation by a Pole, Roman Battaglia. Hess apparently had funds in Switzerland and there were complex plans afoot to keep his location in this country a secret. However, there was nothing in the files that actually detailed the series of events leading to the flight. The fact remains that there is no official explanation of the Hess affair. The absence of any such documentation is hardly likely to dispel the conspiracists.

As an amateur historian, I had doors which might have been open, closed in my face. Whereas John Costello and those I have acknowledged were kindness and patience itself, others were less so. M.R.D. Foot for example, clearly an expert in wartime espionage, sent a dismissive note: 'I know you are building on sand and must repeat to you that no further use will be served by our correspondence.'

The Blair government made a great deal of play in the run-up to the last election over a Freedom of Information Act. Over a year later, there are still only rumblings of one and Jack Straw, the current Home Secretary, has clearly placed it on the political back burner. The British establishment has become obsessed with secrecy. Bombarded by a story-hungry media screaming its 'right to know', the barricades have gone up and the shutters come down. And those of us who merely wish to find out for truth's own sake, to cross the 't's and dot the 'i's of history, are fobbed off with the established riposte, 'not in the public interest'.

So the 'lone flyer' theorists cling to their version, which is as improbable now as it was in 1941. And in doing so, they woefully misunderstand the dilemma of Adolf Hitler, the deviousness and ingenuity of the British Secret Service and the role of Mrs Mary Violet Roberts, the old lady who lured Rudolf Hess to Scotland.

CHAPTER 1

Wings of the Dove

The Swabian city of Augsburg stands high above sea level, forty miles north-west of Munich, between the sparkling waters of the Wertach and the Lech. It is dominated by the gilded spires of Saint Ulrich and Saint Anna and the huge palace of the bishop.

At the northernmost reaches of the Roman Empire in mainland Europe, Augusta Vindelicorum prospered in the Middle Ages as a centre of trade and finance. The Habsburg Emperor Maximilian 1, after whom its fountain-studded main street is named, had his suits of fluted armour made there. And despite the cotton, silk and linen also manufac-tured in the town, it is the steel of war which has formed its backbone through the ages.

Willi Messerschmitt came from further north in the Kaiser's new Germany – Frankfurt am Main – but he settled in Augsburg five years after the Great War and produced his first all-metal plane there three years later. In 1930, he became Honorary Professor of Aircraft Construction at Munich's Technical College and would go on to manufacture the finest German fighter planes of the Second World War. Wings for the Third Reich. Wings for the Führer.

On Saturday 10 May 1941, Bavaria basked in bright sunshine. Hess arrived at the Messerschmitt works in the trademark sleek black Mercedes, swastika flapping in red, white and black on its bonnet. The steel-helmeted sentries would have clicked to attention at the sight of the figure in the front, next to the driver. He wore a plain trenchcoat over his Luftwaffe uniform, but there was no mistaking the shiny black hair, the firm jaw and sloping forehead; no mistaking those dark, firebrand eyes.

Hess entered the central administration block, followed by his adjutant, Karl-Heinz Pintsch, who was carrying a briefcase full of the homoeopathic medicines in which the vegetarian Deputy placed such faith. When Hess re-emerged into the sunlight, the trenchcoat had gone and he stood on the tarmac, shaking hands with the little works crew which had gathered to see him off. He was now in flying boots, Mae West and leather helmet. He said goodbye to Pintsch, to his driver and bodyguard and climbed into the cramped cockpit of the waiting Me Bf 110.

Much has been written about this aircraft, its armaments, its fuel capacity and range, even the code initials on its fuselage. The underside of the Me was a pale blue, to provide sky camouflage against daylight anti-aircraft gunners on the ground below. Its upper surface was mottled grey-green so that to a marauding Spitfire or Hurricane swooping from above, it would merge with the trees of England and Scotland. The aircraft's works number was 3869, its fuselage initials and radio code VJ and OQ.

Watchers on the ground saw the undercarriage fold into the fuselage and the Me circle once before heading north-west into the evening. It was 17.45 on a spring Saturday fifty-eight years ago. No one on the ground saw the plane or its pilot again.

Hess flew north-west over Bonn and, depending on his altitude, could have seen in the cloudless weather the ribbon of the Rhine winding through the great city with the Kreuzberg church and its myriad bridges to the industrial district of Beuel. This place of pilgrimage had been the home of Beethoven, the greatest of German composers.

On north-west, flying still in the safe Luftwaffe-controlled skies of Nazi Germany, over the city of Köln. Marcus Agrippa had camped his legions there centuries before and the powerful medieval merchants of the Hanse had made it a great trading centre. Perhaps Hess saw the Gothic twin towers of the cathedral, spearing 502 feet towards him. Perhaps he knew the flavour of its Rhenish wine and the peace of pleasure steamers gliding past its quays. The British had held Köln for eight years after the war to end wars and its largely Catholic population had remained true to the tottering Weimar state until Hitler's seduction won it over, with the collaboration of its leading industrialists and the Nazi banker Kurt von Schröder.

Twelve months and three weeks later, Köln became the first German city to feel the awesome power of an Allied 1,000-bomber raid. Three bridges sank into the foaming waters of the Rhine. Chemical and tool factories crumbled into blazing ruin. There were 20,000 dead and wounded and three-fifths of the city's survivors crawled away from the wreckage.

Now Hess crossed the Dutch coast somewhere near Harlingen, before banking north-east along the fragmented line of the Friesian Islands that flank the Waddenzee. Then north-west again over the North Sea.

This was the unknown. Fortress Europe was behind him now. His home, his career, his family, his life – all of it ringed by the steel of the Wehrmacht, walled in by the ideology of the jackboot. Now there were no clouds to hide his coming, no fighter escort to guard his back. How utterly alone Rudolf Hess felt in those hours over the North Sea, we can only guess. Light faded and according to most writers he circled off the Northumbrian coast until darkness cloaked him.

British radar installations along the coast (Ottercops Moss was the first) picked up the solitary invader. Far to the south, the heaviest blitz was just beginning on a London already ripped and torn apart, but raiders this far north were uncommon and a solitary aircraft was probably off course and lost.

Winston Churchill wrote of that night:

The worst attack was the last. On May 10 the enemy returned to London with incendiary bombs. He lit more than two thousand fires and by the smashing of nearly a hundred and fifty water mains, coupled with the low tide in the Thames, he stopped us putting them out. At six o'clock the next morning, hundreds were reported as out of control, and four were still glowing on the night of the 13th. It was the most destructive attack of the whole night Blitz. Five docks and seventy-one key points, half of which were factories, had been hit. All but one of the main railway stations were blocked for weeks, and the through routes were not fully opened until June. Over three thousand people were killed or injured. In. other respects also, it was historic. It destroyed the House of Commons. One single bomb created ruin for years.[1]

The unit whose airspace Hess was invading was 13 Group of Fighter Command, relatively starved of aircraft by the need to protect the south-east.* On 10 May, only one squadron was available to intercept 'Raid 42' – 72 Squadron at Acklington, three miles inland from the Northumbrian coast. The only other aircraft which were actually on a routine patrol as the Messerschmitt approached were the Hurricanes of 317 (Polish) Squadron.† The pilots were inexperienced at night flying and probably for that reason were given no orders to intercept the intruder.

* Throughout the war the country was divided into districts by the RAF. Heaviest engaged in 1940 (the Battle of Britain) was 11 Group in the south-east. Because of the tactics of aerial warfare, Fighter Command was more heavily committed than its Bomber equivalent, which came into its own when returning raids on Germany.
† Poland had been overrun by the Wehrmacht using their terrifying blitzkrieg tactics in September 1939. A relative handful of Polish pilots had hurried west to Britain where they were given aircraft and their own squadron for active duty.

72 Squadron had two Spitfires in the air already when Hess's aircraft was picked up on radar at 22.08. A third Spit, flown by Flight Sergeant Maurice Pocock, took off from Acklington fifteen minutes later to join the search, as by now the radar blips were overlapping and Ground Control was frankly confused as to which plane was which. Pocock may well have flown within five miles of Hess, but the Messerschmitt had lost altitude and was flying through the mist of the Northumbrian coast. Given that the Spitfire was not equipped to track aircraft with radar and that a visual sighting was necessary, it is not surprising that even an experienced Battle of Britain veteran like Pocock should have missed Hess.

The same disbelief that had registered at Ottercops Moss now figured in the Royal Observer Corps based at Embleton.* A single aircraft away from a pack was bizarre enough, but it appeared to be travelling fast at less than 5,000 feet, and was a Messerschmitt fighter-bomber. Doubting the evidence of their eyes, the Observer Corps reported Hess's plane as a Dornier 217 bomber.

Whatever it was, the bandit now banked north-west, crossing the Scottish border and flying on to the west coast. Near West Kilbride on the Firth of Clyde, Hess banked east, the hunting Spitfires long lost in the darkness. A greater danger was now on his tail, however. Pilot Officer William Cuddie had been scrambled from 141 Squadron's base at Ayr to the south. He was flying a Bolton-Paul Defiant and Sergeant Hodge was his rear-gunner, scanning the sky above with his eyes on the sights of the four swivel Browning machine-guns. The Defiant had proved disastrously slow in the aerial acrobatics of the Battle of Britain, but as a night-fighter, it was lethal.

* The Observer Corps was a civilian organization set up in 1925. In the war it came under RAF control and was used for aircraft recognition, plotting and height-finding. Its full and part-time members, including women, eventually numbered over 50,000.

By now, Hess was running dangerously low on fuel. Bizarrely, even given the circumstances of the flight, he had neither ammunition for the plane's guns nor a rear-gunner to do the shooting for him. There was nothing magical about Hess's invasion of British airspace. Certainly the lone fighter-bomber was unexpected, so he had the element of surprise, but that only gave him minutes in the air before interceptors were on their way. In 1941, radar only operated at sea and over the coast.[2] Once the Me 110 was over land, it could only be tracked by the Observer Corps. Likewise, the intercepting Spitfires and Defiant had no radar fitted to them. Looking for a lone, camouflaged aircraft in the dark smacked of the proverbial needle in the haystack.

Hess's situation was now critical – something had gone wrong with his plan. In the darkness, he had missed his target. This, according to established theories, was Dungavel House, the country home of the Duke of Hamilton, that night on duty in the operations room at Turnhouse RAF base, twelve miles west of Edinburgh. As confused as anyone by the sudden arrival of the Messerschmitt, Hamilton watched the progress of the raider on the plotting chart.

According to the flight plan which Hess drew later in his long years of captivity, he was actually flying back towards Dungavel from the Firth of Clyde; but then, perhaps to find his bearings from the dim lights of blacked-out Glasgow to his left, banked north-west again. It was here, over Bonnyton and Eaglesham Moor that the Stellvertreter took the only option open to him, lost and out of fuel. He baled out. Wind pressure and perhaps a sticking cockpit slide kept him pinned to his pilot seat. In desperation, he rolled the plane so that he was actually flying upside down and let gravity do the rest. Having blacked out momentarily with the speed of his roll, he now realized the engines had cut out. Scrabbling free of cockpit and canopy, Hess launched himself into the night with no previous experience of a parachute jump and felt himself floating, 'an indescribably marvellous and triumphant feeling' as he wrote later.[3]

The Royal Observer Corps at post H2, twelve miles from Dungavel, saw the billowing mushroom of the parachute silk and heard the whine of an out-of-control aircraft until it ploughed into the ground with a crash of steel and aluminium. It was 23.09 British Double Summer Time.*

It wasn't only the Observer Corps who had seen Hess come down. He landed in a field near Floors Farm, not far from the village of Eaglesham, and a ploughman, David McLean, was the first to reach him. Hess had lost consciousness again and was just coming round for the second time and trying to unbuckle his harness straps. According to Hess, McLean asked him if he was British or German – a rather naïve question perhaps, although the presence of the Polish airforce in the Scottish Lowlands tended to cloud the nationality issue. Hess was calm and collected and replied in perfect English that he was Hauptmann Alfred Horn and that he had an urgent message for the Duke of Hamilton. Hess's alleged reminiscences and the reporting of the local newspaper, the *Bulletin and Scots Pictorial*, give us an extraordinary picture of the next few minutes.

McLean helped the injured Hess, who had twisted his ankle either baling out or hitting the ground, to the cottage he shared with his mother and sister. Mrs McLean was struck by the expensive kid flying boots the German wore, but maybe it was only hindsight, once Hess's identity was known, that made her describe him as 'a man of some standing, used to command'. The Stellvertreter politely declined her offer of tea – 'I do not drink tea at night, thank you' – and drank water instead.

It is a measure of the peculiarity of the situation again that McLean left his mother and sister in the house with an enemy

---

* The Hess flight will be discussed in more detail in Chapter 7.

pilot from a race who, according to the propaganda of the time, did unspeakable things to women and went in search of someone in authority.

McLean quickly ran into others who had seen the parachute come down. Lieutenant Clarke of the Home Guard, whom Hess believed was drunk, was creeping up to the farm buildings with four soldiers and a special constable, Robert Williamson. In the kitchen, Clarke whipped out his Webley Mark V revolver, checked that Hauptmann Horn was unarmed (this precaution had clearly not occurred to McLean) and marched him out to a waiting car. Hess remained totally calm throughout, but obviously believed Clarke to be volatile. In a letter to his wife Ilse he wrote, 'God's finger was truly between his unsteady finger and the trigger.'[4]

The Stellvertreter was driven north to the village of Busby, now swallowed up by the outskirts of Glasgow, and placed in a spartan room belonging to 'C' Company of the 3rd Battalion the Renfrewshire Home Guard. This was a scout hut, and to those familiar with *Dad's Army*, the whole episode might well have come from the classic television series. One of the Guard gave Hess a glass of milk.

There was now some confusion over jammed telephone lines as the whole amateurish communication network swung into action. Politics reared its ugly head too. Hess was transferred to the Battalion Headquarters at Giffnock, but a squabble arose between the Home Guard Commander and the Clyde Sub-Area Military Commander as to where 'Horn' should spend the night. The German's claim to know the Duke of Hamilton and to have a message of some importance for him rang all kinds of alarm bells for the officer of the Argyll and Sutherland Highlanders who had been sent to Giffnock to collect him. Clyde Sub-Area Command were happy for the airman to spend the night in police cells. The final decision was taken by the Military Command who had Hess transferred to the Maryhill barracks in Glasgow, where there was both proper security and a medical unit to attend to his injured foot.

The secrecy which bedevilled the research for this book obscures the story even at this early stage. As part of the routine, Hess was obliged to empty his pockets and an inventory was made of their contents. This probably lies in War Office file 199/3288B which will remain classified until 2017, seventy-two years after the collapse of the Nazi regime which gave them their probable significance. Peter Padfield in *Hess: Flight For the Führer* writes: 'It is difficult to think why the inventories should . . . have been detached from the report [made by the interrogating authorities] and placed in the "closed file".' The likely reason for the cloak of mystery will become apparent.

Major Graham Donald, Assistant Group Officer of Observer Corps based at Glasgow, had driven out with a group of RAF officers to find Hess's plane. Its twisted wreckage was scattered over an acre and a half but, probably because of the low fuel levels in the tanks, the fire which had resulted from the impact had done less damage than Donald expected. The fuselage was clearly that of an Me 110 and the officers could easily read the code painted in white letters along its length. It carried no bombs and no cannon (integral wing guns), and the three empty machine-guns on board were still covered in protective grease.

This forensic information mystified Donald even further. Not only was this a lone fighter-bomber on an erratic and incomprehensible flight path, it was not armed. No one in wartime Britain had yet encountered the notion of the Japanese kamikaze pilots, driven by their 'divine wind' to commit suicide by divebombing enemy targets. Yet a curious atmosphere of suicide certainly haunted the strange flight of Me Bf 110 VJ OQ. Intrigued, Donald and his colleagues drove to Maryhill where they knew the pilot was being held.

The first official to interrogate Hess – interrogations that would become an essential part of the man's life over the coming months – was Roman Battaglia of the Polish consulate in Glasgow. For all Hess's impeccable English in conversation with McLean, the authorities at Maryhill had no knowledge of this and Battaglia was there as an interpreter for the police. Donald, who had visited Munich before the war, had a reasonable grasp of German and noted that 'Hauptmann Horn' looked 'slightly fed up'.[5] Hess had now been in custody for nearly two hours and no one was taking him seriously. It was a pattern that was to stick.

Battaglia assumed that 'Horn' was part of some sort of commando raid and that the parachutist was not alone. In a display of stubbornness that Hess was to exhibit for the rest of his life, he refused to speak English from now on and told both Battaglia and Donald that it was vital he see the Duke of Hamilton for whom he had an urgent message. The inter-rogators and the Home Guard sentries to whom presumably this was translated fell about with laughter.

It was Donald who suddenly changed the mood. 'You look exactly like Hess,' he said. 'That is nothing new to me,' the Stellvertreter replied. 'It's a fact which has embarrassed me often enough.' The idea of a *doppelgänger* – an exact double – was born in that casual conversation and would re-emerge years later, in the Berlin prison of Spandau.

Donald promised that the Duke of Hamilton would get the prisoner's message and that, 'I shall also tell him that your name is Rudolf Hess.' There were further roars of laughter from the Home Guard. Even Hess managed to join in. Donald pursued the link with Hamilton and Hess told him that he had seen the Duke at the Berlin Olympics five years before and that they had a mutual friend.

Hamilton now became the focus of everyone's attention. Squadron Leader Hector Maclean, air controller for the Ayr district, rang Turnhouse first with news of the extraordinary German airman. Getting the Duke out of bed at well past midnight was not calculated to put him in a good mood especially since he had no idea what it was all about. Whether or not Donald contacted Hamilton minutes later with his opinion (at that time his alone) that 'Horn' was Hess is not clear.

It is the curious inactivity of Hamilton – and, further south, Churchill – that should alert percipient minds today. James Douglas-Hamilton (now Lord Selkirk of Douglas) in *The Truth About Rudolf Hess* excuses his father because the Duke had been on duty in the Turnhouse operations room for three consecutive nights of raids and was exhausted. According to the family version the Duke consulted the list he still kept of officers of the Luftwaffe whom he had met in Berlin in 1936 and, as 'Alfred Horn' was not among them, left the matter till morning. This does not explain, however, the fact that he did not send the Turnhouse Intelligence Officer, Flight Lieutenant Benson, to interrogate Hess. This was not only Benson's job, but the perceived wisdom was to do it as quickly as possible while the crashed airman may still be dazed, tired and off his guard.

As for Churchill, the next day when he was told at Ditchley Hall, near Blenheim, that an airman looking remarkably like Rudolf Hess had arrived, the enigmatic warhorse went immediately to a private screening of a Marx Brothers film![6]

Ineptitude on Churchill's part? Complacency? One of those eccentric little Britishisms that now, with the passage of time, seem to encapsulate the Forties? Unlikely. There is no historical parallel to the flight of Rudolf Hess. And the bewilderment of those, like Donald and Hamilton, even debatably Churchill himself, can hardly be wondered at. In May 1941, Adolf Hitler's Third Reich seemed all but invincible. His attempted invasion of Britain – Operation Sealion – may have come to grief in the Battle of Britain because of the tenacity and courage of a small group of gutsy young men and a lot of luck – but elsewhere he was master of Europe. Germany's formidable blitzkrieg tactics had brought much of the continent to its knees. Since September 1939, Poland, Denmark, Norway, the Netherlands, Belgium, Luxembourg, France, North Africa, Yugoslavia, Greece and now Crete had all fallen to the terrifying combination of Stukas from the skies and Panzer divisions on the ground.[7]

Why, given this immense superiority, should the third most powerful man in Hitler's Third Reich fly deliberately into the hands of his enemies? Did he come as an eagle or as a dove? Like much else in the case of Rudolf Hess, the answers are more bizarre than any fiction writer would dare dream up.

CHAPTER 2

Ihre Kämpfe

Rudolf Walter Richard Hess was precisely one of those for whom Adolf Hitler claimed *lebensraum* in the 1930s. As the Third Reich's ambitions for its domain grew and swelled beyond Germany's geo-political frontiers, Hitler laid claim to a number of states because they contained Germanic peoples. Egypt came into the definition.

When Hess was born on 26 April 1894, Egypt was under British rule. Ever since 1878 the supreme European interest in Egypt had been Britain. Whoever controlled the Suez canal, so vital to transworld trade, had to control the desert that flanked it. Only fifteen years before Hess was born, Ahmed Arabi had led a colonels' revolt against the Khedive, the nominal ruler of Egypt who was actually a puppet of the British. At Alexandria, where Hess was born, Arabic batteries were shattered by the guns of the British fleet and at Tel-el-Kebir Sir Garnet Wolseley's army killed 2,000 Egyptians and forced the surrender of 15,000 more.

It was the revolt in the Sudan that led to direct British involvement. Mohammed Ahmed – the 'mad Mahdi' – arose from the southern desert like a sandstorm, wiping out the command of General William Hicks at El Obeid and General Charles Gordon at Khartoum.

It was not until 1898, when Rudolf Hess was a little boy of four, that Gordon was finally avenged at Omdurman. In the last full-blown cavalry charge ever delivered by the British army, a young staff officer called Winston Churchill rode with the 21st Lancers, who earned immortality that day and three Victoria Crosses. British administration of the Sudan was to last until 1952.

It was trade that brought Fritz Hess to Alexandria, the centre of the huge Anglo-Egyptian import/export business. In the mid 1860s, before British domination and before the building of the canal at Suez, the elder Hess had established Hess and Co. with his own business acumen and his new wife's money. There are interesting parallels between Fritz Hess and Aloïs Hitler, the customs officer from Braunau-am-Inn who had fathered the future Führer five years before Rudolf Hess was born. Both were narrow in their outlook, both stern and unyielding, both terrifying figures to their children. Neither father showed any affection to their eldest surviving child and in the psychology of the two Reich leaders, this may explain a great deal. Ernst 'Putzi' Hanfstaengel, Hitler's friend from the early days of the Nazi Party, describes Fritz Hess as having the mentality of a bowling club member.

Young Rudolf attended the German school in Alexandria until he was twelve and was then taught at home by his parents. The Hess villa by the sea was beautiful and in the long years of enforced leisure that Hess was to undergo, he remembered it with fondness:

> ... the garden of Ibrahimieh with its flowers and fragrances and the entire indescribable atmosphere; the horrible 'Chamsin' [the wind that brought sandstorms]; the cool, salty air; the winter storms when the sea would be covered with white foaming peaks out to the horizon; the crying of the seagulls and the listless rhythm of the

waves whose melody we could hear until sleep overtook us. And then there were the long, balmy moonlit nights with the never-ending barking of the dogs in the desert, their voices carrying clearly through the silence of ... our garden on the edge of paradise.[1]

It was here that he picked violets every day and waded out to the rocks in the sea with his little brother Alfred. It was here too that he first learned the names of the stars whose influence was to colour his life. The times with his gentle mother were those he'd remember most fondly. From Landsberg prison in 1923 he wrote to Ilse Pröhl, the girl who would become his devoted wife: 'One's whole youth is incorporated in one's mother. She is part of one's being, one's own original essence ...'[2] By contrast, mealtimes were dominated by his father. Times never deviated and the Hess children, like Victorian children everywhere, were to be seen and not heard.

When Rudolf was fourteen, his father sent him to school in Germany, to the Evangelische Pädagogium in Bad Godesberg-am-Rhein. This was not such a culture shock as might be imagined, because every summer from the time Rudolf was six, his parents took the children to their newly acquired estate at Reicholdsgrün in the Fichtel mountains of Bavaria. At school, Hess excelled at maths and physics and developed a passion for astrology and the music of Beethoven. He also loved German history – before it was rewritten by the Nazis, when presumably he loved it all the more. At Bad Godesberg he was called 'The Egyptian' by his classmates because of his black, oily hair and swarthy skin. In later life, some people thought him Irish for the same reason. Not exactly a model of Hitler's Aryan ideal.

With his sensitivity and intellectual leanings, it was natural that Hess would go on to university, but the influence of his trade-obsessed father altered the course of his son's further education. Instead, the seventeen year old Rudolf was sent to the École Supérieure du Commerce in Neuchâtel, Switzerland, for a year before being apprenticed to a trading company in Hamburg. His life was mapped out for him, in the way it was for millions of other young men of that generation.

A shot fired at the Archduke Franz Ferdinand, one sunny morning in Sarajevo, changed all that.

There was a tragic inevitablity about 1914. In the tangle of alliances and the steamroller of mobilization, Austria declared war on Serbia over the murder of Franz Ferdinand; Russia declared war on Austria according to their principle of pan-Slavism; Germany declared war on Russia in defence of Austria; France declared war on Germany, the old enemy. Britain held out until 4 August when the German invasion of neutral Belgium forced its involvement, as laid out in the Treaty of London (1839).

'The lamps are going out all over Europe;' wrote Sir Edward Grey, the British Foreign Secretary, 'we shall not see them lit again in our lifetime.' But Grey was a realist with more than a hint of prescience. All over Europe, young men rallied to their nation's call. It was flags and bugles and drums and it would all be over by Christmas.

Hess was spending his summer – that golden, forever sunlit summer of 1914 – at Reicholdsgrün with his parents, brother Alfred and little sister Grete, now six. He was twenty years old and rushed to enlist with all the ardour of youth in a cavalry regiment in Munich.

'Now farewell, dear Rudi,' his father wrote to him, caught up in the wave of nationalism and immensely proud of his son's *élan* as were countless others, 'acquit yourself well. We all embrace you heartily and send you most affectionate greetings and kisses. Your Papa.' At Munich, Hess, who, could probably not remember ever being kissed by his father, was turned down by the cavalry who were over-subscribed. On 20 August as the Kaiser's army clattered into Brussels, he enlisted as a private in the 7th Bavarian Field Artillery and was, for reasons which are unclear, transferred to the reserve battalion of the 16th Bavarian Foot. 'Rejoice with me,' he wrote to his parents. The would-be cavalry recruit who joined the artillery was now a foot-slogging infantryman. He only had the airforce to go and would join that before the war to end wars was over.

By 4 November, the day that the Great War spread outwards to include the Turks, who declared war simultaneously on Russia, Britain, France and Serbia, Hess's training was over. He had run through cornfields in full pack, his rifle over his head. He had thrown himself face down in mud, hurled himself at barbed wire, bayoneted defenceless straw dummies that never fought back. Eight weeks of basic training was all that lay between Hess and a miserable death in the trenches. In the particular trenches below Ypres, the shattered, fought-over, shell-shocked town in the cockpit of Europe, some recruits survived for less than twenty minutes.*

Promotion for such a dedicated and quick-thinking soldier was rapid. A university education would have given him the instant rank of Leutnant but without it, he had to start from scratch. They made him Gefreiter (lance-corporal) in April 1915, after the Christmas peace had failed to materialize. The British launched their spring offensive at Ypres, where the Germans used poison gas for the first time. After this battle Hess received the Iron Cross, second class, which allowed him to wear a coloured ribbon buttoned to his field-grey tunic.

In May, as the Allies fought their way ashore in the hopeless killing grounds of Gallipoli and as the first Zeppelins bombed London, Hess was promoted Unteroffizier (corporal). A lull

---

* The cockpit of Europe, essentially northern France, what became Belgium in the early 19th century and had been the Spanish Netherlands, was a recurrent theatre of war from the Middle Ages. The killing fields of Agincourt were only arrow shots from the trenches of 1914-18.

followed for him at the end of August, when Germany and Austria partitioned Poland and the Russians abandoned the mighty fortress of Brest-Litovsk on the Eastern Front. He was sent to the officer training school in the beautiful Westphalian city of Münster, one of the last to hold out to the British Second Army in the *Götterdämmerung* that ended Hess's Reich thirty years later. By October, he was Vizefeldwebel (vice-sergeant), before rejoining the 16th Foot in Artois. As the British Government voted overwhelmingly for conscription, which would eventually help topple the Kaiser's Germany, Hess was dodging machine gun bullets in the battle for Neuville St Vaast.

Disease, as in all wars, compounded the toll of casualties. Hess spent March and April of 1916 as the only patient (an eerie foreshadowing of his later life) in St Quentin hospital with acute laryngeal catarrh. He whiled away the time with chess.

For the Germans as for the French, the stage for the war's catastrophic crescendo was Verdun, the cathedral town on the banks of the Meuse and the key defensive position in the centre of the French lines. Its ring of forts had been constructed to hold back the Prussians in 1870 and, forty-six years later, the same protagonists were once again locked in futile combat, each side contributing to the destruction of the medieval city, each side clinging on. Marshal Joffre, convinced that the spring offensive of 1916 would strike in Champagne, had not kept up the town's defences. Successive German assaults in February and March had been held by heroic resistance, but the combined ferocity of attacks in May and early June, when Hess rejoined his regiment, led to the capture of Fort Vaux to the north-east.

Hess was not a great poet, but his experiences led him to do what Wilfred Owen, Siegfried Sassoon and Guy Appollinaire did far better. He wrote of the trenches before Verdun:

Pitch-Black night
and cold rain without intermission.
In their sunken, mud-filled trenches
the hard-boiled old fighters squat.
Between them smooth, milk-white faces – lads
who a few days before,
garlanded with flowers and singing,
marched away through the streets of home . . .[3]

Years later, Hess made a speech to ex-servicemen in Königsburg in East Prussia. It was translated into a number of languages and struck a pacifist chord among the veterans of 1914–18:

But let us be honest. The smell of death was always in our nostrils. We have seen death in more fearful and mangled shapes than any men before our time. We squatted and crouched in our dug-outs, waiting to be crushed to pieces. We listened with stilled breath as our trained ears heard the hiss of the shell above us, as the mine exploded before our feet. Our hearts throbbed as if they would break to pieces when we sought cover in vain against the deadly rattle of the machine-gun. With our gas masks on we felt ourselves suffocating to death in the midst of the gas clouds . . . Did not each one of us then and there often ask: 'Why all this? Must it be? Can humanity not be spared all this in future?'[4]

Near Fort Douaumont, the next in sequence after Vaux, Hess received the first of the three wounds which punctuated his wartime career. Flying shrapnel from a high-explosive shell embedded itself in his left arm. He was sent to hospital at Bad Homburg and then home on leave. His next posting was to the relatively little-known south-eastern front.

Romania had come into the war on the side of the Allies at

the end of August 1916, causing a certain panic in the German High Command, stretched as they were by now with that worst of Teutonic nightmares, the war on two fronts. Field Marshal Paul von Hindenburg was given command of the army, but not in time to have any effect on the Austrians, always a weaker force, who were defeated by the Romanians on 1 September. On Christmas Day 1916, Rudolf Hess was made platoon leader in the 10th Company of the 18th Bavarian Reserve Infantry, tramping through the mountainous terrain of Transylvania. In July of the following year, he was again wounded, a shell splinter slicing the same arm that had got him invalided out of Verdun. In August the third wound nearly killed him.

Hess would remember, years later, that the sun was bright in the trees and he was leading his platoon through woodland towards a trench. He suddenly saw a Romanian aiming his rifle at him and remembered feeling surprised as the bullet hit him in the chest. Without stretcher bearers or immediate help, he crawled back to his own lines, pistol in hand, bewildered by the shot's impact, but not unduly perturbed.

This wound was to become the focal point of the most absurd of the theories surrounding Hess's flight. When Dr Hugh Thomas was consultant in general surgery to the British Military Hospital in Berlin in 1973, he became convinced that the lone prisoner of Spandau was not Rudolf Hess, but a *doppelgänger*, an exact double. 'There is undoubtedly,' Thomas wrote, 'a difference between records of [Hess's] history in World War I and the torso of the man in Spandau . . . the torso cannot lie.'[5]

Other doctors, like Gibson Graham who examined Hess after his landing in Scotland, and Hurevitz, a New York surgeon who saw him in Nuremberg, agreed that there was no sign of major scarring. Those who did not accept the *doppelgänger* theory – most people in fact – pointed out that Hess's war record saw the light of day for the first time in 1937, when he was Hitler's Stellvertreter and at the height of his fame and power. He would not be the first man to beef up his personal heroism for the glory of the Fatherland and for himself. In fact, we do not even have to assume that Hess was lying. Despite Hugh Thomas's insistence in *The Murder of Rudolf Hess* that a clumsy operation to remove the bullet was carried out by a field surgeon called Suaerbruch, the truth is very different.

Hess was shot with a Russian rifle, possibly a Nagant, with a very small calibre. Normally a rifle bullet would produce a neat circular or oval hole, only slightly larger than its own circumference on impact. The exit wound would be much bigger, made so by the effect of the missile tearing its way out and driving bone debris with it. It is clear from the medical reports of 1917, however, that the bullet missed his heart and spine completely, going straight through his body. The smallness of the calibre would account for the small exit wound in his back. Thomas, Graham and Hurevitz were looking for massive wounds and surgical scars. They were looking for the wrong evidence.

In hospital until 10 December 1917, Hess was promoted to Leutnant in the Reserve and applied to join the Imperial Flying Corps. There was a romance about the 'cavalry of the clouds' which first-hand accounts of the reality of air warfare have done little to diminish. On the ground, it was mud, rats, poor rations and mangled corpses on the barbed wire. But in the air the brightly painted bi- and tri-planes conjured up the romantic duels of Germany's medieval past. It was Wagner, it was Parsifal, it was Siegfried and who more gallant that Manfred von Richtofen, the 'Red Baron', to lead the dragon-flies of death soaring over the trenches?

By 1918 in fact, aerial reconnaisance and aerial combat had attained a strategic importance of their own. And 1918 was the last throw of the dice for the Kaiser's Germany. The Tsar's Russia may have collapsed in the 'robber peace' of Brest-Litovsk, but the Americans, fresh, untried and with seemingly infinite resources, were a new factor in the west. In the spring offensive, the German army swarmed all over the French and crossed the bloody Aisne on the first day. They halted by the Marne, manned by its ghosts of 1914, and turned to face the Americans at Chateau-Thierry. It was a valiant effort, but it was not enough.

Hess's parents were unhappy with his move to the Flying Corps, imagining it to be a far more dangerous situation than the one he had left. His wound healed, his eyesight excellent, he began pilot training in March 1918 and joined Flying School Number 4 at Lechfeld, near Augsburg, on 15 May. The plane he flew was a Fokker D7, the newly designed fighter that had made its debut the previous month in Jagdstaffel 3, the Loerzer Circus.* Arguably the best German fighter of the war, it reached 130 mph in level flight, climbed to 3,300 feet in 1 minute 45 seconds and could reach altitudes of 20,000 feet with ease. It was an easy plane to fly, renowned for its manouevrability, especially coming out of dives. Jagdstaffel 2 scored an astonishing eighty-one kills on enemy squadrons in a mere six days in September 1918. In October and November, Hess flew with Jagdstaffel 35 near Valenciennes. No kills were recorded for him.

With the Central Powers' forces effectively at bay and the leaders exhausted into a political surrender, the war ground to a halt. In terms of combat troops it was, at that point, the bloodiest war in history and Germany's losses were particularly high. Second only to Russia in the size of her army (eleven million men in all), nearly seven million were casualties or prisoners of war by November 1918. Of that figure, 1.8 million had been killed in action or died of wounds. In terms of cash expenditure,

---

* A Staffel usually comprised 9 aircraft and was the smallest combat flying unit. A number of Staffel then comprised a Gruppe, which in turn formed part of a Geschwader. A Jagdstaffel was used during the daytime as a fighting unit, a Nachtjagdstaffel was used at night. The name Circus was a nickname for this particular kind of unit. The British used Squadrons, Wings and Groups in a similar manner.

Germany's figure was placed at $37,775,000, marginally more than the British had spent and far more than any other power involved.

More terribly, Germany was falling apart. Hess wrote: 'It is unspeakable misery. Savage hate lights the eyes of the people, naturally as even now they regard us as the guilty party for the world catastrophe.'[6]

The day before the guns fell eerily silent for the last time, the Kaiser slipped quietly across the Dutch border with his wife, a few servants and whatever he could load into twelve cars. His abdication left Germany to the gangsters.

There was practically no real government. A country that had little experience of democracy was now expected to embrace it fully. A flu epidemic, known poetically as the 'plague of the Spanish lady',* was devastating the German troops who remained at the front, adding to the deep sense of betrayal they felt. It was not they who had surrendered but the faceless politicians back home. For years to come Hitler would spit his vitriol at the 'guilty men' of November 1918 and bemoan the 'stab in the back'.

At Kiel, forge and anvil of the Germany navy which had worked so long and hard, the sailors mutinied. The Liberal Chancellor, Prince Max of Baden, panicked and passed the reins of government to the saddle-maker and Social Democrat leader, Friedrich Ebert. In the general chaos of November, left and right-wing groups armed themselves and soldiers returning home under demobilization orders were given a choice of how to use their new-learned ways of killing.

The success of the Bolsheviks in Russia in the October revolution of the previous year encouraged Communist groups

* Recent research has shown that despite its name, the epidemic began in the United States. Its effects were appalling, yet, perhaps because of the emotional pull of the Great War, it is now almost forgotten.

elsewhere. Using guerrilla tactics the Communists tried to control the key communications buildings in Berlin. Some three thousand soldiers of the right-wing Freikorps faced them on the barricades and bodies littered the streets after confused fighting. 'Their blood,' screamed one Communist paper, 'is on the hands of the new government.'

By March there was famine in Germany. In the major cities the potato ration for adults was 2lb a week, and babies died for want of milk. And while they did, stern-faced gentlemen, the victors of the war that had gone, met in the Hall of Mirrors in Versailles to redraw frontiers and exact their revenge. By June, when the details were published and a battered and bewildered German government put its signature to the multiplicity of documents, the full extent of the punitive peace became apparent. It ran to 200 pages, 440 clauses, 75,000 words. Lloyd George, Britain's Prime Minister for the last two years of the war, prophesied with grim accuracy, '. . . we shall have to fight another war all over again in twenty-five years at three times the cost'.

Most damning of all was the infamous 'war guilt' clause. Count Ulrich Brockendorff-Rantzau, the German Foreign Minister said: 'The demand is made that we shall acknowledge that we alone are guilty of having caused the war. Such a confession in my mouth would be a lie.'[7] Germany went into a week of public mourning and the scale of reparations was fixed at an impossible £6,600,000,000. If there had been no Adolf Hitler and no Second World War, Germany would have paid off the debt in 1992.

Rudolf Hess's experiences in the months after demobilization were at once typical and determining. In May 1919 there was a Bolshevik coup in Munich and a Soviet was set up, spearheaded by Russian Jews. The link between Communism and Jewry was thus reinforced in the minds of Germans everywhere and very possibly in the mind of Rudolf Hess. He joined the Freikorps under Colonel Franz Ritter von Epp, a Great War hero who wore the Blue Max* pinned to his tunic. Epp's hard-hitting, right-wing unit put down the Bolshevik rising with brutality, killing the anarchist Gustav Landauer and massacring Communists in the Munich suburb of Greising. Von Epp's aide-de-camp was Ernst Röhm, a stocky, scar-faced hard drinker and homosexual who had lost half his nose in the war. One of von Epp's paid informers was an ex-lance corporal called Adolf Hitler. It was in the bloody anti-Communism of Bavaria that the Third Reich was born.

More sinister than his membership of the Freikorps, which for an ex-officer, who believed in the greatness of his country was not surprising, was the fact that Hess had also joined the Thule Society, with its headquarters at the Vierjahreszeiten Hotel in Munich. Ostensibly a culture club taking its name from Ultima Thule, the mythical land of the first Germans, it was actually an anti-Semitic organization dominated by an aristocratic elite and founded during the war by the son of a railway engineer, Rudolf Glauer, who called himself Baron von Sebottendorf. The motto of the Thule was, 'Remember you are German. Keep your blood pure.' Its emblem was the swastika, the broken cross that was to spread terror across Europe in the years to come. And the swastika was enclosed with the laurel leaves of victory and the dagger of death.

Hess lived in a hotel, the pension von Schildberg, in the Schwabing suburb of Munich. The city itself was to become the hub of Nazism and was already steeped in history – Schwabing itself was first recorded as early as the eighth century. A thriving

* The Blue Max was the most coveted decoration of the German forces in the Great War. It was an enamelled Maltese Cross but the colour of its ribbon gave the medal its nickname. Its official nomenclature 'Pour Merit' comes from its enamelled inscription.

medieval town, it was known as a centre of the arts by the eighteenth century. Its squares, wide thoroughfares and basilicas complemented its reputation as the home of artists, sculptors and musicians. It was here that Hess met three people who were to dominate his life.

The first was Ilse Pröhl, whom he first saw in April 1920. Her father was an army surgeon and two of her male friends, bright young things of pre-war society, had been torn to pieces in Berlin by the mob during the right-wing rising led by Wolfgang Kapp. The couple worked together for the Nazi Party in the Twenties and backpacked in the beautiful Bavarian mountains. Hess married Ilse in 1927.

The second was Professor Karl Haushofer, a general in the Great War who lectured at Munich University where Hess enrolled, belatedly, as a student. The charismatic Professor became, in the eyes of some commentators on Hess, the father-figure he still needed. He met the Haushofer family, the boys Heinz and Albrecht. The Haushofers were ardent Anglophiles and Albrecht and Hess often strolled together in the English Garden in Munich, speaking English. The relationship and the leaning were to be central to Hess's solo mission.

The third was a small, unprepossessing Austrian with a pale face, protruberant blue eyes and a rather unfetching moustache. Hess said to Ilse Pröhle: 'You must come with me the day after tomorrow to a meeting of the National Socialist Party. I have just been there with the General [Haushofer]. An unknown man spoke, I don't remember his name. But if anyone will free us from Versailles, this is the man – this unknown will restore our honour.'

The village of Braunau-am-Inn is an unremarkable cluster of houses in the Bavarian mountains above the River Inn. Among its inhabitants in April 1889 was the fifty-two-year old Aloïs Hitler and his third wife, formerly his servant, Klara Pölzl. Aloïs stares stonily out of his faded sepia photograph, a man with little hair, hard eyes and the huge walrus moustaches made fashionable then by the Emperor Franz Josef himself. His third son, Adolf, born at six o'clock on the evening of 20 April, would describe his father as a drunken bully and it was to his mother that young Adi clung.

The baby was not strong and earlier births to Klara had not survived, but Adi prospered. When he was four, the family moved to Linz. This was the city which was to fill the future Führer's dreams. Even after he failed to become an architect he would formulate plans to rebuild it entirely and was still working on a scale model in the Berlin bunker in 1945, as his thousand-year Reich came crashing down around his ears.

It was at the Realschule in Linz, which Adolf entered in 1900, that things began to go wrong for him. The Realschule taught sciences and engineering and was demandingly empirical and practical. Adolf's performance was so bad he had to repeat his first year. One of his teachers, Eduard Hümer, remembered, 'He was definitely gifted, but only in a one-sided way, for he was lacking in self-control and he was . . . argumentative, wilful, arrogant and bad-tempered . . . nor was he industrious . . .'[9]

This snapshot of the twentieth-century's bogeyman stayed with him. All the characteristics described by Hümer are discernible in the Führer of the Third Reich. His arrogance was unbounded, his temper awesome and for one of the most powerful (and supposedly busy) men in the world, it is astonishing how often he lay in bed until lunchtime! As a teenager, Adolf became surly, moody, difficult – only really happy when he could escape into his strange fantasy world fuelled by the music of Wagner and the cowboy stories of 'Old Shatterhand' written by Karl May. His mother's death in 1908 devastated him. Dr Bloch, the family physician, wrote later, 'In all my career I have never seen anyone so prostrate with grief as Adolf Hitler.'

Bearing in mind that the young Hitler's best mark in free-hand drawing at school was '4' on a scale that went down to '5', his gamble to become an artist in Vienna at the age of sixteen was a brave one. In Hitler's own words:

> This was for me an endlessly bitter time ... Without support [Aloïs's legacy had been small], compelled to depend on my own efforts, I earned only a few Kronen and often only a few farthings for my labours and this was often insufficient to pay for a night's lodging. For two years I had no other mistress than sorrow and need, no other companion than eternally unsatisfied hunger.'[10]

Although our knowledge of Hitler's Vienna years comes largely from his own book, *Mein Kampf*, written in 1923, there is no doubt that his time in the Austrian capital's gutter was a determining period in his life. The city was perhaps the most beautiful in Europe, with well over half of it given over to woodland and public parks. But like every beautiful city, Vienna had its darker side. Overcrowding was always a serious problem in the working-class areas and the young student's room in the Stumpergasse was a hovel. When almost his only friend, August Kubizek, shared his lodging for a while, he was horrified to find Hitler barely surviving. He didn't smoke or drink. Indeed, his only 'vice' was an addiction to the opera, especially Wagner's works. Kubizek wrote of Hitler's visits to the theatre: 'His violence left him, he became quiet, submissive, tractable. His gaze lost its restlessness ...'[11]

At other times, however, the art student was an outsider, introverted, lonely and desperately poor. Turned down by the Vienna Academy of Art because his work was simply not good enough, he tried to supplement the meagre monthly allowance his father had left him by selling postcards. By December 1909, he had moved so many times he could not remember his previous addresses and reluctantly entered the Asylum for the Shelterless, near the Südbahnhof.

The dreamer who loved Wagner was now concerned with the grim reality of keeping a roof over his head. He could only stay at the Asylum for five nights at a time and by February 1910 had moved again, this time to the Männerheim, the home for single men in the Meldemannstrasse. Here the rules were tough, but at least Hitler had his own table, clothes rack, mirror and bedside lamp. Hitler became prone to speech-making to his fellow inmates at the Männerheim. He dabbled, how seriously we don't know, with the occult and seems to have swung between moods. Often he would rant and rave about the wealthy, cosmopolitan Munich bourgeoisie, at the Marxists who met to discuss the revolution in street-corner cafés, and above all at the Jews, who sometimes bought his postcards and sometimes got in his way as they hawked their own wares in the overcrowded Jewish Quarter.

There is evidence to suggest that Hitler avoided military service for as long as he could. Eventually, in February 1914, the authorities caught up with him in Salzburg and he was examined by an army doctor, whose swift diagnosis was, 'Unfit for combatant and auxiliary duty, too weak. Unable to bear arms.'[12]

All that was to change in August.

The joyful look on the face in the crowd is one of the most memorable photographs of Adolf Hitler; a jubilant young man, laughing, waving his straw summer hat, eyes bright with a nationalistic fervour felt by millions of Austrians and Germans. And in contrast to the young Rudolf Hess, who merely faced a boring career in business, for Adolf Hitler the war was salvation. On 16 August, he enrolled in the 1st Company of the 16th Bavarian Reserve Infantry, the List Regiment. As he trained in Munich and the army camp at Lechfeld, for a time, though neither was to remember it later, he would have been serving with Hess.

Hitler was twenty-five, older than most recruits. He never rose above the rank of corporal, but volunteered for everything and was made Meldegänger, despatch runner. This was a highly dangerous job, because the despatch runners had to run a gauntlet of machine-gun fire and hand-grenades, carrying vital orders from trench to trench at a time when field telephones were notoriously unreliable. At the end of October 1918, for his courage in advancing under heavy British machine-gun fire, he was awarded the Iron Cross, first class.

Nearly two years earlier, in October on the bloody banks of the Somme, a British shell burst in a German dug-out. Four men were killed outright. The only 'slight' wound was suffered by Adolf Hitler, who was hit in the face by a shell fragment. Days later he was hit again, this time in the left thigh, and after two months' convalescence at the Beelitz Hospital near Berlin was back at the Front. In the capital, he had been disgusted by the war-weariness on the faces of the civilians he met and despised the soldiers who had injured themselves to escape the hell of the trenches.

In quieter moments, when the List Regiment was not under fire, Hitler behaved as he had in Vienna, often lost in a silent world of his own. At other times, according to Hans Mend, a comrade, he would rail against the Jews in the army – like Leutnant Hugo Gutmann, who, ironically, recommended Hitler for the Iron Cross a second time some months later.

With five weeks of the war to go, Hitler was wounded for the third and last time. Near Werwick, south of Ypres, where his regiment clung tenaciously to a hill, the British released canisters of chlorine gas. Hitler fell back with the others, his eyes swollen and crimson, his vision blurred, coughing uncontrollably. He lost consciousness for a while and by the time he reached hospital at Pasewalk near Stettin, he was completely blind.

As his sight returned, Hitler came to realize, along with the rest of the world, that the war was over and that, unbelievably, Germany had lost. At the end of November 1918, he went to Munich, straight into the teeth of the Soviet rising led by the Jewish intellectual and drama critic Kurt Eisner. Still a soldier, Hitler spent a boring couple of months sorting gas masks. Food shortages became acute in the city. With a mounting sense of anger and frustration in him, Hitler began to attend political meetings.

The arrival of General von Epp's Freikorps put down the Bolshevik-inspired coup. Hitler, along with several others, was recruited in the spring of 1919 to act as an undercover agent for von Epp. In this context he attended lectures on economics and politics at Munich University and for the first time discovered that he could hold a crowd, especially on the subject of the Jews. All Germany, it seemed, was looking for a scapegoat. Impressed by his oratorical skills, Hitler's superiors appointed him instructor to the 41st Regiment at Lechfeld, where he had undertaken his own training as an ardent recruit five years before. In 1919, four years before *Mein Kampf* he wrote:

> ... there lives among us a non-German, alien race which does not want ... to sacrifice its racial characteristics ... The emotions of the Jews remain purely materialistic ... they dance before the Golden Calf ... They corrupt princes with Byzantine flattery ... They use weapons of public opinion ... Their power is the power of money ... The effect is to produce a race-tuberculosis of the [German] folk.[13]

Hitler's solution to all this corruption?

> Rational anti-Semitism arising out of purely emotional causes finds its ultimate expression in pogroms. Rational anti-Semitism must be directed toward a methodical legal

struggle against them and the elimination of the privi-
leges they possess, which distinguish them from other
aliens living amongst us ... The final aim must be the
deliberate removal of the Jews ....[14]

In Hitler's view, a legitimate monarchy had been overthrown
in Russia by a handful of gangsters led by Lenin and Trotsky
– 'The greatest Jew since Jesus Christ' as a White Russian
general called him in 1920. More crushingly for Hitler, the
'guilty men' of 1918 – intellectuals, Communists and above
all Jews – had swept away the Kaiser in Germany too and
accepted a dictated peace treaty with the enemy by the
summer of 1919. Everywhere, it was international Jewry – the
eternal Jew – that was destroying everything that was fine
and noble for the sake of financial greed. From Hitler's
mouth, this message, recurrent through previous centuries,
found a new generation of adherents in 1919.

On 5 January of that year, the machine-fitter and railway
locksmith Anton Drexler joined Karl Harrar in founding the
Politischer Arbeiterzirkel, the Political Workers' Circle, in
Munich. It was the feeble beginning of a force that would
transform Germany and threaten the world. About forty
strong, the Circle was a curious hybrid of political ideas,
reflecting Drexler's impractical idealism. It was opposed to
profit-making and the laziness of intellectuals, was intensely
patriotic and anti-Semitic. Under its new name of the
Deutsche Arbeiterpartei, the German Workers' Party,
Drexler's friends met in various Munich beer halls. The occu-
pations of the members of the early Nazi Party – the word
'Nationalsocialistiche' was adopted later – were surprisingly
varied: there were soldiers, betrayed and bitter; students,
always ready to embrace a brave new world; railway
workers, desperate to feed their families; engineers, busi-
nessmen, a doctor, a chemist and a painter.

At one of their meetings, on 12 September 1919, was Adolf

Hitler, playing the spy for von Epp. He took the podium after indifferent speeches and so impressed everyone that Drexler gave him his diatribe on the Jews, *My Political Awakening*, to read. Four days later, a still relatively uninterested Hitler joined the Party as No. 55. Here he met the Catholic poet Dietrich Eckart who gave the Nazis their battle-cry 'Germany Awake!' The anti-Semitic Eckart would kill himself with morphine addiction by the time Hitler dedicated *Mein Kampf* to him, but by then he had made the ex-corporal acceptable to polite society, and may have told him to wear a trenchcoat to give a more militaristic appearance to his meetings.

Early in 1920, Hitler decided to make the Nazi party his own. Drexler and Harrar were dispensable and the twenty-five point manifesto that Drexler drew up with Hitler in February was probably his last contribution to the Party. The Party wanted the Greater Germany promised since the days of Bismarck; the Treaty of Versailles was to be torn up; colonies were to be restored; only Germans could hold officer status and officials would be elected by the people; inherited wealth would be abolished; large industries would become profit-sharing; agrarian reforms would take place; profiteers and money-lenders, regarded as traitors to the state, would be executed; education was to be state-run, as was a health service; the regular army would be demobilized and replaced by a people's army; the Press was to be wholly German and subject to strict controls; religious tolerance was to be granted to all Christians but no one else. All this was to be controlled and co-ordinated by a central government whose leaders had to be prepared to die to make the system work.

In Munich the Party gathered numbers, among them Rudolf Hess. In the summer of 1920, when Hess signed on, the black swastika, the *hakencreuz* in its white circle on a red background, appeared for the first time. Hitler spent these months perfecting his public speaking and became, arguably, the best mob orator in history. He stood in front of mirrors, trying this or that posture, clasping his hands to emphasize words, pointing and stabbing the air, raising his arms as if lifting the weight of the world from Germany's shoulders. He stood silently before crowds in various beer halls, his hands clasped, waiting for silence, like a good teacher, until the 'class' was focused on him. He began quietly, hesitating, pacing his words, then building to a climax, thumping his fists, waving his arms, repeating his slogans over and over again to drive home the Party's philosophy. At the first interruption from hecklers, his heavies, not yet in the brown shirts of the *Sturmabteilung*, would swarm through the hall and batter the opposition into silence. By the end of such speeches, which he was to duplicate to audiences of tens of thousands in the future, his listeners were on their feet chanting and shouting; he himself, deathly pale, running with sweat, triumphant. Only his closest confidants – Hess among them – saw that all this was an act. The outpouring of emotion left him utterly unmoved, as he planned, minutes later, the next round in the deadly game he was playing.

A year later Hitler led an organization of 3,000 fanatics and he had coined the title Führer – (leader) – for himself, although it was Hess who popularized it. The bellowed '*Heil*!' had already become the greeting and rallying cry of the Party, now officially the NSDAP. And violence flared increasingly at meeting after meeting. At the Hofbräuhaus on 4 November 1921, Hitler's forty-two heavies, in Bavarian braided jackets, knee breeches and jackboots clashed with a similar army of Communists. After the crash of glass, overturning of tables and cracking of skulls that followed, Hess stood triumphant, his dark, swarthy features bruised and sweating.

The men who followed Hitler might well have been, in journalist Paul Gierasch's phrase, 'the featherbrained, unbalanced type ... flotsam and jetsam of the classes that have lost their footing in the new Germany ...'[15] but they were growing daily in numbers. To their ranks came the drug addict and thug Hermann Goering, of the Richthofen Circus, with his Blue Max and his intimidating swagger; Julius Streicher, the sadistic schoolteacher and Jew-hater who beat and raped his pupils, probably of both sexes; and Alfred Rosenberg, the philosophical engineer from Estonia who accepted the forged 'Protocols of the Elders of Zion'* as proof of an international Jewish conspiracy. He became editor of the Nazi newspaper *Völkische Beobachter*† in 1923.

That was the year that the French army invaded the Ruhr, the heartland of German industry. For four years the country had found difficulty in paying the reparations fixed by Versailles. In the belief that German workers were deliberately shirking, French *poiloux* were posted with rifles and bayonets on factory shop floors. Gustav Stresmann, the new Chancellor of the beleaguered Weimar Government, ordered a policy of non-co-operation. Posters of the day show a sullen German worker with his hands firmly in his pockets stubbornly resisting the probing bayonets of the French and the words 'No! You Can't Force Me!' in Fraktur script.

These workers were in effect on a general strike and had to be funded by the government. The result was hyperinflation. At the end of the war, a loaf of bread cost half a mark in Berlin. By November 1923, it cost 201,000,000,000 marks. A journalist, Egon Larsen, wrote, 'You went into a café and ordered a cup of coffee at the prices shown on the blackboard over the service

---

* The original 'Protocols' were forged by the police in Tsarist Russia to justify their systematic pogroms against the Jews. The 'Protocols' threatened world domination and an international Jewish conspiracy of unprecedented scale.
† The 'People's Observer' was largely a collection of lurid anti-Semitic stories, often involving white slavery and various sexual excesses. In this sense, it was outdone only by Streicher's *Der Sturmer*.

hatch: an hour later, when you asked for the bill, it had gone up by half, or even doubled.'[16] There were riots and looting in the major cities and the left-wing magazine *Simplicissimus* showed a grim cartoon of a mother holding up her naked, starving baby, both of them drowning in a sea of worthless paper money.

Hitler's answer was simply to stage a coup in Munich, take over Bavaria and march on Berlin – a plan that may have been based on the wild romantic march of the revolutionary Gabriele d'Annunzio in Italy four years earlier.* In a flurry of activity on the night of 8 November, Hitler stormed into the Bürgerbraükeller, complete with Goering and his helmeted machine-gunners. At gunpoint he forced Munich's ruling elite to accept him as one of a triumvirate who were going to rule Germany. The other two were Erich Ludendorff, the war hero and former Quartermaster-General who had been the virtual dictator of Germany towards the end of the war, and Ernst Poehner, former chief of police in the city. The actual power in Munich – Gustav von Kahr, head of the Bavarian state government, General Otto von Lossow, the army commander and Colonel Hans Ritter von Siesser, the police chief – had no intention of joining the half-baked corporal, agree with some of his views though they might. They slipped away from the Bürgerbraükeller and organized official resistance to the Nazis for the following day. Hitler would not forget this betrayal – he had von Kahr murdered in 1934.

Hitler's own version of the Beer-Hall Putsch, which he elaborated upon in the years ahead, bore little relation to the truth. In it, with police and army bullets whistling around him, Hitler saves the life of an innocent boy caught in the murderous crossfire. In fact, he was one of the first to run, dislocating his

---

* Gabriele d'Annunzio, an established and rather notorious Italian poet, occupied the city of Fiume in September 1919 in defiance of his own government and of the newly created League of Nations. He became a hero to the Italians overnight.

shoulder as he threw himself to the ground to avoid the guns of Leutnant von Godin's 'Green Police'. Goering was hit in the groin by pavement fragments. Ulrich Graf, Hitler's bodyguard, took five or six bullets. While the dazed and demoralized Hitler made his getaway by car to the house of 'Putzi' Hanfstaengel in a nearby village, Ludendorff walked, head and shoulders above the scattering Nazis, up to the bayonets of the police. They had orders to shoot him, but such was the legendary status of the man that no one dared. He simply walked through the line, batting their rifles aside and waited patiently at the Feldherrn Hall to be arrested. His valet, Kurt Neubauer, caught several police bullets in the head.

Because Rudolf Hess had been given the job of arresting various Munich officials on 8 November, he missed the fiasco of the Bürgerbraükeller. By the time he was ready to ditch his prisoners and get back into action, it was all over. Hess's car was stolen and, to avoid arrest, he climbed the mountains on foot over the border into Austria. Perhaps out of loyalty to Hitler, Hess felt guilty about 'missing the show' and accordingly, in February 1924, gave himself up as a Putsch plotter to the authorities in Munich.

The trial of the Beer-Hall Putschists was as much of a farce as the Putsch itself. Ludendorff was acquitted, Röhm released on condition that he behaved himself; Hitler and Hess received prison sentences that were guaranteed to be no longer than six months. The laxity of the system, the sympathy the judges felt with the Nazis and the social malaise in Germany conspired to give Hitler a second chance. The Bürgerbraükeller became a shrine and the fourteen Nazis who died on 9 November 1923, saints.

CHAPTER 3

The Sleepwalker

Four and a Half Years of Struggle Against Lies, Stupidity and Cowardice was not a title that was going to grip the minds of millions. Accordingly, Hitler's autobiographical rant reached the world as *Mein Kampf* – 'My Struggle'. It was dictated by Hitler first to his chauffeur Emil Maurice, then to Rudolf Hess, in the prison at Landsberg-am-Lech. It was the cushiest stay in prison imaginable, beginning, appropriately perhaps, on April Fools' Day 1924. Hitler had become a folk hero after the failed Putsch and he received letters of support, flowers, wine, cakes and chocolate. The guards fell under the spell of his strange, hypnotic eyes. They saluted him with the soon to be familiar shout of '*Heil* Hitler'. He was already '*Der Führer*' to them as he would be to all Germany.

The majority of political philosophers have long rubbished *Mein Kampf* as the work of an inferior mind, a mish-mash of ill-considered theories. But its message, populist, designed to appeal to everyman's dissatisfactions and couched in layman's language, would be embraced where the *Communist Manifesto* would not. It has been compared with Niccolò Machiavelli's *The Prince* in that it assumes the political elite should necessarily govern by a morality different from that of society, and that the

50

ends most certainly justify the means. At his trial, Hitler had used the dock as a soap-box: 'Pronounce us a thousand times guilty,' he shouted at the judges, 'but history, the goddess of a higher truth and of a better law, will tear down the judgement of this court: for she will find us innocent.'[1]

How much of *Mein Kampf* is Hitler and how much is Hess will never be decided now. The imprisoned Nazis were allowed visitors. Kurt Ludecke maintained links between the Führer and his followers on the outside, like Gregor Strasser and Max Amann who were keeping an understandably low profile after the Beer-Hall Putsch. And Professor-General Karl Haushofer came to see Hess, bringing him books and talking geopolitics.

In 1945, when Haushofer was interrogated by the Allies, he denied that his teachings had given Hitler the concept of *lebensraum*, the urge to spread the Third Reich to the east where the pure Aryans would lord it over the Slavic races, who would become to the Germans what the Israelites had been to the Egyptians. Either to save himself or to save his old friend and pupil Rudolf Hess, who was about to appear in the dock at Nuremberg, Haushofer claimed not to like Hitler, that the man was incapable of understanding the theories he (Haushofer) was advocating. His son, Albrecht, shot outside the prison of Moabit on 22 April 1945, on the orders of Himmler, realized perhaps what his father had done. In one of the last poems he wrote, found on his body, were the words:

> For my father the fates have spoken
> He once had it in his power
> To cast the demon back into the dark.
> My father broke the seal
> But failed to see the evil.
> He let the demon escape into the world.[2]

The consensus now is that Hess was co-author rather than scribe for *Mein Kampf*. Nowhere in the index to the book does Hitler mention Hess, but the Führer did not have the intellectual training or the dogged perseverance to produce something like that on his own. James Murphy, who had translated Hitler's book into English, wrote in 1941 that the sections on the British Empire were certainly written by Hess, rather than Hitler, 'who knew practically nothing about the British Empire in those days.'[3]

If Hess's influence at this stage was considerable, then the importance of his flight to Scotland on 10 May 1941 must be re-evaluated. He was not the faithful, rather impotent lap-dog various commentators have made him out to be – he was Hitler's confidant and abettor. Because of the clever hatchet job done on Hess by his own comrades – Josef Goebbels and Otto Dietrich in particular – after 10 May 1941, the image of the Stellvertreter is of a robotic time-server who could only be trusted with sinecures. It is true that Hess lacked the ruthless dog-eat-dog mentality of Goering and his own number two, Martin Bormann, but that by no means made him politically inept or impotent. As a university man with a better intellectual pedigree than Hitler, his ideas were vital to the Führer, especially in those early days of the Nazi Party.

Albert Speer, who came to know Hess as well as anyone outside his small circle of intimates was ever likely to, regarded him as ambitious. The Nazi creed was as central to Hess's psyche as to Hitler's; he was merely a less emotional and demonstrative personality. As Alan Bullock points out in *Hitler: A Study in Tyranny*, Hess was an officer, providing, with Goering, the junker status that Hitler lacked.* Yet Bullock too dismisses Hess as 'stupid', revealing the extent of the power of Goebbels' propaganda long after the Minister of Enlightenment

* The junkers were the landowning elite of the old Prussia and, despise them though he did, Hitler needed the support of this class.

was dead. And Hess himself, according to Speer's *Inside the Third Reich*, came to believe that he had never got *that* close to Hitler because of an invisible and impenetrable wall that the Führer erected.

A dour-looking Führer was released from Landsberg on 20 December, posing in breeches and trenchcoat by a soft-topped Mercedes hired and driven by Ilse Pröhl. A week later, Hess too was released and the Nazi Party began to rebuild itself. In January the NSDAP was made legal again by the Bavarian authorities, who were obviously not listening when Hitler made a speech at the Bürgerbraükeller the following month: 'To this struggle of ours there are only two possible issues. Either the enemy passes over our bodies or we pass over theirs.'[4]

Rebuilding the Party was more difficult than either Hitler or Hess imagined. Never the strongest of the right-wing organizations, it was almost wholly confined to Bavaria, dirt poor (even without a typewriter in 1923) and its leaders scattered and bickering. Ernst Röhm had virtually broken away and was busy creating another private army, the Frontbann. Outside Bavaria, Gregor Strasser, a chemist who had fought with von Epp's Freikorps and in the Beer-Hall Putsch, was building a North German Nazi group. Heinrich Himmler, later head of the SS and co-ordinator of the Final Solution, was Strasser's number two; and a young journalist who worked on the *Berlin Workers' Paper* was the future Reichsminister of Propaganda, Josef Goebbels. Strasser was a problem for Hitler – he would ultimately be eliminated.

Hess was offered, and accepted, a post at the Deutsche Akademie under Karl Haushofer, which would have meant the comfortable, cosy life of academe together with a reasonable salary. Hess chose instead to become Hitler's private secretary, working largely on the final stages of *Mein Kampf* with Ilse at first, often at Berchtesgaden in the Bavarian Alps. Kurt Ludecke first met Hess eight years later, but his appearance and manner had not altered:

> A man sat in front of me who was not easy to fathom. He had thick, dark hair above a forceful, angular face; grey-green eyes and black, bushy eyebrows. Furthermore, he had a fleshy nose, a determined mouth and a firm, square jaw. He was tall and thin and looked Irish. One could sense a suppressed fanaticism in his eyes, but his behaviour was controlled and calm. I remember him as a domineering personality, which is a compliment that you could give to only a few Nazi leaders. Hess made me feel uneasy. I could not place him and he did nothing to meet me halfway. He was polite, too polite, very aloof; I could not break through his armour.'[5]

This aloofness of Hess's was to be a distinguishing feature throughout his life. He was an educated man with aesthetic tendencies, looking with contempt at thugs like Goering and Streicher, who nevertheless possessed the ruthlessness to oust him as the man closest to Hitler. How close this relationship was, we do not know. There was speculation that, in Landsberg at least, the pair became lovers. When Hess was imprisoned at Mytchett Place in 1941, Churchill heard rumours that Hess was known in homosexual circles as 'Bertha' and 'Fraulein', but this seems to be born of the same music hall tradition that counted the testicles of the collective Nazi leadership. Goering was known to make gibes about Hess and the name 'Bertha' seems to have been bandied about by him. In the early days of the Nazi Party, with Röhm's homosexuality quite blatant, rumours of all sorts circulated. It is true that Hitler and Hess used the familiar term '*du*', but so did Hitler and Röhm; and Hitler had Röhm murdered. From 1924 onwards, at least in public, Hess was always meticulously formal and respectful towards the Führer.

What the Party really needed was adversity. A successful, economically vibrant Germany led by a successful Weimar Government would not do at all. And in 1924, that seemed to be happening. The French pulled their troops out of the Ruhr and the Americans came up with the Dawes Plan which would ease the impossible reparations situation.* If Stresemann's Weimar Government could effect economic miracles – with a little help from its friends – who needed Hitler and his untried Nazis?

The answer for Hitler was to appeal to the masses and use his astonishing ability for oratory to achieve it. He outmanouevred Strasser early in 1926 by making other Nazis realize that Strasser's socialistic Drexler-influenced ideas of nationalizing industry were only a short step from Bolshevism and thus the international Jewish conspiracy. Strasser backed down for the first time in a slow decline that would end with a bullet through the back of his neck from Reinhard Heydrich on 30 June 1934, the 'Night of the Long Knives'. So from early 1926 onwards Josef Goebbels put his considerable propagandist talents at the disposal of Hitler.

The Führer and Hess courted rich industrialists openly in the increasing affluence of the later Twenties. And if the well-known anti-Semitic millionaire Henry Ford turned down their begging letters, there were many Germans who did not. Emil Kirdorf, director of the massive Rhenish-Westphalian coal company, lent his support as did the chairman of United Steel, Fritz Thyssen.

Although heads would continue to be broken on street corners and the number of Röhm's brown-shirted stormtroopers grew with a steady menace, Hitler's new way was to infiltrate

---

* Under the terms of this agreement, drawn up by American banker Charles Dawes, the United States lent Germany £45 million in order to stabilize the economy. The Reichsbank was reorganized to control inflation and the need for Germany to make a surplus on exports was established.

democratic government and wait to ambush it from the inside. Goebbels summed it up in 1928: 'We become members of the Reichstag in order to paralyse Weimar with its own assistance. If democracy is so stupid as to give us salaries for this work, that is its affair. We do not come as friends, nor even as neutrals. We come as enemies . . .'[6]

In 1928, the Nazis' grip on the Reichstag was as weak as 12 out of 491 seats. The rise in the Party's fortunes would be directly linked to the massive unemployment that resulted from the Wall Street Crash of October 1929.

The sponsorship that Hess had obtained first from wealthy individuals like Helene Bechstein, Gertrude von Seidlitz and 'Putsi' Hanfstaengel, then from heavy industry, enabled the Nazis to set up a luxurious headquarters – the Brown House in the Briennerstrasse in Berlin. With its oak-panelled rooms and marble memorials to those who fell in the Putsch, it was a far cry from the succession of hovels and workhouses Hitler had lived in as an impoverished student in Vienna. It was from here that the Führer launched his political campaigns of 1930–33.

Hess's role in the seizure of power by Hitler was crucial but is not well documented. When it was clear that Hess's mission to Scotland had failed in May 1941, his name was systematically removed from the records. It is likely also that much documentation was deliberately destroyed. As the link between the Führer and industrial support and between the Führer and the intellectual community – what was left of it anyway – Hess was pivotal in Hitler's success.

On 1 December 1933 he was appointed Reichminister Without Portfolio. He was already a Gruppenführer (Lieutenant-General) in Himmler's black-shirted SS, the elite private army whose motto was 'Loyalty is my oath' and whose devotion to Hitler was absolute. He was still Hitler's right-hand man, but increasingly, with responsibility for internal Party organization, was working on his own or acting as something of a buffer between Hitler and other Nazi leaders. As Stellvertreter, Hitler's official Deputy, he lived in a magnificent mansion in the Wilhelmstrasse in Berlin.

It is difficult to summarize the extent of Hess's powers in the Thirties. He was responsible for policy decisions at the highest level as Party and State became synonymous. Hitler was clearly happy, as an essentially lazy and inconsistent administrator, to leave a great deal of work to his Deputy. Hess advised on important public appointments and could overturn court rulings on dissidents (dwindling in number in the Germany of the 1930s) who opposed the state. He could formulate legislation without recourse to the Reichstag at all and was at the centre of a vast amount of information, secret and otherwise. Which all makes nonsense of the assertion by some that in 1941 Hess had no idea of Hitler's plans to launch Operation Barbarossa against Russia. The Gestapo, the secret police of the SS; the Research Office, in fact a wire-tapping agency; the security services of Himmler and Heydrich; the Abwehr, the counter-intelligence units run by Admiral Canaris and his Ausland organization (which co-ordinated Nazification of Germans living outside Germany): all these poured a steady stream of information through Hess's offices on the Wilhelmstrasse.

Peter Padfield believes that it was the elimination of opposition from within – the Night of the Long Knives on 30 June 1934 – that changed Hess's slavish devotion to Hitler. Even the man's signature, Padfield believes, became more depressed. Most dangerous to Hitler's position as Chancellor in the early Thirties were the ever-restive SA and their Chief of Staff Ernst Röhm, who saw the Führer's assumption of power as a mere step on the road rather than the cul-de-sac it actually was. Röhm clearly had designs on the War Ministry and intended to interpopulate the Reichswehr (the German army) with his own stormtroopers. We do not know the extent of Hess's involvement in the purge that followed, but when Hitler struck it was with a sudden ruthlessness that surprised all but the few centrally involved. On 15 June Hess broadcast to the nation on German radio, now of course totally in the hands of the Nazis: 'Woe to him who breaks faith, and thinks to serve the revolution through rebellion. Woe to him who clumsily tramples the Führer's plans in the hope of quicker results.'[7]

By June 21 a list of 'Unwanted Persons' was drawn up. Röhm's name topped it. There was no shortage of men queuing up to kill him. First, Max Amann, Hitler's sergeant in the List Regiment during the war offered – 'The biggest swine must go. I'll shoot Röhm myself.' Hess was next – 'No, that's my duty, even if I should be shot afterwards myself.'[8] In the event it was Theodor Eicke, the concentration camp inspector, who shot Röhm in his cell. Henceforth, the SA was small, powerless and wholly devoted to Adolf Hitler. When war came in 1939, most of the SA were given the job of training the German Home Guard.

1934 was undoubtedly the year of ultimate triumph for the Führer. The Enabling Law gave him the title and absolute power for life, the Long Knives coup eliminated his most serious rivals and the death of Hindenburg saw thirty-eight million Germans vote for Hitler to succeed him as President. Hitler was now also Supreme Commander of the Armed Forces and the Reichswehr, which became the Wehrmacht, swore a binding and sacred oath of 'unconditional obedience' to him by name. The dead sound of their chanting in the flickering torches at army bases all over Germany has a haunting echo down the years.

Hess's unique position as Minister Without Portfolio allowed him to indulge various interests and gave him wide-ranging powers. Nowhere was this more apparent than in the various Ausland organizations he orchestrated. At his headquarters in Berlin, Hess built up an impressive organization to run the

Ausland system. Split into thirty-two separate departments, each one dealt with a different facet of the organization's work. For instance, Department 21 dealt with culture; 31, run by Rudolf's brother Alfred, handled international commerce, involving tenders and contracts passed to Berlin by the scattered groupings. Hess appointed Ernst Willielm Bohle as Gauleiter to administer the organization on a day to day basis. Bohle was, like Hess, an Auslander himself. Born in Bradford, England he was, again like Hess, technically a British subject and even retained his British passport for several years.

Now in a position to help his old friends, Hess appointed Professor Karl Haushofer to head the VDA, the People's Alliance for Germandom Abroad, as it accorded with the old man's expertise in geopolitics. In domestic affairs, he had his fingers in all sorts of pies: the law, now of course a Nazi construct; education, where history and biology were rewritten to perpetuate the Aryan myth for the rising generations; employment; finance; technology, which was split between autobahn construction under Fritz Todt and aircraft production under Willi Messerschmitt; health, which was largely a team of civil servants checking Jewish lineage; and an intelligence organization, which is at the heart of what happened in 1941.

Under him was the pushy, aggressive Martin Bormann, a former SA leader whose ability to assume subservience and shift allegiances meant that he escaped the purge of the Long Knives. An apparently loyal and undeniably efficient number two, the 'brown eminence' was simply amassing money and power. Hess's flight to Scotland gave Bormann his longed-for opportunity to slide inexorably into the Stellvertreter's shoes.

There is little doubt that Hess had no personal ambitions for power. Karl Haushofer said in 1945 that Hess was not exceptionally clever, but the disillusioned old man might have been trying to cushion his old student's ride to the scaffold. Nowadays, the consensus is that Hess's devotion to Hitler was a weakness, that only a relative moron could be such a lap-dog. This might in part reflect how the modern-day gut-reaction towards notions of loyalty and devotion is perhaps more cynical. But it certainly misunderstands the importance of Hitler to the Germany of his day. With hindsight, we know that he was leading his nation to destruction, but in the Thirties he was still the Messiah, the strongman longed for by Germans everywhere who would avenge Versailles and make Germany great again.

There is also little doubt that Hess was set apart from other Nazi leaders. Naturally shy, curt and formal, he had a dry sense of humour that few understood. He became more obsessed by mysticism as the Thirties wore on, prone to inexplicable stomach cramps relieved occasionally by incomprehensible homoeopathic remedies. A strict vegetarian, he so annoyed Hitler by bringing his own food to the Berghof, the Führer's summer retreat at Berchtesgaden, that Hitler stopped inviting him for meals.

Hess's mysticism is obscure. In many ways a romantic, his upbringing by his mother in the scented gardens of Egypt may have put him on track for a lifetime's obsession with the stars and astrology. He took note of his dreams, even telling Albert Speer years later in Spandau that the whole flight to Scotland came to him in a dream. His mentor Haushofer had similar dreams, seeing Hess striding through the ringing halls of ancient English castles, bringing peace between nations. That he was different and obsessive about his diet cannot be doubted, but to imply, as some have, that all this contributed to Hess's eccentricity and ultimately his madness, is to twist the facts. Interestingly, his stomach cramps, almost certainly the result of stress, were treated in 1940 by Felix Kersten, Himmler's masseur, whose boss suffered exactly the same problem. Himmler's involvement with the occult was altogether of a different nature.

Hess also became the acknowledged 'conscience of the party'. This was taken by those outside his staff as a sign of weakness and was a perfect motive for his flight in May 1941. Schwerin von Krosigk, Finance Minister in the Thirties, wrote: 'Therefore even at Party rallies he always wore only the brown shirt without orders or decorations, thereby making a doleful impression beside Goering's bird-of-paradise hues.'[9]

In this, Krosigk is demonstrably wrong. In Weimar in 1936, Hess was wearing the same orders as Hitler. At a party meeting at the Luitpoldhalle three years earlier, he is wearing his SS black, as he is again at the Sportpalast in Berlin in 1937. If anyone appeared regularly in sombre, civilian clothes, it was Goebbels; and to compare Hess unfavourably with Goering in matters of uniform is absurd. The Reichsmarshal was unique in always looking like a walking Christmas tree.

The bottom line of all this is that clearly the more ruthless and ambitious of the leading Nazis – Goering, Himmler, Heydrich, even Bormann, though he had the sense to wait – were pushing Hess to one side. But the oft-inferred corollary of this – that the man who flew to Scotland in 1941 was an outsider, out of touch with what was actually happening in Berlin – is nonsense. Nowhere is this more apparent than in the Jewish question.

The Nazis' catalogue of arbitrary and repressive measures against the Jews, particularly as enshrined in the Nuremberg Laws, is extensive and well-documented.[10] Systematic subordination, disenfranchisement, demoralization and imprisonment, and eventually, violence and terror, gathered pace through the 1930s. But even after the first of the Nuremberg Laws was enacted in September 1935, most people both within and outside Germany, Jewish and non-Jewish, could not accept or did not take in the true significance of Nazi policies. The increasingly restrictive decrees were introduced and executed in such careful increments and with such insidious propaganda that the first Nazi pogrom in November 1938 still came as a horrific revelation to many.

In retaliation for the way his family had been treated by the Nazis, a Jewish student burst into the German embassy in the French capital and shot the first official he could find, Ernst von Rath. This sparked off the infamous Kristallnacht, the Night of Broken Glass. The *New York Times* German correspondent wrote on 11 November:

> A wave of destruction swept over Germany today. Huge crowds looked on ... Generally the crowds were silent and the majority seemed gravely disturbed by the proceedings. Only members of the wrecking squads shouted occasionally, 'Perish Jewry!' and 'Kill the Jews!'[11]

Over 7,000 shops were looted throughout the night and well into the next day. In an orgy of destruction, 191 synagogues were burnt down. At least a hundred Jews died and an estimated 30,000 were sent to the camps. A communal fine of one billion marks was fixed on German Jews for the murder in the Paris embassy. Goering was furious because of the cost of replacing so many windows – 'They should have killed more Jews and broken less glass.'

By December, Economics Minister Walther Funk closed down Jewish business entirely. From now on, Jews were not part of the economic life of the country and since all their assets were simply taken by the Nazis, the necessary adjustment was slight. In the year war was declared, Jews were required to hand in precious metals and jewellery. At the end of April, mass eviction took place and the ghettoization of millions began. Jews were banned from theatres, cinemas, lecture halls; they even had to hand in their wireless sets.

Hess's involvement in all this seems to have been total. His personal signature was at the bottom of much of the official documentation that implemented Hitler's Jewish policy. Being the 'conscience of the party' did not mean that it was his duty to curb Hitler's vicious racial excesses. On the contrary Hess, bound by his loyalty and devotion, was the last person to do so. His attempts to drive a wedge between the Führer and Streicher, the greatest Jew-hater of them all, probably had more to do with personal jealousy than with any recoiling from anti-Semitism.

Conversely, in his personal dealings there is no evidence that Hess was overtly anti-Semitic. In his relationship with the Haushofer family, in particular, Hess seems to have been playing a double game. The professor's wife was Jewish, yet Hess and Hitler both owed the professor a great deal. Moreover, his son Albrecht Haushofer was one of Hess's best agents with an unrivalled knowledge of all things British and he was to play a vital role in Hess's decision to fly to Scotland. As long as Hess was Stellvertreter, he could protect the Haushofers, conveniently ignore the blood-slur and allow Albrecht to keep his college lectureship in Berlin.

In 1933, Hess signed protective letters for Albrecht and Heinz Haushofer which in effect made them honorary Aryans. Before this, Martha and her family had considered emigration as the anti-Semitic tide rose. Authorities are vague on the position of the Haushofers, especially Martha, in the Jewish context. Wolf Hess says that his father issued a 'letter of safe conduct' for the whole family, protecting them against persecution; he does, however, use the phrase 'so called' which may imply that the safe conduct letter was no guarantee of their safety. Douglas-Hamilton says that the protection was only extended to the Haushofer sons, Albrecht and Heinz, and this makes a certain sense in that Albrecht in particular was of more use to Hess than his parents.

Hess's key role in foreign policy may well have been his under-standing of Britain – and this, apart from his early childhood in British-run Egypt, was the result of his link with the Haushofers and their Anglophile attitudes. Again, the link is a vital one in explaining Hess's flight, but in the meantime, Hitler had more pressing interests: a piece of paper and a continent to tear up.

CHAPTER 4

The Peacemakers

When Winston Churchill's government failed to produce any satisfactory explanation for the arrival of Rudolf Hess in Scotland in May 1941, the initial reaction was one of annoyance, first in Parliament, then in the Press. Today, the media would not tolerate such silence, but in the 1940s it was perhaps more generally accepted that governments were allowed secrets, especially during a war.

A detailed response from the Government was never forthcoming and that has led to endless speculation, most neatly summarized by A.P. Herbert, writer, politician and member of the Naval Auxiliary Unit.

> He is insane. He is the Dove of Peace.
> He is Messiah. He is Hitler's niece.
> He is the one, clean, honest man they've got.
> He is the worst assassin of the lot.
> He has a mission to preserve mankind.
> He's non-alcoholic. He's a 'blind'.
> He has been dotty since the age of ten,
> But all the time was top of Hitler's men.
> (Indeed, from all the tales he had to tell,
> Joe Goebbels must be slightly touched as well.)
> He is to pave the way to Britain's end.

He is – as dear old Lindbergh was – a 'friend'.
He's fond of flying. He was racked with fear.
He had an itch to meet a British Peer.
He thought that Russia was a crushing bore.
He simply can't stand Hitler any more.
In such rich fancies I am not engrossed,
For this is what appears to matter most –
He came unasked, an enemy, a Hun;
And nobody was ready with a gun.

The consensus now is that Hess flew in search of a peace party, a group of influential people who saw good reason in 1941 to believe that peace with Germany was not only desirable, but the only sane policy to be followed. Did such a group exist? In order to answer that question, we have to understand the nature of Anglo-German relations before war broke out.

It is with the upper echelons of British society that Rudolf Hess seems to have been preoccupied, and it is at that level that a relevant shared history can be traced. With the Hanoverian succession of 1714, the first 'German' king took his place on the throne of England. The genealogy is complicated. James I's daughter Elizabeth married Frederick, the Elector Palatine (in effect ruler of the Rhineland) in accordance with the marriage customs of the early seventeenth century. When James' grandson, James II, fell foul of leading politicians because of his ostentatious Catholicism and other excesses, he was ousted by what was actually a parliamentary coup, not unlike the one Hess hoped might have ousted Churchill in 1941. Leading Whigs and Tories invited James' daughter Mary to take the throne in his place. Mary accepted, on the condition that her husband William, Statholder of the United Provinces (now the Netherlands) rule as her co-monarch. The constitutional reign of William and Mary produced no living heirs and the throne slipped sideways to Mary's sister, Anne.

Whether through the hereditary Stuart disease of porphyria or some other cause (some historians have suggested the very unlikely congenital syphilis), all seventeen of Anne's children died before her and so the throne passed to her nearest blood relative, Sophia, Electress of Hanover. Sophia was a sparkling and vivacious woman who would probably have made an excellent queen but as she too predeceased the gout-ridden Anne, the throne devolved on her son, George.

There was nothing sudden about this arrangement. Queen Anne's succession had worried politicians for years and a formal invitation had been made, again by Whigs and Tories, to secure George as England's king. Lady Mary Montagu described George as 'an honest blockhead . . . more properly dull than lazy' but in fact, he detested work and detested England. While dallying with his German mistresses, listening to the music of the court composer, Handel, or riding to hounds, he allowed power to slide from the monarchy into the welcoming hands of Robert Walpole and the Whigs. George refused to speak English, although he probably could, and spent six months of every year in his native Hanover, where he died of a stroke near Osnabruck, allegedly after an indigestion attack from eating melons, on 12 June 1727.

The later Hanoverians did rather better. George II at least spoke English; George III was born in England and, in his extraordinary devotion to duty regarded his position of king as more important than his position as Elector of Hanover. All the Hanoverians were anxious to defend the little German state however, using British troops and British taxes to do so. The Hanoverian connection was finally severed in 1837 on the accession of Victoria. According to the Salic Law which then operated in Europe, a woman could not inherit the Electorate.

The German connection, however, continued. In 1840, Victoria chose Albert of Saxe-Coburg-Gotha as her consort. Victoria's mother was German and the princess was brought up almost exclusively under her influence. It was no doubt partly this that created Victoria's unusually competent understanding of European affairs when most Englishmen followed the 'terrible m'Lord' Palmerston's lead and shouted loudly at foreigners in English. There is no doubt either that Albert was an unpopular choice in England, as it was widely believed that the head of a small and obscure German state without democracy or parliamentary tradition, would quickly assume the role of dictator and demand to be made king. In fact, Albert was a thorough-going committee man and worked hard in the twenty-one years of life left to him to win the hearts of the English.

Albert and Victoria's eldest son was Bertie, within the family, and on the stage of history, Edward the Peacemaker. He was a cosmopolitan roué, with a notorious eye for the ladies and a tendency according to some commentators to give the letter 'r' the guttural German sound he had inherited from his father.

There is of course nothing sensational in any of this. In an age of democracy, industrial revolution, increasing education and political development, the influence of the monarchy on its people is arguably very slight. But the influence of the monarchy on the aristocracy – and on politicians – is far greater. The abdication crisis of 1936 is a clear example of that.

By the time of the First World War, the three branches that had intermarried within the royal family Anglicized themselves to emphasize the rift between Germany and Britain. The anomaly about 1914 was of course that three of the protagonists' monarchs – George V of England, Nicholas II of Russia and Wilhelm II of Germany – were cousins. The weakness of these relationships, even in totalitarian states like Tsarist Russia or the Kaiser's Germany, is evident – the war happened anyway, despite their links of blood. So George V became 'Windsor' rather than Coburg (only the loaf remains to honour the association); his queen, May of Teck, became Cambridge;

and the Battenburgs, the Mountbattens (the marzipan cake alone survives to bear witness). Anglo–German royal blood links carried little weight in the *realpolitik*-ing between the wars.

Among the aristocracy the marriage pattern was more parochial. Dynastic families there were – today the Spencers might be a good example – but they married among themselves to double the size of their estates or to gain another seat in the Commons, not to forge international alliances. Their most common links with Germany a century ago were visits to the spa resorts to take the waters. Again, royalty set the tone – Edward VII was a frequent visitor to Marienbad.

What may have pushed some members of the British aristocracy towards a rapport with Germany was the rise of Bolshevism in the East and its ramifications for an anxious British aristocracy.

With the Liberals ever weakening under Asquith and Lloyd George, forced into coalitions with the Conservatives, the Independent Labour Party was approaching fast on the rails of government as a potential third and ultimately successful party. The Tories may have won the election of 1922, but the most significant new group in the Commons were the 'Red Clydesiders' and the colour that identified them with Lenin's Bolsheviks had a sinister significance for a large number of the 'old England'. The illegitimate Glasgow crofter's son, James Ramsay MacDonald, became leader of the Labour Party that same election month and among the telegrams of congratulation sent to him was one that would have struck an alarmist chord with the gentry – 'Labour can have no truck with tranquillity.'

The writing may also have been on the wall the following year, when in the jockeyings for position as leader of the Conservatives (Stanley Baldwin replaced Andrew Bonar Law) the King did not, as was the custom frequently in earlier periods, ask a member of the Lords to head a government. The

election of that year – in which Hitler staged his abortive
Putsch in Munich – produced an astonishing result. The
December poll gave the Tories 258 seats, but Labour emerged
as Britain's second party with 191 over the Liberals' 159. In
January, a carefully top-hatted Ramsay MacDonald accepted
the king's request for him to lead a government – only twenty-
four years after the new party was created.

Although a minority government that would have difficulty pushing through anything but bland legislation, eleven
of the twenty-man Cabinet were, like the Prime Minister
himself, of working class origin. And there must have been a
deafening outcry in obvious quarters when the Foreign
Office, that most reactionary and public-school dominated
institution, was told to start work an hour earlier! And
Winston Churchill who had so far in his twenty-four-year
political career dithered between Conservative and Liberal
and back again, warned, 'The enthronement of a Socialist
government is a serious national misfortune.' One of the
oddest recruits to join MacDonald was Oswald Mosley, a
wealthy ex-Tory, and the son-in-law of that bastion of Empire,
Lord Curzon. 'You stand forth,' he wrote to MacDonald, 'as
the leader of the forces of progress in their assault upon the
powers of reaction. I ask leave to range myself beneath your
standard.'[1]

By the end of that extraordinary year, however, Labour was
out in a welter of corruption and intrigue. On 12 September it
was leaked to the Press that MacDonald had 'reluctantly' taken
possession of a Daimler car and £30,000 worth of shares in the
McVitie and Price biscuit company. 'I only technically own
them,' was his rather limp excuse. Plans to give financial aid to
Bolshevik Russia were far more serious and gave real ammunition to those already convinced that MacDonald was working
for Moscow. The Zinoviev letter clinched it. Shortly before
polling day, a letter purporting to come from Grigori Zinoviev
of the Russian Politburo, exhorting the tiny British Communist

Party to rise up in revolution, hit the papers. The letter was undoubtedly a forgery but the mud stuck.* After the country went to the polls on 31 October, Labour was still the second party, but at a mere 151 seats to the Conservatives' 258. For a while, at least, the threat of Bolshevism seemed to have been faced down.

But the threat was never far away in the minds of the aristocracy. By October 1925, a total of twelve Communists had been charged under the 1797 Incitement to Mutiny Act. 'We cannot be smashed,' they claimed, 'We shall continue to fight against the coming capitalist offensive.' It was the following year however that saw the Communist call grow louder. 'Not a penny off the pay, not a minute on the day,' thundered the miners against the Royal Commission's findings that wages must be cut to make the ailing coal industry more competitive. On 4 May, *Daily Mail* workers refused to print an article by their editor, Thomas Marlowe, which claimed that the Trades Union Council's support of the miners was an act of revolution against the Government.

The General Strike of nine days which followed is the only one in British history. It was not truly general, in that the professions largely refused to join and the Government was supported by the armed forces and the police. What the strike did, however, was to show the potential for class revolution as never before. Stockbrokers, lawyers and students manned lorries and trains to keep vital supplies moving. The majority of those queuing up to join the Special Constabulary were likewise men of the middle classes, and whereas it might be seriously stretching a point to equate these loyalists with the street thugs

---

* One man who claimed to have written it was Sidney Reilly, whose real name was Sigmund Rosenblum. A Polish Jew from Warsaw, he had a chequered and fascinating career as an 'ace of spies' before his last operation to the USSR in 1925. He was to disappear inside Communist Russia a year later.

of the SA, the General Strike ended before any heads needed to be broken. The point was underlined by the reaction to the strike with the Trades Dispute Act of the following year, designed to curb the extent of strikes and the power of the TUC. 'This means,' said the Labour party grimly, 'the battle of the century and serious conflict of class.'[2]

With hindsight we can of course find no real threat of Bolshevism in Britain in the 1920s. Ramsay MacDonald's Government was pledged to housing improvements and reducing unemployment, not instituting the proletarian regime of Karl Marx. The miners and their supporters who struck in 1926 were concerned for the roofs over their heads and the bread in their children's mouths, not with international working class solidarity. But there was no hindsight for the aristocracy, gentry and even some of the comfortable middle class at the time. Even in safe little England, the Bolshevik threat seemed real enough.

In Europe it was. In 1922 the lantern-jawed blacksmith's son Benito Mussolini became 'Il Duce', the leader of the growing Fascist Party in Italy. A rash of Communist-led strikes led big business to fund the Fascists, who promised to stop them. Mussolini's black-shirted Squadristi beat up Communists in the streets, breaking strikes and heads with equal relish. This new 'Radicalism of the Right' was gaining ground in Italy's confused and weak parliament with thirty-five seats by the end of that year. Long before Hitler came to power in Germany, Mussolini was the strongman who would stand as a rock against the all-engulfing tide of Bolshevism.

Two years later, another citadel of ancient power collapsed when King George II of Greece was deposed by his own parliament. This was not exactly a surprise – the Glucksberg family were hideously unpopular – but the Kingdom of the Hellenes was now in the hands of referendum-loving Republicans. The British aristocracy, no less than George V, shuddered. And on 14

April 1931, King Alfonso of Spain, honorary colonel of the British 16th Lancers and a frequent visitor to this country, lost his throne too in the tide of Republicanism. Who knows what alarmist dissent he spread among royal and aristocratic circles when he and his family arrived in London? When Alan Bennett puts the following words into the mouth of one of his fictional characters in *Forty Years On*, he is parodying a very real feeling of the time: 'The tide is flowing fast against monarchy in Europe. Scarcely a week passes but a throne falls. Mr Baldwin thinks it may be our turn next.'

When Hitler came to power in 1933, his dreams of halting the Bolshevik tide could start to become reality. 'We stop the endless German movement to the South and West,' he wrote in *Mein Kampf*, 'and turn our gaze towards the land in the East. If we speak of soil in Europe today, we can primarily have in mind only Russia and her vassal border-states.'

Those in Britain who feared Communism liked what they heard and heard what they liked. Again, we must not fall into the trap of hindsight. The appalling racial policy and the death camps were a thing of the future – not until 1945 would the dreadful evidence come to light in the West, although some would argue it was there to see earlier if looked for hard enough. In 1933, Hitler was another bulwark against Communism and, geographically, a useful buffer state between 'us' and 'them'. And if Hitler's dreams of *lebensraum* were directed eastwards, all the better – it would check Communist westward expansion and was well away from Britain.

Even the Jewish situation was not totally out of keeping with British attitudes in the early Thirties. The aristocracy and gentry, secure in their estates and finances despite the advent of death duties (assuredly *not* a Communist plot, having been introduced by a Conservative government in the 1890s) were not exactly vulnerable to the Jewish/Freemasonic financial conspiracy which Hitler, Streicher, Goebbels and Goering warned against. Even so, an almost throwaway remark by the Marquess of Tavistock, a prominent pacifist during the war, is telling:

> We should not forget, also, that even in our boyhood the German Jew was a byword for all that was objectionable ... Even in our own country there are thousands of quite respectable people, normal and reasonable in other respects, who have a most venomous hatred against the Jews and would certainly become Jew-baiters of a kind if they had Hitler's power and opportunity. Indeed, there may be a bit of the Hitler even in ourselves ...[3]

It may be that the middle classes also took the 'threat' seriously and believed the fabricated nonsense of the 'Protocols of the Elders of Zion' as a blueprint for world financial domination by Jewry; and among the aristocracy, the Duke of Northumberland seems to have believed every word of it. In areas where Jews proliferated, such as the East End of London, the grim reality of racism was never far away. The population of Whitechapel and Spitalfields was over 90 per cent Jewish in the first quarter of this century.

There is no doubt that what made Hitler and his new regime attractive to some Britons after 1933 was the economic miracle he was working. After the most crippling military defeat and within only years of the worst economic crisis in recorded history, Germany was envied by the world as a phoenix rising from the ashes. Many wealthy Britons travelled to Germany, as they or their parents had before the Great War, not a few of them to see what the Führer was doing with his Third Reich. It was undoubtedly impressive and even those hardened veterans who looked upon Germans as 'the Hun' and 'the Boche', the enemy of 1914–18, must grudgingly have admired Teutonic industrial and financial know-how rather as we do today. Public works schemes produced autobahns, thirty years before such roads appeared in Britain. High employment was being achieved, (unbeknownst to visitors, because of the clandestine munitions programme), at a time when it remained a grim problem in Britain. There would be no Jarrow marches in Germany, not because such a thing was outlawed, which it was, but because economically, it was not necessary. Unemployment in Britain nearly doubled in the fourteen months up to August 1930, whereas in the Fascist state of Italy and the Fascist-oriented state of Germany, it actually fell – and this in the teeth of the Slump.

Even Churchill, so soon to become the great champion of anti-Nazism on the world stage, was impressed by Mussolini. 'If I had been an Italian, I am sure that I should have been wholeheartedly with you from start to finish in your triumphal struggle against the bestial appetites and passions of Leninism.'[4] A few years later, he was snarling about the bestial appetites and passions of Hitler and Mussolini.

What motivated the British aristocracy, gentry, and Government is what motivates any state at any time – a sense of self-interest and self-preservation. An impressive, gutsy resurgence by two of Europe's underdogs, Italy and Germany (and the British have always loved underdogs and supported them) was bound to impress and as long as those countries could be controlled, they seemed infinitely preferable in the self-preservation game to the vast steamroller of Communist Russia, believed by many to be behind the Bristol riots of October 1931 when armed mobs battled with police.

A good summation of pro-German (and pro-Italian) views is provided by G. Ward Price, a director of the *Daily Mail*, in *I Know These Dictators*, published for the Right Book Club in 1937. Pre-Munich, the whole tone of the book is one of hope that Hitler can be controlled, but if he cannot, the blame lies squarely, Ward Price believes, with the governments of Britain and France. Ward Price was clearly a Germanophile and enormously impressed by the economic and political miracle that Hitler had brought about. To wrench a country from bitter discontent and defeat into one of pride and power in seven years was indeed miraculous. Ward Price is particularly scathing of the French, who persist, he says, in throwing in their military lot with the Russians for the encirclement of Germany, even though Stalin's Russia is the avowed enemy of democracy. His solution is for us to pull out of our links with France immediately and foster good relations with Germany.

He quotes Hitler at length on his consistency in arguing for a greater Anglo-German understanding. Hitler had studied maps of London and would be able to find his way about should he ever land there. His favourite film, which he once watched three nights running, was *Lives of a Bengal Lancer*. Despite the fact that Gary Cooper and the whole production was American, the story was set in that bastion of British Imperialism, the Raj. '1750 to 1', roared the film's posters, 'Always outnumbered! Never outfought!' It was based on a book by Francis Yeats-Brown, himself an ex-lancer, and starred such true blue Brits as Sir Guy Standing and C. Aubrey Smith. It was from films like this that Hitler was beginning to glean a little of the language and Kannenberg, his steward at the Chancellery in the Wilhelmstrasse, often entertained the Führer with English songs of an evening, to the accompaniment of an accordion. The first official dinner-party that Hitler gave at the newly decorated official residence was an intimate affair at which the only four foreign guests were British members of the Right Club – Viscount Rothermere, the newspaper baron; his son, Esmond Harmsworth; founder of the Anglo-German Fellowship, E.W.D. Tennant; and Ward Price himself.

This was the first time Ward Price had met Hitler and he was clearly impressed. He noted how, at the same Olympic Games state banquet at which Lord Clydesdale (later the Duke of Hamilton) was present, Sir Robert Vansittart stood laughing and joking in his glittering Grand Cross of St Michael and St George with the Stellvertreter, Rudolf Hess, in a simple khaki tunic with the plain Iron Cross.

A great coup for those with pro-German sympathies was the acquisition of the Mitford sisters to the cause. The six daughters of Baron Redesdale were a formidable group. The eldest, Nancy, would become a successful novelist in the Forties and Fifties. The youngest, Deborah, married Andrew Cavendish, later Duke of Devonshire, in the year of the Hess flight. But it was the middle sisters, Diana, then Lady Guinness, and Unity Valkyrie, who grabbed the Hitler headlines.

'No one could sit long,' drooled Ward Price, 'in the same room as Miss Unity Mitford without noticing her. Her golden hair, fair skin and blue eyes attain the highest standards of that Nordic beauty which Germans especially admire.'[5]

Unity had been attending art classes in Munich in 1934 and used the same restaurant near Hitler's modest little flat where he used to lunch. He asked her over for coffee and an odd relationship began. Both Mitfords regularly appeared at Nazi rallies, proudly wearing the swastika lapel badges given to them by Hitler himself. 'There is no more human trait in Hitler's character than the pleasure he takes in the light-hearted company of these typical young Englishwomen of today.'[6]

Ward Price was surely stretching credulity a little when he refers to the Mitfords as 'typical' in any sense, but he may be right when he claims that it was from them that Hitler learned a great deal about England and the English.

Unity was still in Germany when war was declared. The 'Storm Troop Maiden' as the Nazis christened her, walked into the English Garden in Munich and put a bullet through her head. Astonishingly she survived and the newspapers of the day show a pale, wild-eyed young woman carried by stretcher from the cross-channel ferry at Folkestone on 30 January 1940, her hair trained carefully over the gunshot wound in her right temple. She was the second beautiful girl around Hitler to shoot herself. On 18 September 1931, Geli Raubal, the future Führer's niece and the only woman he is said to have loved, wrapped one of her uncle's Walther 6.35mm revolvers in a damp towel to muffle the sound and put a bullet through her heart. Unlike Unity, she did not survive. Those closest to Hitler agreed he was never the same again.

Ward Price catalogues Hitler's rise to power, careful to understand, but not necessarily condone, all his actions. He glides smoothly over the Jewish problem and explains the Night of the Long Knives by Hitler's need to avoid civil war in Germany. He drip-feeds the superiority of the German people: ' "Team-work" in national affairs receives much lip-service in Britain . . . The Nazis not only preach this ideal, but achieve it . . .'[7] Even the German landscape is better: 'The derelict, thistle-studded, water-logged fields of the British countryside have no counterpart in Germany.'[8]

But it is in his comments on Hitler's views on foreign policy that Ward Price is more fascinating. The Condor Legion[9] dropped its bombs on Spain, he says, because if the Bolsheviks took the country, France would be next and that would leave Germany surrounded by the most deadly enemy of mankind, 'and Bolshevist rule would have reached from the Amur River to the Rhine'.[10] The 'political leprosy' of Bolshevism was only being kept out of British India by the eternal vigilance of the Japanese. 'The day may yet come,' Hitler once told Ward Price, 'when Britain will thank God that Germany has a strong army to defend Europe against Soviet Russia.'[11]

He maintains that there are good relationships among the *people* of both countries – it is only the vacillating and suspicious *Government* of Britain that has kept Hitler at arm's length. In particular, the Anglo–German Fellowship here and the Deutsch–Englische Gesellschaft in Berlin were making great strides forward.

The Fellowship was founded by E.W.D. Tennant 'and a small group of Englishmen with intimate knowledge of German affairs' on 2 October 1935. Its secretary was T.P. Conwell-Evans and its headquarters were near Sloane Square in London. In 1937, it had only 700 members, but the quality of those 700 cannot be denied. They were all professional or industrial leaders, three of them directors of the Bank of England and sixty of them members of one of the Houses of Parliament.

Hitler had written to Rothermere in May 1935 stressing the need for greater co-operation. In that it led to the Anglo–German naval agreement, it worked:

> I believe that my consistent mental attitude, my invariable principles and my unshakeable resolution will in the end succeed in enabling me to play a great and historical part towards the re-establishment of sound and permanent relations between the two great Germanic nations.
>
> Such an agreement between England and Germany would represent the weighty influence for peace and commonsense of 120,000,000 of the most valuable people in the world. The historically unique colonial aptitude and the naval power of Britain would be combined with that of one of the first military nations of the world.[12]

He had indeed been consistent. The international dreams in *Mein Kampf*, written twelve years earlier, follow much the same line: 'National destinies are firmly forged together only by the prospect of a common success in the sense of common gains, conquests; in short, of a mutual extension of power.' And he would go on being consistent. Even after the declaration of war, Hitler spoke to the Reichstag on 6 October 1939:

> I have devoted no less effort to the achievement of Anglo-German understanding, nay, more than that, of

an Anglo-German friendship. At no time and in no
place have I ever acted contrary to British interests . . .
I believe even today that there can only be real peace
in Europe and throughout the world if Germany and
England come to an understanding.

Goering, bemedalled and extrovert, had hunted foxes with
Halifax, the British Foreign Secretary and rival of Churchill. He
knew several members of the British aristocracy quite well,
something most of them were probably anxious to play down
after the outbreak of war. Ward Price's summary of Goering's
conversations have an uncannily familiar ring to them:

> 'We respect and like the British race,' he has said to me
> repeatedly, 'You are akin to us by blood and we wish
> to see you a strong and powerful nation . . . With our
> two countries in agreement, the peace of Europe
> would be on unshakeable foundations. Who could
> stand against the British fleet and the German army?
> There is nothing on earth about which Britain and
> Germany need quarrel. We should even be prepared to
> guarantee British interests in every part of the globe.
> But you must respond by conceding to us the position
> on the Continent to which we are entitled by our
> national qualities and situation, just as you are entitled
> to maintain British standards and influence
> throughout your great world-Empire.'[13]

This was precisely the peace deal that Hess brought with him
in May 1941. It was exactly what Goering had told Ward Price,
exactly what Hitler was consistently telling the world. Yet
Ivone Kirkpatrick, the Duke of Hamilton and Lord Simon, all
of whom were sent to interrogate Hess in May 1941, dismissed
it as the product, ultimately, of a disordered mind. The
western powers were still keeping Hitler at arm's length.

Exactly at what point admiration for Germany's economic miracle gave way to appeasement is difficult to pinpoint. Hitler left the League of Nations. Britain barely raised an eyebrow. Mussolini invaded Abyssinia in his desperate quest for an overseas empire to resurrect the glory that was Rome. His bombers rained death down on natives armed with spears and shields and when the Abyssinian Emperor Haile Selassie made his dignified plea to the League, nobody listened. Sir Samuel Hoare, the Foreign Secretary, whose name would feature in some people's versions of the Hess story six years later, went further and in the Hoare–Laval Pact, Italy was to keep the best parts of the little African kingdom it had conquered. Leaders of all the major churches condemned Hoare as a cynical opportunist, but it was clear from the start that several of Hoare's Cabinet colleagues were perfectly happy to go along with the pact until Anthony Eden, then Minister for the League, forced a showdown. Stanley Baldwin, the Prime Minister at the end of 1935, gave Hoare an ultimatum – apologize or go. Hoare went in what Baldwin called 'an error of judgement'. Months earlier, however, the Government had signed an accord with Germany which enabled Hitler to rebuild his fleet. One Paris newspaper asked the question: 'Does London imagine that Hitler has renounced any of the projects indicated in his book *Mein Kampf*? If so, the illusion of our friends across the Channel is complete.'[14]

Churchill was still almost a lone voice in 1936, the year that saw Hitler invade the Rhineland, when he spoke of –

> the lamentable weakness into which our defences have been allowed to fall. Errors, feebleness, vacillation there have, no doubt, been in the current policy of the government, but the underlying cause of our impotence is the improvident neglect of our defensive strength in years when every other great nation was arming sternly and resolutely.[15]

By the time Neville Chamberlain became Prime Minister in 1938, the only road left, short of the total war so dreaded by Britain and France, was appeasement. He was old-fashioned, not yet attuned (unlike Hitler) to the power of the media, and he still believed in honour and pledges, especially in foreign policy. But underneath the apparently duped exterior, there is some evidence to suggest that he never trusted Hitler and may have been working secretly behind the scenes to oust him from power. Goebbels in his diary remembered the Prime Minister as being 'ice cold', the 'English fox' and, in the short term at least – before the Pyrrhic nature of the victory became apparent – it was Chamberlain, not Hitler, who was the winner at Munich.

Furthermore Chamberlain was Prime Minister when the Venlo affair took place. The idea was to inveigle a senior Wehrmacht officer, with anti-Nazi leanings, to London in an attempt to arrange a coup to oust Hitler.* Chamberlain's involvement in this is unknown, but if he was privy to it, it stands in marked contrast to the image of an appeasing lamb to the slaughter which still attaches to him. Information on this is scanty at present and may well lie in the same locked files which gather dust in Whitehall and tell the real story of the Hess flight; but at the time, certainly, none of it leaked.

The aristocracy and gentry, those impressed by the Hitler miracle, followed their Prime Minister's lead at face value. Chamberlain knew as did Churchill, fuming in the wilderness in the late Thirties, how woefully unprepared Britain was for war. Fear, self-preservation, self-interest – these are the motives which best explain the existence of a peace party in Britain on the eve of Hitler's war.

Oswald Mosley is perhaps the best-known, yet most enigmatic 'fellow traveller of the Right' in pre-war Britain. When he died in 1980 he was, nevertheless, described as a brilliant,

* The Venlo affair is discussed in more detail in Chapter 5.

flamboyant and handsome politician. Mosley was an aristocrat, educated at Winchester and Sandhurst, commissioned in the 16th Lancers, who became Conservative MP for Harrow in 1918. By 1922 he was an Independent and two years later spectacularly joined Ramsay MacDonald's Labour Party, only to be defeated at the polls. Successful in 1926, he represented Smethwick and was Chancellor of the Duchy of Lancaster in 1929 and 1930. That was the year he founded the New Party, appalled at the rise in unemployment and the 'spineless apathy' of the Socialists.

Mosley's plans to reduce unemployment included huge borrowing, which was wholly unrealistic in the economic climate of the time. His New Party spoke of 'vitality and manhood' and promised to transform Parliament 'from a talk-shop to a workshop', but every one of his candidates failed at the polls, and the Labour Party was at pains to distance itself from him. In September 1931, Socialists pelted Mosley with stones and chased him through the streets of Glasgow.

By now his British Union of Fascists was becoming a reality. His visit to Italy in April 1933 had a profound effect on him and he and his followers adopted the black shirts from then on. Contrary to Mussolini's *fascisti* however, British Fascists pursued virulent anti-Semitism and delighted in the running street battles with the Left which characterized the SA in Germany. At the end of that April, seven Mosleyites found themselves in the thick of an angry crowd in Piccadilly Circus. The boycott of Jewish shops in Germany had just been announced by Hitler and Mosley was determined to show his solidarity, unimpressed by other Fascists' lukewarm support of the Nazis' move. The Jews of Whitechapel retaliated with anti-German posters until the police removed them. While the Nazis burnt Communist literature and 'Un-German' books, like Erich Remarque's classic *All Quiet on the Western Front*, in their celebrated orgies of pyromania, Mosley's blackshirts and the Jews met to crack heads in the East End.

Whereas the gangsterism of both the SA and the SS were

officially sanctioned in Germany, the British official line was to oppose strong-arm, bully-boy tactics with ever grimmer determination. By early 1934, Mosley was demanding a 'modern dictatorship' armed with the very powers – the Enabling Law – that Hitler was introducing into the Reich. A fascist rally at Earl's Court, attended by 2,000, caused serious alarm in Westminster. Casualties were numerous and a monstrous regiment of judo-trained women began to beat up females in the crowd. 'Red agitators from the ghettoes' were blamed by Mosley for starting the violence. Sir Kingsley Wood warned that 'certain movements in the country might very well shake parliamentary government in the future'.

In October 1936 Mosley's 7,000 descended on the East End; lorries were overturned, a tailor and his son were thrown through a plate-glass window. In repeated mounted charges by the police, eighty people were injured and eighty-four arrests were made. The Government responded with a Public Order Act three months later which was effectively the death knell of the British Union of Fascists. Although the organization was not banned, marching which was likely to provoke disorder and the wearing of uniforms was, at least temporarily, outlawed.

In Liverpool in October 1937, the ban lifted, Mosley was busy again. This time 'Britain's Hitler' was hit by a well-aimed bottle in the second fist fight in a week. Using coster barrows as barricades, the Mosleyites had already marched through South London. A quarter of the marchers were women. In both rallies – and in many ways this single act helps to explain why neither side took root in Britain – both Fascists and Communists stood to attention to sing the National Anthem. Only their salutes were different.

Unsurprisingly, Mosley strenuously opposed the waging of war on Germany in 1939 and unsurprisingly too, he was watched like a hawk by a country obsessed with the existence of an active fifth column and arrested in May 1940 under

Regulation 18B.* Thirty-three others, belonging to organizations which 'have had associations with the enemy' were also
interned, among them Captain Archibald Ramsay, President
of the Right Club and MP for Peebles, and John Beckett, secretary of the British People's Party. All this of course was in
response to the westward thrust of Hitler's blitzkrieg, driving
the British to Dunkirk by the end of the month. Three thousand German-born citizens were interned and adult male
aliens of whatever nationality had to follow a strict curfew
and report daily to the police.

Ultimately, the violence associated with the BUF played a
major part in its failure. Those in influence who shared their
ideals abhorred the violence which so often marred the meetings, so the BUF was never going to attract the upper class
power base it needed. The events at Olympia represent something of a watershed in this respect, as prior to the meeting
violence had been much less prevalent.

In 1933, Hess assisted with the setting up of the Ausland
organization which was eventually to reach forty-four countries. Within each country there were further subdivisions. In
Britain the head office was in Cleveland Terrace, London, but
there were subsidiary offices in Birmingham, Liverpool,
Glasgow and Belfast. Altogether there were some 600 groups
throughout the world, the greedy fingers of the Reich ever
reaching out. As James Murphy writes in *Who Sent Rudolf Hess?*
'This meant that every domestic employee of German nationality and every German clerk employed in a bank or counting
house was bound to register with the local Nazi group.'

Not until 1940 were these aliens rounded up and interned. For
seven years therefore, a vast amount of information was transmitted back to Berlin. For example German translators passed
pending patent applications to their local group, who passed them

---

* Regulation 18B was part of the Defence of the Realm Act which
was designed to eliminate potential *agents provocateurs*.

on to the Ministry of Trade in Berlin, enabling German technology to stay half a step ahead. Although there is doubt about the effectiveness of this intelligence gathering (after all, the central thesis of this book is that Hess could be *misled* by disinformation), the second aspect of the Ausland organization was highly effective. Every German non-resident paid three shillings a month to the Nazi Party back home. Even allowing for a third of this amount to defray local expenses, Murphy calculated in 1941 that the annual contribution pre-war was a staggering £6 billion.

As opposed to the formal Foreign Ministry apparatus of state, with its embassies and diplomats, Hess's people were far more ubiquitous, ensuring an almost blanket coverage at street level, not unlike Dansey's Z System* in various European countries, flexible and informed. The loyalty of the Auslanders was assured by potential or actual threats against their German-based relatives, a principle adopted first by Italian Fascists who had a similar organization.

A list of rules was drawn up for them. Every Auslander had to obey the laws of his host nation and he was never to interfere, even in conversation, in the politics of the country whose hospitality he enjoyed. He was to remember at all times that he was a member of the Nazi Party, to do credit to the movement and to Germany and to be 'just and honourable, courageous and loyal' in all things. Every Auslander was 'a front-line fighter' for the ideals of the party – ideals he must know and understand. Cohesion and total support of National Socialism were essential. Books and periodicals were to be read, the local group should be close knit and single-minded in its purpose. But the simple fact was that after 1940 the Auslanders were in jail and in no position to liaise with Hess.

On the surface, Mosley would have been an obvious candidate to back Hess. But Mosley was not released until 1943 and

* See Chapter 5.

anyway it was the next layer down that Hess was interested in – not out-and-out Fascists, who were too few in number and not in any positions of influence in Britain, but the 'fellow travellers of the Right', whose existence is all the more shadowy because the travellers did a rapid U-turn with the outbreak of war.

So who made up this group of influential aristocrats, which Hess believed was waiting in Britain in 1941 to engineer a peace deal?

Nearly all the leading British protagonists in the case of Rudolf Hess owned property in the Lowlands of Scotland and were living within a fifty mile radius of one another on 10 May 1941. And perhaps it was not a random decision that the Luftwaffe made on the night of 13 August 1940 to drop parachutes, wireless transmitters, photographs, maps and lists of addresses of prominent people in this very area, as though to encourage insurrection against the Lowlanders' political masters south of the border.

Central to the Hess story is Douglas Douglas-Hamilton, the Marquess of Clydesdale who became the Duke of Hamilton and Brandon in 1940. 'What do you tell your wife,' he asked Churchill in May 1941, 'if a prostitute throws her arms around your neck?'[16] The prostitute of the Hess affair never quite left him and despite Churchill's attempt, both in the House and the Press, to exonerate him, rumours never quite disappeared that Hamilton had been responsible for Hess's arrival.

Born into an ancient and distinguished family in 1903, Hamilton was one of the most famous men in Scotland before the war. Educated at Eton and Oxford, he was Scottish middleweight boxing champion at a time when the public schools and universities still taught and prized such skills. He became the second-youngest MP in the Commons in December 1929 and was possibly uniquely distinguished in being a friend of both Ramsay MacDonald and Winston Churchill. The common interest of all three men was aviation and in the early Thirties Hamilton was an instructor with the Auxiliary Air Force. In the year that Hitler came to power, Hamilton was selected as chief pilot on the attempt to conquer Everest by air. His skill and powerful physique made him a natural choice and he succeeded admirably.

Hamilton travelled to Germany on several occasions. On one of them, in February 1935, he was forced to land because of bad weather at Mannheim and was detained in a locked room, only being released after a thorough interrogation. Mannheim, like Willi Messerschmitt's works at Augsburg, was a secret flying school for the Luftwaffe. Richard Griffiths in *Fellow Travellers of the Right* devotes a whole section to the role of aviation in mutual respect between Britons and Germans, each genuinely impressed by the other. Ever since 1913, when the Schneider Trophy was first contested, the two nations had been rivals. Obviously in the Great War, their flying skills were honed by the need to reconnoitre, fight and destroy, but after the war, aviation once again became friendly. Hess flew in races such as 'Round the Zugspietze' in the Thirties and the sport can be compared with the rich and rather eccentric round-the-world ballooning craze which has developed again today.

Hess believed he had met Hamilton via aviation. In 1936, both men were in Berlin for the Olympic Games. On the ground, the hero of the day was undoubtedly the 'Ebony Antelope', Jesse Owens, who gained Hitler's displeasure by winning so many medals at the expense of his Aryan super-heroes. It was at the banquet given for the International Committee on 11 August that a meeting may have taken place. Hamilton was at the table of Robert Ley, the German Labour Minister, and Hess was elsewhere in the room. Whereas it is certain that Hamilton met Hitler, Goering and von Ribbentrop, there is doubt over a direct link with Hess. 'Chips' Channon, MP and socialite in the 1930s, was under the impression that the two knew each other but since both Hamilton and Hess later denied it, there seems little point in challenging the matter. A casual couple of hours over claret and coffee hardly made Hess and Hamilton conspirators in any venture, especially five years before their paths were to cross again. By then they had a go-between.

Hamilton was, however, no stranger to German politics and his links were many in the 1930s. He visited the South Tyrol in 1936, annexed by Italy after the Great War, but heavily populated with Germans. Hitler was wooing Mussolini at that stage and had no wish to jeopardize that relationship until he was holding all the cards. The assumption has been made that Hamilton was a member of the Anglo-German Fellowship, which held regular dinners and functions and produced its own newspaper. James Douglas-Hamilton maintains that his father attended only one such dinner and was never a member. The organization was innocuous at first, but its later dinners had swastika-decorated tablecloths and gave prominence to pro-Nazi speakers.

It is Hamilton's letter to *The Times* of October 1940 that has led many to believe in the man's complicity with Germans in general and perhaps Hess in particular:

Sir,

Many, like yourself, have had the opportunity of hearing a good deal of what the men and women of my generation are thinking. There is no doubt in any quarter, irrespective of party, that this country had no choice but to accept the challenge of Hitler's aggression against one country in Europe after another. If Hitler is right when he claims that the whole of the German nation is with him in his cruelties and treacheries, both within Germany and without, then this war must be fought to the bitter end. It may well last for many years, but the people of the British Empire will not falter in their determination to see it through.

But I believe that the moment the menace of aggression

and bad faith has been removed, war against Germany becomes wrong and meaningless. This generation is conscious that injustices were done to the German people in the era after the last war. There must be no repetition of that. To seek anything but a just and comprehensive peace to lay at rest the fears and discords in Europe would be a betrayal of our fallen.

I look forward to the day when a trusted Germany will again come into her own and believe that there is such a Germany, which would be loth to inflict wrongs on other nations such as she would not like to suffer herself. That day may be far off, but when it comes, then hostilities could and should cease, and all efforts be concentrated on righting the wrongs in Europe by free negotiations between the disputing parties, all parties binding themselves to submit their disputes to an impartial equity tribunal in case they cannot reach agreement.

We do not grudge Germany Lebensraum, provided that Lebensraum is not made the grave of other nations. We should be ready to search for and find a colonial settlement, just to all peoples concerned, as soon as there exist effective guarantees that no race will be exposed to being treated as Hitler treated the Jews on November 9th last year [sic.]* We shall, I trust, live to see the day when such a healing peace is negotiated between honourable men and the bitter memories of twenty-five years of unhappy tension between Germany and the Western democracies are wiped away in their responsible co-operation for building a better Europe.

Yours truly, Clydesdale.[17]

---

* Hamilton is referring to the grim events of the Kristallnacht. This occurred in 1938 and not, as he implies, 1939.

This letter can be, and has been, misconstrued. It was reported on German radio the same day. Perhaps the Haushofers heard it. Perhaps others, nearer to home, read the original. Perhaps it struck a chord, produced the spark of an idea. We shall return to the enigmatic Duke of Hamilton.

Hastings William Sackville Russell, the 12th Duke of Bedford, provides a stark constrast. The family seat of the Bedfords is Woburn Abbey, which was home to much of the extraordinary plotting in the Hess story. In common with many aristocratic families, young Russell grew up away from his parents, who were aloof and remote. His mother, Mary, discovered flying late in life and made record flights to India and the Cape in 1929 and 1930. She disappeared over the North Sea in 1937. The Duchess found her son 'a cold and unloving little creature' and he was a disappointment to both parents. As a boy at Norris Castle in the Isle of Wight, the future 12th Duke remembered that 'Queen Victoria called and I was commissioned to offer her a plate of buns'. He was at Woburn when taught how to kiss Queen Mary's hand so as 'not to make a noise like the orfes eating a piece of bread'.

Yet Russell was always a nonconformist, and was bullied whilst at Eton. His solution, predating the Appeasement mentality of his adulthood, was to buy the bullies off with his generous 'tuck' allowance – 'If thine enemy hungers, feed him.' Churchill's comment on Appeasers was that they resembled those who fed crocodiles in the hope that they would be eaten last.

The Marquis of Tavistock (as the heir to the Bedford estates is known) refused to enlist on the outbreak of the Great War as he had hated his time with the Territorials and 'by some blunder on the battlefield [might] perhaps sacrifice the lives of my men needlessly'. The 11th Duke threatened to disinherit his son and wished never to see him again as a result. Uninterested in sports and games, the traditional pastimes of the younger aristocracy, he at least shared his father's passion for rare birds and animals. He disliked the vast, cavernous Woburn Abbey and preferred to live in Crowsholt, a house in the village nearby. His real love, however, was Cairnsmore, a country seat in Galloway that his parents had leased soon after he was born. When war broke out in 1939, this was the Duke's residence.

By that time Bedford was regarded as another notable eccentric. He had done a great deal of charity work in the depressed Thirties, but his loud and frequent espousal of 'social credit' and the British People's Party lost him considerable credibility. It is likely that Bedford's admiration for Germany at this time stemmed from its apparent economic miracle. The doctrine of social credit, propounded by a Scot, Major C.H. Douglas, advocated the use of a 'national dividend' or 'money for nothing' so that surplus goods might be bought and consumed. (Such a scheme was being promoted in Alberta, Canada in 1935 where a Social Credit Party was in power.) In Germany, Dr Hjalmar Schacht, Hitler's Minister of Economics, was carrying out the sort of scheme that Bedford had in mind. 'His creation of credit,' writes William Shirer, 'in a country that had little liquid capital and almost no financial reserves was the work of a genius, or – as some said – of a master manipulator.'[18]

Bedford formed the British People's Party in the summer of 1939 and contested a by-election at Hythe with the likes of John Beckett, formerly a Mosleyite, and Ben Green, a former Labour MP. At the outbreak of war, Bedford adopted a firm pacifist position. Hitler had re-armed, he said, '. . . because he suspected that the financiers and politicians of the democracies would never, of their own free will, allow Germany economic justice, and in this belief he was probably quite correct.'[19] More damningly, he wrote, 'The decision of our Government and of President Roosevelt to pick a quarrel with him [Hitler] was a tragedy.'[20]

Had Bedford not been a peer of the realm, he might well have been interned as a conscientious objector or under the 18B Regulation and Defence of the Realm Act.

When Rudolf Hess was discussing with his friends the Haushofers the possibility of a peace mission to Britain, the correspondence that survives refers to 'old Ian Hamilton or the other Hamilton'. The 'other Hamilton' is probably Clydesdale; 'old Ian Hamilton' is General Sir Ian, a hero of the Great War.

Ian Hamilton was born the son of a captain in the 92nd Foot, the Gordon Highlanders, who were stationed on the island of Corfu, in January 1853. With his father in the army and his mother a Gort (John Gort was Chief of the Imperial General Staff in the late 1930s) a military career was inevitable. Before admission to Sandhurst however, Hamilton spent some time in Dresden in the care of a General Dammers, where he became fluent in German. The sycophantic *Celebrities of the Army*, published in 1902, records his military career. He served on the staff of Lord Roberts – 'Bobs' of Kandahar – at Madras; on the Nile expedition to relieve Gordon at Khartoum; and commanded a brigade in the Tirah Campaign in which Lieutenant Winston Churchill first saw action. In the Boer War, he commanded a Mounted Infantry Division, apparently with great courage.

Hamilton's Waterloo, however, was Gallipoli. Churchill's gamble on the 'soft under-belly of Europe' paid off against the Italians in the Second World War, but a similar assault on Turkey in 1915 met with stiffer resistance than was expected. Hamilton was the commanding officer, but the planning had not been thorough enough and amphibious operations were then in their infancy. The result was appalling casualties and a humiliating withdrawal. No one at the time realized how close we had come to breaking through to Constantinople, the ultimate target. It was just as well – the irony of the near-success makes the loss of life all the more galling.

Still deeply respected as a gallant soldier, Hamilton became an active promoter of the British Legion, and president of its Scottish division in 1931.

The letters he wrote to *The Times* and the books he produced were increasingly pacifist in tone, advocating a rapprochement with Germany. His main concern was to avoid the suffering of the last war, which he had seen only too closely at V Beach and in Suvla Bay.* This was a sentiment widely held in inter-war Britain, when maimed and crippled ex-servicemen were an everyday sight. Hamilton played host to visiting Germans through the Legion and in that capacity visited Munich in 1938 where he was fêted by Rudolf Hess at his family home. He went to meet Hitler and spent the night at the Berghof. He is shown, deep in earnest conversation with Hitler, at Berchtesgaden in the August of 1938 on the cover of the *Anglo–German Review* for that month. In 1939, Hamilton was living at Lennoxlove House in Lothian, now the home of the Duke of Hamilton.

The 8th Duke of Buccleuch was among the major landowners in the country. His principal estates lay in the hunting county of Northamptonshire and at Drumlanrig Castle in Dumfries. Walter John Montagu-Douglas-Scott was born in 1894 and like so many peers' sons attended Eton and Oxford. Before he inherited the title of Buccleuch in 1935 he was MP for Roxburgh and Selkirk, and Lord Steward to the King. According to Cambridge historian John Costello, Churchill dismissed him from this post in 1940, probably because his insistence that peace should be negotiated was becoming too loud and frequent. Certainly, lords like Buccleuch and Brocket, who had visited Hitler, could be placed in the 'self-interest' category among the British

---

* Both hotly contested landing areas in the Gallipoli peninsula.

peerage. These men were not Nazis nor even Nazi sympathizers; but they may genuinely have doubted whether by 1940–41 Britain was militarily capable of winning the war.

The 7th Duke of Montrose is almost a carbon copy of Buccleuch. His education followed the same pattern – Eton and Oxford, arguably themselves bastions of the Right. Some historians believe that Montrose was actually a member of Archibald Ramsay's Right Club, though this now seems doubtful. His ancestral home was at Anchoar, Drymen, near Glasgow, within a few miles of the spot where Hess's plane ploughed into the heather.

When discussing Anglo–Nazi connections at this time the figure of Prince Edward, Duke of Windsor, is hard to ignore. His and Wallis Simpson's unfortunate flirtation with the Third Reich has given rise to a multitude of speculations as to their activities before and during the war. The Duke's involvement in the Hess case is tangential. He was staying near Lisbon when peace moves were being suggested which might have meant Hess flying to neutral Portugal rather than hostile Scotland. There is no hard evidence to suggest that this ever took place, except for one telegram now regarded generally as a forgery.[21]

When Lord Simon wrote his memoirs, many years after interviewing Rudolf Hess, he had to admit a grudging sympathy for a man who had so misunderstood the temper of the British people. Ian Hamilton, Bedford, Buccleuch and Montrose were eccentric pacifists perhaps, but they did not approve of the Hitler regime once war had been declared. They were, to a man and woman, patriots and proud of their British heritage. The point is that it was in someone's interests to pretend to Rudolf Hess that they were not.

CHAPTER 5

The Spymasters

'The whole point of a secret service is that it should be secret.'
This line from Compton Mackenzie's spy novel *Water on the
Brain* may be a blinding glimpse of the obvious, but in these
days when Britain's secret service is dogged with 'whistle-
blowers' and we know the name of the man who runs it and he
advertises for spies in the newspapers ... It wasn't quite like
that in 1941.

The two principal agencies of the secret service at the
outbreak of the Second World War were MI5 and MI6. MI5
was the 'home' service, MI6 dealt with foreign matters. At that
time there was an urgent need to expand MI5. Undoubtedly
since 1933 there had been a shift of emphasis; the Communist
threat had been superseded by the Nazi one, but both needed
watching, thus increasing the tension in MI5. Nigel West esti-
mates that in September 1939, the organization had some
seventy-five staff working out of their headquarters at
Millbank. They were responsible for the country's internal
security, which meant monitoring 71,600 registered aliens and
attempting to trace many more who were not registered. A
quiet, but nevertheless urgent, recruitment campaign began,
targeting largely the sharper brains in the City rather than the
more youthful and maverick cohorts from the universities. It
was from this influx that the secret protagonists of the Hess

case emerged. The outbreak of war also saw a geographical move for MI5 to enable it to accommodate its new staff.

Ten days before war was declared, the younger 'Borstal' inmates of Wormwood Scrubs were removed to Feltham and the War Department (in fact MI5) moved in. The heavy iron doors were far from suitable for an office full of scuttling bureaucrats and private, whispered conversations echoed from floor to floor in anything but total secrecy. The joke abounded that the conductor of the No. 72 bus that ran past the front gates would shout out 'All change for the Scrubs and MI5'.

The solution was the smaller, and far more secluded Victorian mansion at Latchmere House in a cul-de-sac off Ham Common. Already owned by the War Department and intended as a convalescent home for officers after the horrors of the Great War trenches, it came to be used by MI5 to interrogate suspected enemy agents. Latchmere House was given the official name of Camp 020 – the Roman numerals XX for 20 giving rise to the term 'double cross'. Agents were to be 'turned', to be used against the Germans by feeding them disinformation fed to them subtly by their interrogators at MI5.[1] It was here that the 'Hanging Committee' met, in circumstances still shrouded in mystery. They alone, without consideration of habeas corpus, defence counsel or a jury for the defendant, decided the fate of spies. Only one man was acquitted – fifteen others died by the rope at Wandsworth or Pentonville and a sixteenth, Josef Jakobs, a German officer, was shot by firing squad at the Tower.

In May 1940, one year before the Hess flight, Winston Churchill kissed rings at Buckingham Palace. One of his first acts as Prime Minister was to fire Vernon Kell, then head of MI5. The man's 'retirement' had been trumpeted before, in the Twenties, to lull subversives into a sense of false security, but this time, it was for real. Why Churchill sacked him is unknown – it may simply have been a mistake. There was an element of schoolboy games about MI5, an amateur spirit smacking of pranks in the dorm, of which the new Prime Minister disapproved. Kell was of retirement age – as of course was Churchill – and suffered from asthma, but there is no evidence that his efficiency was in doubt. Peter Padfield conjectures that Kell was simply too set in his ways – 'a terrific anti-bolshevik' whereas what Churchill wanted was a terrific anti-Nazi. Certainly, three days before the Kell bombshell was dropped, Oswald Mosley of the British Fascists, Captain Archibald Ramsay MP of the Right Club and Admiral Sir Barry Domville, leader of the Link, were all arrested under Regulation 18B and held without trial.*

MI6, or the Secret Intelligence Service (SIS), as an external operation, gathered information via what today would be called listening posts, in many countries. During the Twenties and Thirties MI6 had set up a large number of 'passport offices' throughout Europe and around the world, which served as a front for a whole host of secret observational activities.

As the Nazi grip on Europe extended, these passport offices lost all credence. The deluge of refugees and mass migration of Jews swamped the offices with the actual work which was their cover – agents found themselves buried in paperwork of visas, work permits and a whole variety of travel documents. Financial irregularities in certain offices had not helped the situation and by the late 1930s there was a desperate need for flexibility. This was provided by Claude Dansey, an ambitious intelligence officer from MI5.

Professor Hugh Trevor-Roper describes Dansey as 'an utter shit, corrupt, incompetent, but with a certain low cunning'. Edward Crankshaw, an agent who was MI5's Russian expert in the first war, called him 'the sort of man who gave spying a bad name'. Dansey's solution – known as the 'Z System' – was to

---

* The Link was an organization founded by Domville in 1938 to promote closer relations between Germany and Britain. It produced a journal *The Anglo-German Review*, the circulation of which probably never exceeded 400.

plant trusted friends in key countries under the cover of working for legitimate international companies such as Menoline Limited. By 1938, the Z System was established throughout Europe. The Venlo fiasco destroyed it.

Major Richard Stevens (a new operative in charge of the passport office in The Hague), and Captain Payne Best (using the cover of an import-export business at 15 Nieuwe Vitleg, one of Dansey's Z operations) walked into a trap neatly laid for them by the Abwehr, the German secret service. They let Stevens and Best believe that there was an anti-Hitler faction at work in the upper echelons of the Wehrmacht, which wanted the Führer out of the way and a junta of officers to run the Reich.* It was a curious inversion of the Hess affair two years later. At a meeting in no-man's land between Holland and Germany at the town of Venlo, the British agents were kidnapped at gunpoint and their chauffeur killed.

Questioned, though apparently never tortured, first in Dusseldorf, then in Berlin, Stevens in particular seems to have given the Abwehr a great deal of covert information. The chumminess and old boy network of recruitment among SIS operatives meant that all of them knew a great deal about the whole institution rather than merely their own part of it. The amount and detail of information that the pair parted with is astonishing; names, code-names, telephone numbers, addresses, even down to the fact that Stewart Menzies, soon to be the new head of MI6, pronounced his name 'Mingis' in the Scots way. The Abwehr believed that more could have been acheived if the seizure of Stevens and Best had not taken place so soon, but there had been a bomb attempt on Hitler's life in his beloved Bürgerbraükeller in Munich and the Führer

---

* Ironically, of course, this mirrored fact. As the war dragged on and the tide turned against Germany, various key members of the Wehrmacht such as Rommel and von Stauffenberg literally took their lives into their hands to attempt Hitler's assassination.

believed Himmler's own propaganda that the British, in fact probably Stevens and Best, were behind it.

This could have been Hitler's excuse to march into Holland – the neutral Dutch were collaborating with the recalcitrant, shifty British. The Dutch capitulated in five days. Richard Deacon (Donald McCormick), spywriter and himself involved in British Intelligence during the war, says, 'By the time the Germans had invaded the Low Countries in the spring of 1940, Britain was left with practically no effective Intelligence service in Europe.'[2] He goes further, claiming that Stevens and Best had virtually destroyed an entire organization in a single afternoon.

Into those bleak days stepped Stewart Menzies, 'Churchill's Spymaster', who was appointed to head MI6, as 'C', weeks after the Venlo incident took place. A cavalry officer and no-nonsense Scot, his vast experience in Intelligence work by 1939 got him the job, although Churchill, on the appointment board, may well have preferred a naval man (Churchill was at that time First Lord of the Admiralty). In the early days, there is little doubt that Menzies suffered from his association with the appeasement years of Chamberlain. He was also linked with the Venlo affair, as he 'ran' Stevens and Best. More interestingly, he was linked with the Hess affair.

The Naval Intelligence Division (NID) – the naval branch of the secret service – recruited outside the services. In the whirlwind foreign policy of the outbreak of war, fresh minds were needed, minds not constrained by the conventions of Intelligence work. Cipher breakers, propagandists, forgers, all of them played their part and nowhere more deviously than in the game of black propaganda played with increasing expertise as the war went on. NID's most famous catch was Ian Fleming (renowned in the Cold War years as the creator of James Bond) from the London stockbrokers Rowe and Pitman. But more crucially for this story among the recruits to the Secret Services was Walter Stewart Roberts, listed in the

Foreign Office files as having served from 1940–48. He is a shadowy figure, as are many of the men involved with Rudolf Hess, and we can only speculate precisely why Roberts was recruited before he went on to become Deputy Director-General of Political Intelligence in 1946.

Certainly, he had all the right credentials. He was an old Etonian and a schoolfriend of Stewart Menzies. He was a Cambridge graduate with all the kudos that that entailed. His cousin Patrick had been a high flyer in the Foreign Office. He was a successful City stockbroker with the firm of Silverston. And, perhaps in some ways the most important of all, his cousin and his aunt, Mrs Violet Roberts, were personal friends of Professor-General Karl Haushofer and his family, who in turn were friends of Rudolf Hess, the Stellvertreter. On such contacts does espionage turn; on such contacts are wars won.

Air Intelligence was the newest branch of the pre-war secret service. With the international camaraderie that flying invoked, Air Intelligence's head, Frederick Winterbotham and his German agent, William de Ropp, were able to mingle with the Nazi elite. Winterbotham met Hess on several occasions later and wrote in *Secret and Personal*: 'I found a certain depth of character and level of intelligence which was often missing in other Nazi leaders. There was a latent sensitivity in place of the ruthless efficiency of the Goerings and the Himmlers . . . His flight to England [sic] during the war was quite in character.' At the outbreak of war, Winterbotham became responsible for liaison among the various departments of the secret service, the go-between for Menzies and the odd, quirky group of intellectuals who became the 'Ultra' code breakers at Bletchley Park.*

---

* All enemy codes obtained from whatever source were processed at Bletchley. Thanks to Naval Intelligence rather than the SIS, the Ultra group were usually marginally ahead of Enigma, the German code-breaking machine.

Prior to Churchill's appointment as P.M. Chamberlain had commissioned Maurice Hankey, Minister without Portfolio, to prepare a report on the state of the complex, overlapping and rather disorganized department that Menzies had inherited. This report, submitted to Churchill, the new broom in his first month in office, led to the creation of a new Intelligence unit that would 'set Europe ablaze'. Churchill wanted agents in Europe to pierce what he called 'the veil of the unknown'. But that veil descended over the machinery created in the summer of 1940 here in England and it is that veil that has screened the truth of the Hess case from researchers for so long.

The organization which was to 'set Europe ablaze' in Churchill's phrase was the Special Operations Executive (SOE), previously operating in two separate divisions, SO1 (concerned with 'words') and SO2 (concerned with 'deeds'). In the confusion of the time and since, SO2 has become synonymous with the entire organization, because this is the more exotic element, the dropping of astonishingly brave agents behind enemy lines to wreak whatever havoc they could.

M.R.D. Foot, SOE's official historian, writes:

> Unhappily, deception was plunged in the deepest secrecy at the time and has not been much illuminated by later disclosures ... SOE is often accused of having played a part in one or other of the deception schemes that had to form a large part of British strategy – had to, because the post-war governments had followed their electorates' wishes too closely and had left the country under-armed to face its actual Axis opponents on real battlefields.[3]

Foot found, when he produced his work on SOE thirty years ago, 'a state of authentic confusion'. There was no central registry, papers had been removed and destroyed by fire. Richard Deacon was prepared, unlike some historians who cling to a blind faith in 'a paper trail' of hard evidence, to take this situation to its logical conclusion: 'The truth about SOE will not be easily established even when the files are fully available to all researchers.'[4]

The work of SO1 in particular is shrouded in mystery. Richard Deacon merely says that 'the propaganda division of SOE was situated at Woburn'. Anthony Cave Brown, in 795 pages on Stewart Menzies, does not mention SO1 at all. Even Professor F.H. Hinsley, in the definitive history of World War Two Intelligence, makes only two single line comments on the unit.

Rather more detail is provided by Ellic Howe, a printer whose talents were used within SO1. The Electra group, incorporated in SO1 and based in the building of the same name along the Victoria Embankment, had been set up before the outbreak of war to provide both 'white' and 'black' propaganda outside the remit of the newly created Ministry of Information. The general feeling was that a fifth column may well have been operating in the country, establishing links with the Germans by radio, submarine landings at night or a thousand and one other communication methods that fear is heir to. The Ministry of Information was yet another example of the vital need for the Government to keep a grip on the psychological war. After all, as the posters said, 'Careless talk costs lives.'

To wear down the British spirit, which the Mass Observation Unit (a sort of early market research in morale) gloomily saw was at best indifferent and at worst depressed, 'Radio Caledonia' sought to stir up Scotsmen to a separate peace. It was done by a German with an appalling Scots accent and played 'Auld Lang Syne' as a signature tune. Such radio propaganda also encouraged Englishmen to write demoralizing chain letters and boo Churchill whenever he appeared on newsreels in the cinemas. One woman who said that Hitler was a better ruler than the Prime Minister went to jail for her candour.

'White' propaganda refers to the sort of posters that are reproduced today by the Imperial War Museum and the Blitz Museum in London – 'Be Like Dad, Keep Mum', 'Digging For Victory' and so on. Leaflets printed by Ellic Howe rained like confetti from bombers in the early months of the war over Germany, until it was realized that such flimsy propaganda efforts were hardly worth the loss of even one plane or one man.

'Black' propaganda, however, was another thing altogether. As Howe says in *The Black Game*, 'There were various shades of negritude, ranging from dense black to grey . . . but subversion – the disruption of the enemy's will and power to fight on – was the common factor in all the output intended for German ears or eyes.'

Even though SO1 was part of the Political Intelligence Division (PID) of the Foreign Office, its strategies and schemes were entirely secret. 'Nothing perpetrated by the black specialists,' writes Howe, 'could possibly be acknowledged by HM Government as being of British origin. Indeed, the black operators could do a great many things that would have been absolutely impossible for respectable white propagandists.'

The Electra House team, headed by Sir Campbell Stuart, of the Committee of Imperial Defence, comprised: Captain R.J. Herbert Shaw as Head of Section; Lt. Colonel Reginald Dallas Brooks, Liaison Officer between SO1 and other Intelligence units; Robert Walmsley as the German expert; and four journalists who presumably could be relied upon to create disinformation for Germany's benefit. They were Anthony Gishford, Cecil Sprigge, Valentine Williams and the Honourable Leo Russell. There is every reason to suppose that these men were chosen for their knowledge of European affairs.

Gishford, a friend of Campbell Stuart's, worked for the group of newspapers owned by Lord Camrose – the *Sunday Times* and the *Daily Telegraph*. Cecil Sprigge was the *Manchester Guardian*'s Italian specialist, Russell was the advertising director of

Illustrated Newspapers Ltd and Valentine Williams wrote for the *Daily Mail*. He was also, interestingly, the author of a spy novel, *The Man With the Club Foot*. Only Robert Walmsley was an outsider, in this strange, quirky old-boy network from which spies traditionally have been recruited. Ellic Howe notes that in the files he consulted for *The Black Game* is a note that Walmsley 'wrote a "Dear Sir" letter stating his qualifications' [as a German expert]. Such an approach was highly unusual in such organizations at such a desperate time.

Electra House was too central to be safe. Despite the actual lull of the 'phoney war', the assumption was that aerial bombing would start immediately and at the suggestion of Leo Russell, Electra House, its personnel and typewriters moved forty-three miles north-west to his relative's country home at Woburn Abbey. There was a deep irony that the house of the eccentric, pacifist 13th Duke of Bedford should be used to help win a war of which he disapproved. Indeed, it was specifically guaranteed that the tenancy would only take place if SO1 kept to the stables and did not set foot in the house itself. There was, of course, no danger of Bedford bumping into a black propagandist. He was living at Cairnsmore, his house in the Lowlands of Scotland.

SO1's personnel grew rapidly to sixty, a surreal situation in which all kinds of black propaganda were being dreamed up against an enemy that had yet to fire a shot. 'The atmosphere of the early days,' Walmsley remembered, 'was one of bustling amateurishness, and with one exception, almost complete ineffectualness.'[5]

In case the convolutions of the Hess lure seem too preposterous for the traditionalists to accept, the recent opening of Whitehall files make it quite clear that ludicrous ideas were not only entertained and discussed, but written down and classified. One particularly droll idea which I found among the available papers of SO1 was the plan to project offensive messages on to clouds over Germany by way of specially adapted searchlight beams. The scheme was only called off after the firm which had the technological capability for this, one based in Watford, put in an impossibly high tender for the work!

Some of the more bizarre assassination ideas in 'Operation Foxley' for instance involved poisoning Hitler's tea; as he was known to be a 'milk-first' man, any toxic discoloration would not be noticed. Then there was the possibility of impregnating his clothes with lethal bacteria – about 'a millionth of a gram' would prove fatal.

Among the more lurid examples of information-gathering was the file dated 18 July 1942 and marked 'Adults Only'. In this, Christian Weber, the Munich Gauleiter, features prominently with a marked penchant for naked girls on horseback. On file are tales, allegedly from deserters and captured agents, of girls strapped naked on a huge roulette wheel and obliged to have sex with the SS officer at whose position around the table the wheel stopped. Himmler is reported to have organized cult activities with opera singer Ursula Deinert. An officer named Ley regularly procured girls for senior SS men. Willie Brockman kept a number of teenaged boys on tap in East Prussia for his sexual pleasure, often dressing them as girls. Admiral Conrad Albrecht watched through a peep-hole as his sailors queued up to make love to his mistress. Dr Theodore Auer, German consul in Casablanca in the Forties, regularly cruised the beaches in search of Arab, French and even Jewish boys, thus neatly breaking every rule in the Nazi book. Sudeten evacuees who happened to be pre-pubescent and female found their way into the clutches of an officer named Brentman.

All this information was collected with a mixture of prudish shock, impish schoolboy humour and an inevitable air of 'I told you so.' How much of it was true is debatable, but all of it was useful in the black propaganda game. Material like this, exposing and shaming the Nazi elite, was produced to be disseminated among the Wehrmacht rank and file.

Even though the structure of SOE was essentially developed by Dr Hugh Dalton, the Labour Cabinet member who was Churchill's Minister of Economic Warfare, an increasing suspicion was growing in Cabinet among the Labour group, spearheaded by Clement Attlee. This was not helped when Churchill made his private secretary, Brendan Bracken, Minister of Information in 1941. Referred to as 'the Tory Thug', he typified the breed of man on whom Churchill relied. A public schoolboy himself, although his time at Harrow was hardly distinguished, Churchill naturally veered to the old-boy network from which SOE took its recruits, amateurish though he may have found them. They were unaccountable and what we have with SO1 in particular is a clique within a clique, in itself ' a riddle wrapped in the mystery inside the enigma'.*

The public-school image was one that Hitler, in particular, detested: 'The whole system is calculated to rear men of inflexible will and ruthless energy who regard intellectual problems as a waste of time but know human nature and how to dominate other men in the most unscrupulous fashion.'[6] Next in line as an example of pernicious Britishness came the Boy Scout movement (clearly a rival to the Hitler Youth!): '. . . for England [it] represents a camouflaged but powerful instrument of British cultural propaganda and an excellent source of information for the British Intelligence Service . . .'[7] One wonders how many of SOE had been Baden Powell's boys in their youth.

What do we know about the practitioners of the 'black art' at 'CHQ' or 'The Country' as Woburn was called? The outsider, Walmsley, was sent for on 17 March 1939 by a 'Major Douglas' who invited to meet him in response to his job application. Douglas was actually Major Lawrence Grand, an army officer

---

* Churchill's description of Soviet Russia.

running 'Section D' (for 'Destruction'), a sabotage unit within SIS. Walmsley was asked to suggest examples of black propaganda that Douglas could use. He suggested tampering with Foreign Office speeches and forging Nazi literature from Germany to its various Auslander organizations, which, had it ever been adopted, would have damaged one of Hess's particular interests. Grand wrote of his new protegé, 'He is considered to be the best German leaflet writer in the United Kingdom. He will shortly be coming to see CS [Campbell Stuart] and would be at our disposal in war.'[8]

On 18 April Walmsley met Stuart for the first time and was offered a job. He worked on the leaflets which Ellic Howe later printed on the outbreak of war, but much of his work seems to have been looking for policy direction in Nazi propaganda. When war was declared, Walmsley was one of a few of the team who were ordered to meet at the Sugarloaf Hotel in Dunstable. He drove there in an old Morris banger he had recently bought for £15, prior to moving on to Woburn where ten housemaids, four waitresses, two counter hands and two kitchen porters supplied by Joe Lyons catering company looked after the team.

Dallas Brooks, who would end his career as a Major-General, represented the military wing of the group and stayed at Electra House when the others moved to 'The Country'. An Australian, he returned home long after the war as Governor-General of Victoria. Percy Winner, a journalist attached to the the Office of Strategic Services (OSS)* summed up Brooks in this way: 'He is a formal, rather stuffy, not overbright individual who is immensely vain and susceptible to flattery. He carries out his tasks with a good deal of efficiency but completely lacks imagination or an awareness of the problems of political warfare.'[9]

---

* Political Warfare Executive's American counterpart.

Robert Walmsley, who knew him far better, found him on the contrary to be 'an immensely able political soldier'. Winner's gossipy comment is not untypical of many commentators on both sides of the Atlantic who occasionally found the 'special relationship' between Britain and the United States a little hard to stomach. The fact that Brooks was Australian is irrelevant. He was working for British Intelligence and the verbal sneering of Percy Winner is the exact counterpart of those less cultured GIs who regularly got into scraps in village pubs with their 'Tommy' allies.

But at Woburn, two brighter lights were burning. The first was Richard Crossman, a dazzling Oxford intellectual who had spent the years of the Slump in Weimar Germany with the underground Communist press. From 1934 until 1937 he spent part of each year in the Third Reich, studying Nazism and making radio broadcasts. One wonders how closely Josef Goebbels and the Abwelhr watched him. On his return, Crossman abandoned academe and became assistant editor of the left-wing *New Statesman*. Hugh Dalton, who knew Crossman in this period, thought him 'one of our best propagandists to Germany'. But he was also opinionated, described by one contemporary as 'an hornet's nest all to himself', and unpopular. In the small, hot-house environment of Woburn, he could have been a disaster. Superiors at Whitehall gave him orders by phone and rang off before he launched into a rage. In particular he could not stand Reginald 'Rex' Leeper of the Foreign Office Press Office, referring to him with contempt as 'an almost illiterate civil servant'.

Hugh Gaitskell, the future Labour Party leader, knew Crossman at Winchester and found him 'brilliantly able, immensely energetic and overwhelmingly ambitious'. Hugh Dalton agreed – 'He is loyal to his own career but only incidentally to anything or anyone else.' He was made head of the German section until he was sent (to get him out of the way?)

to Algiers in May 1943. In the end, he was the Prime Minister who never was, passed over for promotion in politics by both Attlee and Gaitskell after the war, and probably the most genuinely able of Harold Wilson's Cabinet in the 1960s.

The other, altogether more controllable genius, was Denis Sefton Delmer, a thick-set, balding specialist whose line, according to Ellic Howe, was 'the blackest of black propaganda with the Germans on the receiving end and no holds barred'. He joined SO1 at Woburn in the month of the Hess flight, a modest man with, according to Walmsley, a 'Rabelaisian nature and ... a Falstaffian corpulence'. He yelled at people with the best of them, but he respected other people's opinions, was a good judge of character and knew what would work. On his desk, perhaps in case he lost sight of the ultimate goal, was a captured Nazi sign which read *Hier sind Juden unerwünscht* ('the presence of Jews is undesirable'). Sefton was born in Berlin of Australian parents in 1904 and moved to London when he was thirteen. At Oxford he read History and rowed for Lincoln College. His German was brilliant, even to class inflection and regional dialect. He landed a journalist job in 1928 writing on Beaverbrook's *Daily Express*. He met Hitler in his five years in Germany and possibly Hess. In the hectic whirlwind that led to the war, Sefton Delmer seemed rarely to be absent. He was in Spain during the civil war, in Berlin during the Munich crisis, met Unity Mitford in Prague and was in Warsaw on the day blitzkreig came to that doomed city.

Over lunch in Boodle's,* Valentine Williams – 'a neat, compact man with thick black curly hair, a humorous crinkly red face and laughing blue eyes' – offered Delmer a job, but nothing happened and he found himself in neutral Lisbon in November 1940, in effect working for MI6 under cover as an *Express* journalist. While there, Leonard Ingrams, the 'Flying

---

* The prestigious gentlemen's club in St James's, founded in 1762.

Banker' who had known him in Berlin, invited him back home in January 1941. More of that in the next chapter. In his book, *Black Boomerang*, Delmer describes his first visit to the ballroom at Woburn and his meeting with the motley crew who made up 'the top team of Britain's psychological warfare'. There were university men, diplomats, officers of the armed forces, journalists, ad men and car salesmen – all of them, in their different ways, highly experienced at shooting a line.

Above all there was Rex Leeper, the department's boss. Delmer, who had known him since before the war when he was Press chief at the Foreign Office, thought he looked like an 'old-time papal secretary – tall and spare with [a] thoughtful, concentrated face'. Their fathers had known each other at Melbourne University. Specifically, Delmer's job was to write and broadcast black propaganda from Woburn under the call sign 'Gustav Siegfried Eins' (George Sugar One). As we shall see, it is likely that the Woburn team had altogether bigger fish to fry.

Walmsley had said it, indirectly, cryptically, infuriatingly, already: 'The atmosphere of the early days was one of bustling amateurishness and, with one exception, almost complete ineffectualness.' *With one exception*? That, I contend, was the astonishing, wholly successful plan to lure across with false hopes of establishing links with an active peace party, Hitler's right-hand man.

CHAPTER 6

Plots, True or False

Plots, true or false, are necessary things,
To raise up commonwealths and ruin kings.
Absalom and Achitophel
John Dryden

March 1940: the fourteen-week war in the freezing snows of Finland was over – a defeat for the Finns. Along the defences of the Mannerheim Line however the fabled Red Army had taken a series of batterings. Only the weight of numbers prevailed and Stalin's army now stood exposed in a weakness Hitler must have watched with secret delight. On the sixteenth day of that month, the first British civilian, a Scot, was killed in an air raid – a signal that the 'phoneyness' of the war was about to come to an end. At the town of Auschwitz near Krakow in Poland, Heinrich Himmler ordered the building of a concentration camp. In Hollywood, Vivien Leigh won an Oscar for her Scarlett O'Hara in Selznick's *Gone With the Wind*. And in England, Peter Fleming, the elder brother of the more famous Ian, was laid up in bed and wrote a book called *Flying Visit*. It was dedicated to his son Nicholas with the inscription 'in the hope that this book, when he comes to read it, will be no longer even remotely topical'.

Fleming was both an assistant editor at *The Times* and a war correspondent in Norway during that year. His entries in biographical dictionaries talk of his Eton and Oxford education and the racy, unconventional travelogues he produced in the Thirties. *Flying Visit* however was either one of the most extraordinary coincidences in history or it was the germ of an idea – an idea of the kind that might well appeal to the black artists at Woburn. In this work of 'what if' fiction, Adolf Hitler, Führer of the Third Reich, flies to Britain, parachuting out of his plane, to seek a peace treaty. 'The war would stop,' predicts the book's narrative voice, 'The bells would ring. Everybody would sign a piece of paper . . . Then, get to work on Russia . . . build up reserves . . . and then, in 1943 perhaps, he would show the British what it meant to incur the enmity of Germany.'

Peter Fleming served later with SO2, helping with 'deeds' in the same cause that he had waged with 'words' up to that point. Brother Ian served in Naval Intelligence, whose work constantly overlapped with other secret service units because of the liaison officers, like Dallas Brooks of SO1. What a tangled web they wove . . .

In the same month that Peter Fleming was allowing his imagination to take wing, the Marquess of Tavistock, later the 13th Duke of Bedford, published the first report of his peace mission. Lecturing at the Kingsway Hall to an all-party audience in April, Tavistock assured his listeners that 'Peace is possible now!' Tavistock was used to self-publicity and from his Scottish estate at Cairnsmore in Galloway struck up a friendship with the man he dubbed an 'Anarchist–Socialist' – Guy Aldred, who ran the Strickland Press in Glasgow. The pair produced most of Bedford's pacifist literature, debunking the 'warmongering' of Churchill's Government with articles entitled 'Why Blunder On?', 'The Financiers' Little Game' and 'Why Not Think?' After the war, Bedford wrote his autobiography, *The Years of Transition*, which outlined his pacifist views and the conduct of the War Cabinet.

During the seven years spent researching this book I placed several advertisments, always on 10 May, in the leading dailies asking for information, however indirect, on the flight of Rudolf Hess. In 1995 a response came from Allan Page, a conscientious objector at the outbreak of war. Such men had to appear before a tribunal and each case was treated on its own merits. For Allan Page, his alternative duty was at a sewage works in London, but the works were bombed and Page found himself convalescing in Stranraer with an old family friend, Dennis Rokeby.

Rokeby was an interesting figure on a number of levels. The family name was in fact Rebsch and Rokeby's father was a German diplomat who defected to England in 1916. The family had long Anglo–German associations – an earlier Rebsch was in service with Albert of Saxe-Coburg. Dennis himself was a high Anglican priest, which may well have produced some interesting pulpit clashes with his Lowland Scots congregation! Before the war, Rokeby and Page had compiled a unique photographic record of the railway network throughout Britain. Such a collection was pure gold to Luftwaffe pilots and bomb aimers. The damage that a smashed rail system could lead to did not bear thinking about – so on the outbreak of war, the photographs were confiscated.

Rokeby was also a committed pacifist and became a friend of the Duke of Bedford in this context. The vicar's parish at Stranraer was no more than twelve miles away from Cairnsmore and the two met there frequently. According to the current owner of Cairnsmore, the authorities were highly suspicious of the Duke of Bedford, who was placed under house arrest along with Rokeby and Page, during a meeting on 29 May 1941. Allan Page smuggled letters out – to whom and why is uncertain – while the police were actually in the house. The house arrest was not mentioned in the Press at the time. It came to me from Page and is printed here for the first time. His role in the Anglo-German story is vague and unsatisfactory, but it helps focus on the Duke of Bedford and illustrates the fine distinction sometimes made (and sometimes not) between pacifists and Nazi sympathizers by the wartime authorities. Incidentally, another friend of Rokeby's, from his Oxford days, was Hugh Gaitskell, then Hugh Dalton's right-hand man in SO1 and for a time at Woburn with the black propagandists.

While Page stayed at Stranraer, Rokeby had two other lodgers: ladies who worked in the local censor office handling mail from neutral Eire, which was used as a halfway house for post passing between Britain and mainland Europe. One of the lodgers was Isobel Forsythe, daughter of a Far East businessman. Well-travelled on the continent, Isobel moved in diplomatic circles, including the 'Fascist set'. Her fluent German had made her an obvious choice for censorship work. Was this, then, how the Duke of Bedford came to hear of a German peace proposal in the January of 1940? The trail of evidence has only one link missing – the Irish connection. Bedford's Irish contact was John Gregg, ' . . . a man,' according to Bedford, 'of exceptionally humane and enlightened outlook [who] had travelled in Germany, was married to a young German wife and was acquainted with the members of the German legation in Dublin.'[1] The legation in turn had been in touch with 'the highest authority in Berlin'.

Bedford got hold of these peace proposals and intended to publish them via the British People's Party literature and, no doubt, appropriate letters to *The Times*. In the end, friends persuaded him he should show the proposals to Lord Halifax, Chamberlain's Foreign Secretary, instead.

In summary, the terms suggested a 'reconstituted Czech state' (the old Czechoslovakia, the terms contended, had been manipulated by Britain and France) provided that state would remain neutral. Poland was also to be 'reconstituted' and independent, with outlets to the sea and to the River Vistula; she was of course also to be neutral. Relations between Germany and Austria were regarded as internal – there may be an Austrian plebiscite, but there was to be no external interference. Germany would disarm as long as disarmament was multilateral. She would rejoin the League of Nations as long as the League was fairer than it had been and was not dominated by Britain and France. Germany wanted her colonies back, or if that was not acceptable, an alternative method of obtaining vital raw materials. In connection with the 'Jewish Question', Germany was only too willing to help, with other nations, to find a 'national home' for the Jews.

Halifax and Bedford met on 24 January and the Foreign Secretary was sceptical. All Hitler's speeches in the Reichstag were adamant – Poland was now German, and the 'statements of Herr von Ribbentrop* and Dr Goebbels [are] that the German war aim is [Britain's] complete destruction'. Bedford conversely bemoaned the fact that Halifax and Churchill were rattling their own sabres in Hitler's direction on every conceivable occasion. Exasperated, Bedford asked permission to go to Dublin to verify the proposals of the German legation himself. Halifax's reply reads like a line from *Mission Impossible*: 'You will understand, of course, that there could be no question of your going in any official capacity or of your being entrusted with any mission from myself.'[2] Halifax, who had hunted with Goering, who was Chamberlain's co-appeaser and loathed Churchill, was now calling the Nazis 'blackguards' and a 'set of gangsters'. Bedford, on his part, excused the 'atrocious' words of both Hitler and Ribbentrop – 'no statesman's manners are worth a war'.

He went to Dublin, with or without Halifax's blessing, and met Herr Thomsen of the German legation, who assured him

---

* Joachim Ribbentrop (he added the 'von' to give himself more class) was a rich and successful champagne salesman who had been German ambassador to Britain in the Thirties and was, by 1940, Hitler's Foreign Minister.

that Gregg was wrong in thinking the peace proposals authentic. Bedford believed that it was the sabre-rattling of Halifax that had caused this volte-face.

There are a number of explanations for these peace proposals. They could have been a piece of German black propaganda, invented by someone in Admiral Canaris's Abwehr to sow as much discord and chaos as possible – in which case the ruse was fairly successful. Or they were a figment of John Gregg's imagination and we have no idea what his agenda was. Or they were genuine but the Germans had realized that an open declaration of these proposals was not the way to deal with the British. Bedford had thought better of publishing them – John McGovern, the pacifist Independent Labour MP for Glasgow went further and passed the information to the *Daily Express* who networked the thing to all the leading papers. On 4 March, *The Times* reported an exchange in Parliament between R.A. Butler, speaking for the Foreign Office, and a backbencher, G. Strauss:

BUTLER: 'No special facilities were given to Lord Tavistock to visit Dublin. On his return he published certain proposals which, it was claimed, represented the terms on which the German Government would conclude peace. These proposals had been previously communicated by Lord Tavistock to Lord Halifax. Apart from whatever may have been the merits or demerits of the proposals, there was no evidence to show that they emanated from the German Government or that they could be regarded as authentic. I notice that the German legation at Dublin has officially repudiated these proposals.

STRAUSS: Is an ordinary citizen free to go to the German legation in Eire wihout let or hindrance, and how does the Under–Secretary reconcile the latter part of his answer to the fact that Lord Tavistock still maintains that he received this document from the German legation in Dublin?'

BUTLER: Statements have been issued on behalf of the German Government and the German legation in Dublin. With regard to the first part of the supplementary question, that is a matter for the authorities and officials in Eire.[3]

And that, officially – although not, as will be shown, behind the scenes – is where the matter ended. The first issue which leaps to mind about this incident is whether Bedford was acting legally in approaching the German legation. In some circles this could be construed as sleeping with the enemy and Bedford's anti-Semitic remarks in some of his pacifist literature added fuel to that fire. Second, in allowing him to go to Dublin at all, what exactly was the position of Halifax? Was he trying to run with the fox that was Appeasement while still baying for blood with Churchill's hounds? The 1939 Emergency Powers (Defence) Act did not cover home-grown subversives, but was designed to deal with aliens, especially the influx from refugee Europe after 1938. The law was not amended until 23 May 1940 to include anyone who has 'sympathies with the system of government of any power with which His Majesty is at war' – in other words, the essence of Regulation 18B. The Passenger Traffic (Northern Ireland) Order 1939 said, 'A British subject shall not proceed from the United Kingdom to a destination outside it, or from Northern Ireland to Great Britain, or from Great Britain to Northern Ireland, except with the leave of an immigration officer.' Technically, since we must assume the Duke obtained such permission, he was not breaking the law.

Halifax's position was more complex. He wrote to Lord Lothian, then Ambassador to Washington in 1940, that 'peace feelers come almost every day'. Chamberlain and Halifax, however, were in an impossible situation in early 1940. Hitler had already proved that his solemn word meant nothing. Chamberlain had gone to war with him in September 1939, so why sue for peace in March 1940? All he could hope for was for the resistance movement in Germany to overthrow Hitler and perhaps Chamberlain could do a deal with his successor. The problem with this was that despite plots on Hitler's life, the resistance movements in Germany remained small and disunited; in the words of Emmi Bonhoeffer 'stones in a torrent'.* And in 1940, the torrent was too great.

As ever, Churchill spearheaded the anti-peace campaign. He was horrified in November 1939 when Queen Wilhelmina of the Netherlands and King Leopold of the Belgians offered their combined services as mediators. In the House he defiantly attacked pacifist Lords Brocket, Ponsonby, Londonderry, Darnley and Buccleuch who pointed to the unfairness of the Diktat of 1919. Beaverbrook and Halifax lunched quietly with their critics, canvassing support, watching, waiting.†

Why should we assume the peace proposals to be genuine? The answer lies in the timing. On 9 April, Hitler invaded Denmark and Norway simultaneously. A month later Holland and Belgium, whose royals were so anxious to act as peace brokers months earlier, fell to the terrible stampede of blitzkrieg. Perhaps all this could have been forestalled or averted by peace with Britain. Perhaps Hitler and Ribbentrop were giving the West one last chance to come to their senses. But Hitler was already planning Operation Barbarossa. He and Stalin had made uneasy bedfellows in the Nazi–Soviet Pact. The drive of the Reich eastwards would come sooner or later – it had been prescribed since *Mein Kampf*. Hitler needed Russia's

* The wife of the Lutheran pastor and philosopher Dietrich Bonhoeffer, resistance fighter, hanged in 1943.
† More detail on Beaverbrook's role in the Hess case can be found in Chapter 9.

steppe-lands and Slavic labour force and raw materials. And to obtain that efficiently he needed a quiescent Britain.

By May 1940 the scene had changed entirely. Blitzkreig had rolled west, smashing the passport office system of intelligence gathering as it came. Churchill took over from Chamberlain and assembled his ramshackle coalition team – Attlee as Deputy Prime Minister to keep Labour quiet; Halifax, the ditherer, at the Foreign Office; Beaverbrook, the media man and Ernest Bevin, the Trades Union boss, were dragooned in. Twelve days later, in a constitutional act unprecedented in parliamentary history, the Emergency Powers Act gave Churchill and his Cabinet virtually unlimited power. He could now legitimize the stance he had taken for years: 'You ask what is our policy? It is to wage war by sea, land and air, with all our might and all our strength.'[4] And then he moved against the Right.

Captain Archibald Ramsay was the founder of the Right Club, which Peter Fleming in *Invasion 1940* calls, 'a small, seedy clique of anti-Semites whose dedicated members went round in the blackout sticking up handbills which proclaimed "This is a Jews' War".' Ramsay was admirably suited by his background to lead such an organization, although he was not a Nazi. Discreet and not given to the provocative marches of Mosley's Fascists, the Right Club had aroused the suspicions of MI5 who infiltrated the organization with Joan Miller. Her secretarial skills were employed to type the pamphlets denouncing the 'Jews' War' that Ramsay circulated; while her espionage skills enabled MI5 to discover that Ramsay's assistant, Anna Wolkoff, was meeting regularly with Colonel Francesco Maringliano, a naval attaché at the Italian Embassy. This was embarrassing for MI5 because both Anna's parents, White refugees from Tsarist Russia, worked for them as interpreters!

What Joan Miller had discovered was a can of worms. For months the Germans had been reading top secret communications passing between Churchill and Roosevelt via the American embassy in London. The third contact for Wolkoff and Maringliano was Tyler Kent, a cipher clerk at the embassy. In the early hours of 20 May, bowler-hatted men from M15 raided Kent's flat at 47 Gloucester Place and arrested him and Anna Wolkoff. Here was enough evidence to hang them both. Cipher cables, Government documentation and a red leather-bound book containing the names of the Right Club's members. Ramsay had given this list to Kent rather than leave it at his own address because he supposed that the clerk's diplomatic immunity would save him from MI5's scrutiny. Only with reluctance had Ambassador Joe Kennedy given permission for the raid.

Under interrogation Kent admitted he had passed the ciphers to Wolkoff, but in the belief that she in turn was passing them to Ramsay for evidence that Churchill and Roosevelt were conspiring to prolong the war. It is no secret now of course that bringing America in, with its huge resources in men and *matériel*, was precisely what Churchill wanted. For him, Pearl Harbor must have seemed divine intervention.* Wolkoff was imprisoned for her German sympathies and Kent was sent to jail in the Isle of Wight.

This Right Club link has no direct relevance to Rudolf Hess (although Anna Wolkoff had actually met him in Germany in 1939) but Vernon Kell's diary tells us that 'Kennedy's confidential reports to Roosevelt were reaching the office of Nazi Party Chief Rudolf Hess'. The importance of the connection is that Hess knew, contrary to the view of some writers, that Churchill's position was unshakeable – there would be no peace with him in charge – and because of the work of Wolkoff, Kent, Ramsay and who knew how many more, that there *was* a fifth column operating in Britain.

* There is a recently suggested theory that Churchill withheld vital information from the Americans in December 1941 so that the Japanese attack would take place as planned, thus forcing Roosevelt's hand.

The Home Secretary, John Anderson, now moved against Mosley. His name is inextricably linked with the air-raid shelters hastily sunk to face the 'phoney war' and he did not suffer fools – or potential traitors – gladly. Thirty-three members of the British Union of Fascists were arrested under Regulation 18B, as was Ramsay, despite his loud protestations of parliamentary privilege. John Beckett of the British People's Party also went to jail, but the Duke of Bedford did not – probably, as he himself surmised, because it would appear 'bad form' to the Americans for the British to be locking up their own aristocracy. The British peerage must appear united in its grim determination to resist Hitler's tyranny.

By the time Churchill authorized Dalton to set up SOE on 1 July, these divisions, which were to be concealed from the Americans, were becoming apparent. The strain of the war was beginning to tell. In the Commons a cross-party group of about thirty MPs, backed by a further ten in the Lords, rallied under Labour MP Richard Stokes, who looked to Lloyd George as a possible replacement for Churchill. Among these men there was no talk of capitulation. The German threat must be repulsed, but then a peace must be made, as the only true winners of the war would be America and Russia. Two months earlier, the military theorist Basil Liddell-Hart had advised that we should, 'Come to the best possible terms as soon as possible . . . we have no chance of avoiding defeat.'[5] But the all-important security posts in the Cabinet remained firmly in the hands of Churchill's Tories.

M15 was under the auspices of Anderson at the Home Office and M16 under the Foreign Office, still skippered by Halifax. It did not help that so much of the recruitment to both services came from the City, with its old boy network and the wearing of the school tie. By appointing Hugh Dalton as head of SOE, Churchill had achieved a political master-stroke – the Minister of Economic Warfare was, after all, a socialist. By placing Dalton in charge he reduced the suspicions of the Socialist Cabinet Members regarding intelligence matters. These suspicions had been harboured from the formative days of the Labour Party, when the intelligence agencies had paid great attention to their activities and members.

An organizational chart dated February 1941 shows how SO1 had settled in at Woburn. In overall charge was Rex Leeper, with his flat, unemotional voice, his thoughtful face and, according to Sefton Delmer, 'one of the subtlest political brains I had met'.[6] Below him was Christopher Warner, head of the Northern Department at the Foreign Office, then Dallas Brooks as liaison and Valentine Williams as assistant to Warner. Under them came various department heads and Walter Stewart Roberts. Roberts is described as 'Establishment and Finance Officer'.

In fact, Roberts seems to have been much more than a book-keeper. He was born in 1889, the son of Ernest Roberts, a brilliant mathematician who was one-time Master of Gonville and Caius, Cambridge. Educated at Eton, he studied at his father's college before entering the Civil Service. We do not know why he left. Perhaps it was the money that drew him to Stand 3 at the Stock Exchange where he eventually became a partner of J. Silverston and Co. at 4 Copthall Court. There is some confusion over Roberts' service details. *Who's Who* lists him on the Foreign Office files from 1940 to 1948. For the first six years, he was Director of Finance and Administration (which accords with Ellic Howe's memories of him) but in 1946 he is referred to by the rather grander – and altogether more intriguing – title of 'Deputy Director-General of Political Intelligence'. The Foreign Office files themselves however do not carry his name until 1946, the year he unaccountably added the Stewart to his name (Stewart was his grandfather's Christian name). He returned to the City with a CBE in 1948 and died of natural causes in 1974.

In November 1940, the year in which Roberts was recruited to SO1, he dined with Robert Bruce Lockhart, who would become Director-General of Political Warfare and receive a knighthood in 1943. Was this mere politeness to invite a new man to dinner? Or was Roberts something more than a book keeper? At the time of the dinner, Bruce Lockhart was the British representative to the Provisional Czech Government in exile. Hugh Dalton wrote constantly to Roberts between then and January 1941 and most of the retained correspondence concerned a German national who had been employed at Woburn. Either Roberts was also a personnel officer or his opinions were highly valued by his superiors – and Dalton reported to Churchill.

The team at Woburn was growing and a formal management structure, complete with regular meetings, was established. From 31 August 1940, weekly meetings were held every Saturday, in which the command structure was regularly present, minus Roberts himself. Dalton dropped in from time to time, but curiously, on Saturday, 10 May 1941, the day of the heaviest bombing of the blitz and the day of the 'flying visit' of Rudolf Hess, there were not one, but *two* cabinet ministers present. Anthony Eden, now Churchill's. Foreign Secretary, was there too. Yet the minutes of the meeting were routine, ordinary. And after that meeting, no further minutes were kept. A memo of 16 May said that in future it was 'not desirable' for minutes to be kept. Why?

Perhaps the answer lies between the lines in the minutes of that very ordinary meeting on 10 May. Leonard Ingrams, the Ministry of Economic Warfare's liaison officer said, 'We should encourage the Germans to attack Russia by misleading Hitler and by hinting that large sections both in Britain and the US who preferred to see the overthrow of the German regime might be prepared to force through a compromise peace.'[7] Is this Ingrams, tongue in cheek, having a joke at SO1's expense? For I believe that this is precisely what SO1 had been doing since July or August 1940.

Why were Eden and Dalton there together? One possibility is that the imminence of a heavy air raid had somehow filtered through and key Cabinet personnel were being advised to get out of the capital that night. Churchill himself was at Ditchley Mall, the country house in Oxfordshire. (By May 1941, Luftwaffe bomber navigational beams could be intercepted and the work of the Ultra codebreakers was beginning to bear fruit.) There is nothing in either man's diary of the time to suggest this – only the most succinct of factual entries, logging the visit.

My submission is that the Foreign Secretary and the Minister of Economic Warfare were waiting for news that Rudolf Hess was captured or dead. The staff of SO1 had the technical and intellectual ability to pull off even a coup as fantastic as this. Any study of the Foreign Office files of this period gives an overriding impression that Germany and the German psyche were understood very well. Both SOE and its American equivalent, the OSS, had been working on a full psychological analysis of Hitler. F.A. Voigt, of SO1, formerly the *Manchester Guardian*'s Berlin correspondent, had come to this conclusion in 1939: 'The greatest, by no means inconceivable, danger would be a military coup d'état which would make Germany seem respectable by ridding her of the gangsters and offering a "just" peace and a front against Bolshevism.'[8] So there was no point in Churchill following Chamberlain's line in hoping for a revolt to unseat Hitler from within.

But what of the reverse? There were four men in Britain, in almost any combination, who I believe could have arranged the illusion of a 'peace party' powerful and convincing enough to lure Hess over. The first is Ian Fleming.

Fleming was born into a wealthy merchant family who had originally made their fortune in nineteenth-century Dundee. In the 1920s, when Ian and his brother Peter were boys, the family was well established in England and the Fleming sons were educated at Eton (so often the training ground of Intelligence men in that period). Serving with the Grenadier Guards for a time, the younger Fleming went to work with the City firm of Rowe and Pitman. According to his latest biographer, Andrew Lycett, the 'world's worst stockbroker's social graces far outweighed his financial acumen'.

In 1939, he was approached to join Naval Intelligence, largely on the strength of his domineering mother's relationship with Montagu Norman, Governor of the Bank of England. At NID, Fleming quickly established himself, amidst the piles of bumf, as an ideas man. The rumour may be unfounded that Admiral Godfrey, Director of Naval Intelligence, is supposed to have said that Fleming would be better at his job than he was, but certainly responsibility came his way thick and fast. Of particular relevance was his work in liaison, where he met Dallas Brooks of SO1, effectively his opposite number. Another man who knew Fleming well was Donald McCormick, who also wrote under the pseudonym Richard Deacon. He linked Fleming closely with the Hess affair in his book *British Secret Service*.

Nowhere was propaganda blacker than dealing with the black arts themselves. Although Ellic Howe dismisses it, Hitler, Hess and Himmler were all fascinated by the subject and within the framework of the SS (even the runic symbols themselves) the occult had a lurking significance. In prison at Landsberg, Hitler had once seen the moon through the clouds of the night sky and he said to Hess, 'You know, Rudi it's only the moon I hate. For it is something dead, and terrible and inhuman. And human beings are afraid of it ... It is as if in the moon a part of the terror still lives which the moon once sent down over the earth ... I hate it! That pale and ghostly fellow.'[9] This is a rare example of the inner terrors of Adolf Hitler which only the inner circle were allowed to witness. That he should have confided it to Hess is doubly significant – Hess was Hitler's right-hand man in the Landsberg days and the future Führer knew the man's fascination with the heavens.

McCormick admits that the use of astrology in Intelligence was a long shot, although arguably less so than the apparent plan to drive Hitler insane by exposing him to vast quantities of pornography!* But again, it was central to an understanding of

---

* This is another of the almost laughable ideas that emanated from secret service quarters (this time the American OSS), along with a scheme to infect the laundry of U boat crews!

at least three leading Nazis' psyches. Godfrey believed that Hitler's astrologers predicted that everything Hitler wanted to achieve 'must be done by the end of February 1941 . . . after March 1941, Hitler's luck will be out.'[10] (There is in fact no evidence that Hitler ever visited an astrologer himself, although Himmler and Hess may well have done.)

This flirtation with astrology sounds in itself a flight of fancy, but remember that the Nazis were all-powerful in Europe and the British had their proverbial backs to the wall. Accountable to no one but Dalton and Churchill (and the Prime Minister as a young man had also consulted astrologers), what had the black propagandists to lose? Fleming himself was probably cynical about the whole thing, but realized that Hess in particular took it all very seriously.

According to McCormick, the real instigator of the Hess plot was a Russian-born American called William Otto Lucas, who went by the unlikely aliases of William van Narwig and Bill Findearth. With an uncanny ability to infiltrate both the Reichschancellery and the Kremlin, Lucas sounds a little too good to be true. According to Fleming, only Naval Intelligence would even talk to him and eventually decided they could not use him or his ideas.

Fleming had read the file on Barry Domville, Director of Naval Intelligence in the late Twenties, and knew of the existence of the Link, banned after the outbreak of war. Why not pretend to the Nazis that the Link had been reorganized as a latently powerful underground organization, poised to oust Churchill and his dogs of war and pave the way to a negotiated peace? The next step was to contact a gullible Nazi leader and leak this information to him. Invasion plans might then be shelved and all sorts of scenarios might result.

If one believes McCormick, Fleming did plan along these lines. In which case he must have been a maverick working largely on his own, outside the ken of Naval Intelligence. This had to be so because Churchill's policy was just the reverse. It would have been a huge loss of face for him to back-pedal on the defiance of Germany he had always shown, but he *could* have done that and *could* have made a separate peace with Hitler via Hess in 1941. If Churchill had never entertained the idea of a negotiated peace, it speaks volumes for his pugnacious character, but perhaps less for his common sense. In fact, despite assurances to the contrary, Stalin continued to believe that this was precisely what *had* been going on. Churchill was a warmonger, pledged to bring the Americans in, pledged to beating Germany into the ground. To this end, despite the advice of Sir Charles Portal of Bomber Command, the Prime Minister insisted on bombing Berlin, which in turn he knew would stiffen the resolve of the British people to fight on.

Fleming confided his plan to a Swiss friend who was an astrologer and to a confidant in 'another branch of British Intelligence'. The plan had three aims: to convince the Nazis that the Link had been revived and that the 'peace party' in Britain was real; to manipulate Hess as the most gullible Nazi leader, by feeding him bogus astrological predictions; and to establish contacts with other occultists with German connections. To mock up the reformation of the Link, stories had to be planted via neutral countries – Berne in Switzerland and Lisbon in Portugal were chosen. In the latter, the Café Chiada was the most fruitful watering hole for agents. For Fleming, the scalp he sought was Admiral Canaris, chief of the Abwehr, whom no doubt every member of British Intelligence regarded as a *bête noire*. Wilhelm Canaris was an enigmatic figure, paranoid about Communism, yet opposed to Nazi brutality. He was not particularly competent either and there is every reason to believe that the Abwehr could not hold a candle to British Intelligence. Even so, he was unlikely to be swayed by horoscopes. Rudolf Hess was another matter.

Ever since his mother had talked to him about the stars in the

Egyptian garden at Ibrahimieh, Hess had been fascinated. At
boarding school he read voraciously. At university under Karl
Haushofer, himself a student of the occult, he had dabbled
further. Letters to Ilse and other members of Hess's family
make this clear. His inborn fatalism was wound up inextricably
with his astrology. Schwerin von Krosigk, later Minister of
Finance in Germany, wrote that Hess 'lived in unreality, he
believed in dream-readings, prophecies and astrology'.

When Josef Goebbels was given the awkward task of
telling the German people over the air what Hess had done
on 10 May 1941, he said, 'Recently he had sought relief [from
"severe physical suffering"] to an increasing extent in various
methods practised by mesmerists and astrologers.'[11] Hitler
gave the same message to his Gauleiters face to face: 'For the
rest it appears to me that this step was most strongly induced
by the astrological clique whose influence Hess has
surrounded himself with. It is time, therefore, to make a
radical clean sweep of this astrological rabble.'[12]

Peter Padfield quotes Robert Cecil who wrote *The Myth of
the Master Race* as saying, as though this was either Hess's
incentive or his downfall, that on 10 May 1941, there were six
planets in Taurus, a portentous configuration. However,
Hess made no astrological comments during his long years
in captivity, though was clearly fascinated by space exploration.

The point is that Fleming believed, along with many others
on this side of the Channel, that Hess *was* obsessed with plan-
etary influences and proceeded accordingly. Fleming's friend
Aleister Crowley told him of Hess's apparent preoccupation
with the occult. Another friend was Ellic Howe, who, despite
his reticence in *The Black Game* had, as a master forger to SO1,
the task of faking a German astrological magazine. According
to the astrologer Nicholas Campion, Howe 'cast the horoscope
for the time at which Hess took off from Germany. It was most
inauspicious . . . largely because six planets were in the house of

death [odd then that Hess should outlive all the Nazi leaders!] and two other points were strong: the fixed star Algol (which leads one to lose one's head) and the evil degree Serpentis.'[13]

McCormick has no details of the precise wording of the horoscopes, but clearly, they had to accord with what Hess was used to reading, or he might become suspicious. To that end, Crowley was utilized, as was Louis de Wohl, a Hungarian who had escaped Nazi persecution.

Ellic Howe tells us that de Wohl was used by SOE to publish bogus, doom-laden predictions for leading Germans in a lecture tour of the United States. He left in the month that Hess flew. According to Howe his reward for this black propaganda was presumably cash and the right to a commission in the British army, for which he longed. Reputedly he was often to be seen parading around Whitehall in a khaki tunic he was supposed to keep secret!

As far as Crowley's involvement with Hess goes, his son Amado believes that Fleming and 'the wickedest man in the world' underwent a ritual in Ashdown Forest, which the elder Crowley subsequently referred to as 'the firework display'. This was a 'long and complex high ritual' at which Amado, a boy at the time, remembers a crowd of robed figures and a dummy in Nazi uniform sitting on a throne. McCormick certainly believes that rituals like these were actually used to influence Hess's actions.

In Germany, the '*Aktion* Hess' was a systematic rounding up of all those close to the Stellvertreter, especially astrologers. Top of the list was Karl Ernst Krafft, a Swiss who claimed (unwisely as it turned out) to be Hitler's astrologer in 1940–41. His fate remains unknown. According to McCormick, another was Ernst Schulte-Strahaus, Hess's astrological adviser.

Was Ian Fleming, then, the instigator of a plot to lure Hess to Scotland? Sefton Delmer, who knew him well, says, 'As an idea, inducing Hess to fly . . . by means of astrological hocus-pocus and the bait of the Duke of Hamilton was something that might have appealed to Ian Fleming, or even to have been conceived by him. I am quite ready to believe that.'[14]

Fleming always denied any involvement, as did his brother Peter, believing that 'the elaborate ruses were [never] carried out or even planned'. It was Fleming however who suggested, when Hess landed and his identity was known, to let Aleister Crowley interrogate him. 'If it is true,' Crowley wrote in a letter to the Director of Naval Intelligence on 14 May 1941, 'that Herr Hess is much influenced by astrology and magick, my services might be of use to the Department . . .'[15]

In the end, the Department turned him down.

The whole theory that suggests Fleming's involvement in the Hess case comes from Donald McCormick, who died last year. An enigma in his own right, he is not regarded today as particularly faithful to the facts. Having said that, his work in Intelligence meant that he was close to his sources and had access to information either still classified or long ago consigned to the incinerator.

Sefton Delmer is another possible protagonist and his passing of the buck to Fleming is typical of the man. Those who knew Delmer regarded him as a brilliant black propandist and after the war he was considered so tricky as to be suspected of being a double agent for the Russians.

In *My Father, Rudolf Hess*, Wolf Hess is well informed on Sefton Delmer. This is not surprising, because the Australian journalist-cum-black propagandist befriended the Hess family after the war and entertained Wolf at his London club. And Wolf Hess is fairly contemptuous of SO1:

> 'Black propaganda, on the other hand, represented a completely new concept of secret psychological warfare. It operated by using the most evil means, such as lies, deceit and forgery. Its methods were distinct from those

of the Secret Intelligence Service, the Ministry of
Information and the Foreign Office, as well as those of
Special Operations 2, which itself did 'not balk at
bribery, blackmail and murder.'

Wolf Hess believes that as the Special Operations units developed into the fully fledged Political Warfare Executive, it
became a 'surrogate British Government', 'a secret underground state whose behaviour was not subject to the control
of Parliament and the public'. Perhaps he is right. Hess also
believes that Delmer's ability to understand the subtleties of
the 1930s German mind gave him the potential to lure Hess
to Britain. Delmer also had close links via his journalism to
Beaverbrook and even Churchill.

Eleven days after Hess landed, Delmer began transmitting
his 'Gustav Siegfried Eins' broadcasts: 'Like the whole clique
of crack-pots, megalomaniacs, wire-pullers and drawing-
room Bolsheviks who call themselves our "Führers", [Hess]
had nerves too weak to withstand the crisis.'[16] Almost alone
of British propagandists, Sefton Delmer was doing what Josef
Goebbels expected – he was making capital out of Hess's
arrival.

There is certainly a controlled anger in *Black Boomerang* at
the chance lost with Hess once he had been captured. When
Beaverbrook, the appeaser, had interviewed the depressed
Stellvertreter, the encouragement he showed bucked Hess up
enormously. He told one of his guard officers how much he'd
enjoyed the conversation. Delmer believed, and he was probably right, that if Beaverbrook had gone in again, smiling,
talking over old times in Berlin, Hess might have been
prepared to talk.

As it was, Beaverbrook was not allowed to return. '[Hess],'
wrote Delmer, 'was allowed to shut himself off once more in the
pose of apathy which was ultimately to degenerate . . . A great

opportunity in the war of wits had been bungled.'[17] The whole episode post-11 May was 'a miserable farce' and sending the 'sly German-hater' Ivone Kirkpatrick or the 'polished but frosty' Lord Chancellor (Simon) against Hess had been pointless. Interestingly, Wolf Hess believes that it was actually Beaverbrook and not the Duke of Hamilton, that his father had flown to see.* It is likely that Dallas Brooks' role in the Hess lure was merely one of liaison. His military credentials made him indispensable if we are to assume that Hess's flight would have to be monitored, but not intercepted, by the RAF to make it work.

The next possible instigator of the plot is the enigmatic Leonard Ingrams. Sefton Delmer describes him thus:

> ' . . . he looked the part of the mysterious Mr X to perfection. He was tall and athletic . . . and his eyes and mouth had just the right expression of drawling sardonic pity for the world around him. Victoria, his wife, a member of the influential Baring family, was his devoted slave. So too were her brothers, and so for that matter, was I.'[18]

Here we have homage indeed. If a man like Sefton Delmer could wax lyrical about Ingrams, then he was most probably the intellectual mastermind behind the Political Warfare group. Ingrams was an ideas man and he clearly had the charisma to make the ideas work, bulldozing opposition when he found it. More so than Rex Leeper, Leonard Ingrams was regarded by many as 'the boss' at Woburn. Ellic Howe wrote: 'I find it difficult to believe that these dirty tricks [black propaganda] were either conceived or engineered by the innocents at Woburn or the small Section D group . . . However they could certainly

* See Chapter 9.

have originated in the fertile mind of Leonard Ingrams, who was [Electra House's] liaison officer at the Ministry of Economic Warfare.'[19]

When Delmer began the regular broadcasts to Germany under the call-sign 'Gustav Siegfried Eins', Ingrams' wry suggestion was that the initials actually meant Gurkensalat One (Cucumber Salad One). It was Ingrams who chose Corporal Peter Seckelmann to be the 'voice' of GS1. Seckelmann was one of that small band of non-Nazi Germans who horrified Hess's Auslander organization by refusing to be part of it. Their knowledge of things German and their command of the language were indispensable to SO1.

Leonard St Clair Ingrams was born in January 1900. His education prepared him perfectly for subversive espionage: Shrewsbury School was followed by Pembroke College, Oxford and a commission in the Coldstream Guards. From 1924 he worked as the European representative for the Chemical Bank and Trust Company of New York. His fascination with aviation – he owned a Puss Moth – earned him the nickname 'the flying banker'. Moving between his office at the Ministry of Economic Warfare in Berkeley Square, his club (Boodle's) and 'the Country' (Woburn) he was ideally placed to mastermind the Hess operation.

Richard Ingrams (former editor of *Private Eye* and newspaper columnist) was only thirteen when his father died, aged fifty-three, in Germany and his memories of him are not cherished ones. Sent to boarding school at eight, which he hated, most of the younger Ingrams' holidays were spent with his mother. 'My father was an aloof figure and although I was his favourite, my brothers . . . and I were all scared of him. He had a terrible temper.'[20]

Ingrams senior has acquired a reputation for anti-Semitism, based on his alleged membership of the Anglo–German Fellowship. According to Richard Ingrams his father never attended the Fellowship's dinners, but he admits that Leonard was pro-German in the 1930s. 'He was a merchant banker,' Ingrams junior remembered in 1995, 'who became involved in the secret service, but it was terribly hush-hush.'[21]

After the war and before Nuremberg, Ingrams was sent to interview Goering, giving us a hint perhaps of the esteem in which he was held by Churchill's Government. In the immediate post-war period, the Reich Fieldmarshal was second only to Hitler in terms of power and guilt.

I believe that either alone or in combination, Ian Fleming, Sefton Delmer and Leonard Ingrams dreamed up a plan as serpentine as anything Fleming would dream up after the war for his books. The vital fourth man was the Director of Finance at Woburn, Walter Stewart Roberts – because he had a well-connected aunt . . .

Mary Violet Roberts can have had no idea of how she would be involved in one of the most intriguing episodes of the war. Her involvement was first chronicled in 1964 by Heinz Haushofer, the younger son of the professor, Karl, who was Hess's mentor at Munich University. He describes her as 'the daughter-in-law of Lord Roberts of Kandahar' and David Irving in *Hess: The Missing Years* accepted this: 'A Mrs Violet Roberts, daughter-in-law of the former British Viceroy of India, Lord Roberts of Kandahar . . .' Likewise, in *The Truth About Rudolf Hess*, James Douglas-Hamilton writes, 'Mrs Roberts was apparently the daughter-in-law of Lord Roberts of Kandahar who had been Viceroy of India. She had married Ainslie Roberts and was his widow.' Actually only part of this is true.

Lord Roberts was Kipling's general – 'Bobs' Bahadur – and the poet laureate of Empire wrote about him twice. After Roberts's lifetime of service to Victoria, from the Indian Mutiny to the Boer War, the poet wrote:

> 'Now they've made a-blooming Lord
>   Outer Bobs,
> Which was but 'is fair reward –
>   Weren't it, Bobs?
> So 'e'll wear a coronet
> Where 'is 'elmet used to set;
> But we know you won't forget –
>   Will yer, Bobs?[22]

And when the Field Marshal, probably the most popular soldier of his day, died in France in 1914 –

> He passed in the very battle-smoke
> Of the war that he descried.
> Three hundred mile of cannon spoke
> When the Master Gunner died.[23]

But the Master Gunner only had one son and his name was not Ainslie. It was Frederick Hugh Sherston Roberts and he won the VC on 15 December 1899 for his part in saving guns of the Royal Artillery in the attack on the besiegers of Ladysmith. Mown down by murderous infantry fire, he died in the action, aged twenty-six. And he was unmarried. Lord Roberts's other children were girls – Aileen Mary and Ada Edwina. Aileen never married and took the title Countess of Kandahar in 1914. She died thirty years later. Ada married in 1913, becoming Mrs Lewin. Neither of these was the mysterious Mary Violet, whose name begins to peep from between the pages of various documents as we delve deeper into the Hess case.

Why Heinz Haushofer should have made the spurious link with Lord Roberts we do not know. A blinkered obsession with English aristocracy was characteristic of leading Nazis in the 1930s, but as Haushofer came from an Anglophile family who had known the Roberts' for nearly forty-five years it's an unlikely explanation. James Douglas-Hamilton, whose wires also seem to have been crossed, nevertheless got other biographical details right. He records that the son of Mary Violet and Ainslie Roberts, Patrick Maxwell Roberts, was killed in a car crash in 1937 and worked for a time in the British Embassy in Berlin. From this it was possible to research the enigmatic lady further.

Mary Violet Maxwell was born on 5 September 1864 at Ferozepore, India. Her father, Patrick Maxwell, was a captain in the Bengal Staff Corps and her mother Louisa, the daughter of a naval officer. Maxwell was promoted to major in 1865 and lieutenant-colonel six years later, before returning to England and settling in Bath, the home of many retired Indian Army officers. Violet's future husband, Herbert Ainslie Roberts, was born a few months before her at Swinshead in Lincolnshire, the son of a local doctor who produced a family of outstanding academics. Herbert himself graduated in Mathematics at Gonville and Caius, Cambridge, in 1887 and took up a teaching post at Bath College where he met Violet.

The couple married in 1894. Their only son, Patrick Maxwell, was born a year later and the family moved to Cambridge in 1898, where Herbert wrote a treatise on elementary dynamics. The family prospered – Herbert's brother Ernest became Master of Caius in 1903 and the death of Violet's father left her comfortably off. She and Herbert built a mock Tudor house (then very fashionable) at 33 Storey's Way, Cambridge with the help of architect Baillie Scott (now a listed building).

It was most probably between September and November 1899 when the Roberts met the Haushofers. In those months, Karl Haushofer visited England. The archive material is sparse, but we know the General met Joseph Chamberlain (father of Neville), very much the 'coming man' in British politics and at that time Colonial Secretary in Lord Salisbury's Government. Although a meeting cannot be proven in 1899, the Roberts's visit to Germany in 1925 seems to have renewed an old acquaintanceship rather than forged a new one. The Haushofer papers make it clear that the families had met before the outbreak of the Great War. Exactly how and when is not clear.

Violet and Herbert's son Patrick, after Eton and Trinity College, Cambridge joined the Foreign Office in 1910 and was posted to Berlin in October 1924. A further move was on the cards for Patrick – he would become third secretary at the British legation in Warsaw in August 1925. Two diary entries from Martha Haushofer's papers show that Patrick and his parents visited Hartschimmelhof, the Haushofer home, on two separate occasions in the summer of that year. It is certain from this that Violet and Herbert were as friendly with Albrecht, the Haushofer's eldest son, as they were with his parents. The common ground between the families is obvious. Both had sons moving in diplomatic circles in their respective countries – and Patrick was temporarily based in Berlin. Herbert Roberts, in his capacity as secretary to the Cambridge Foreign Science Students Committee, had the same fascination for geography as Karl Haushofer, even if this did not extend to geopolitics. It was while Patrick Roberts was in Berlin that the professor was visiting his former student Rudolf Hess in Landsberg.

There appear to have been no further meetings between the families before Herbert's death in 1932. (No papers are available from the Roberts family and the Haushofer files were probably vetted very carefully by the Americans immediately after the war.

Two years after the death of Herbert Roberts, Karl and Albrecht Haushofer travelled to England. Whether they met Mrs Roberts during their brief stay in July 1934 is not recorded, but the Haushofer papers make clear they certainly went to Cambridge where the seventy-year-old widow still lived at Storey's Way. The house had been renumbered by this time and Violet was on the point of moving to a much smaller house in Madingley Road where she employed a caretaker and part-time gardener.

We now know exactly where the old lady was in 1937 when tragedy struck and her son Patrick was killed in Greece – she was living with him there at the time. A brilliant young man with a promising diplomatic career ahead of him, he had been posted after Warsaw to Belgrade, Istanbul, Addis Ababa and finally Athens. He was a passenger in a car which crashed near Ikali, a village outside the Greek capital. The dead man's grant of probate gives his mother's residence (in March 1938) as 36 Queen's Gate, London SW7 –an elegant Kensington address. In fact, this rather fine Georgian terraced house belonged to Violet's nephew, Walter, the future Financial Director of SO1.

Patrick's role in the Hess story is twofold. Not only was he clearly a friend of Albrecht Haushofer, but also in his short-lived career with the Foreign Office he made important contacts. Most obvious were Rex Leeper of the Political Warfare Executive and Anthony Bevir*, who was later a 'fixer' for Churchill and the Prime Minister's private secretary. With Patrick's death the secret service connection focuses on Walter Roberts and it was no doubt via him that the link between his aunt and Rudolf Hess was established as being worthy of exploration by SO1.

The other vital relationship exploited by Ingrams and his fellow conspirators at Woburn was that between Albrecht Haushofer and Lord Clydesdale, later the Duke of Hamilton. They met at the Olympics in Berlin in 1936 and Clydesdale remembered him as a ponderous, clumsy man whose head seemed too small for his body. A fascinating conversationalist, it was clear that Haushofer was not only not a Nazi, but not afraid to ridicule the Nazi elite. He had his largely British audience in stitches over dinner one night mimicking Ribbentrop, but he could find nothing remotely funny about Goebbels. ('Goebbels is a poisonous little man, who will give you dinner one night and sign

---

* Bevir was a named beneficiary in Violet Roberts' will. She died in 1958

your death warrant the next morning.'[24] In fact, another of
the elite, Himmler, would sign Albrecht Haushofer's death
warrant.)

The two met again in February 1937 when Clydesdale was
skiing in the Austrian Alps. They did not talk politics at the
old man's lovely Bavarian-style house at Hartschimmelhof,
but four days after the visit, Rudolf Hess arrived and was
fascinated to hear more of the exploits of the man who had
conquered Everest by air.

Three months later, Haushofer was in London, partly at
the request of the Royal Institute of International Affairs at
Chatham House where he gave a lecture on 'Raw Materials
and Colonies: A German Point of View'. The talk was well
received, although Haushofer's allegory of the unfairness of
the Treaty of Versailles was a little unnerving to some of his
audience. Over the next few days at Clydesdale's London
home he was open enough with the peer to rail against the
stupidity and intransigence of von Ribbentrop, then still
ambassador to London. In June he was back again, concerned
at the growing extremism of his country's foreign policy and
on his way to a diplomatic visit to Japan.

Unable to attend Clydesdale's Edinburgh wedding to
Elizabeth Percy in November, Haushofer nevertheless wrote
a congratulatory letter: 'On Thursday then, my thoughts –
and a very strong feeling of friendship – will accompany your
steps in St Giles Cathedral – and perhaps the spirit of history
will have a little fun in my mind . . . Please imagine what
might have happened a few centuries ago: the heir of
Douglas captured by the Percys . . .'[25] Not only is this letter
evidence of the men's friendship, but of the depth of
Haushofer's grasp of British history and with it, an understanding of the British psyche.

He came to Britain once more before war made this impossible, and although he saw Clydesdale, a meeting with
Halifax at the Foreign Office never happened because the

Foreign Secretary had no 'window' in his day. James Douglas-Hamilton believes that his father and Haushofer met for the last time ten days before Haushofer drew up a vitally important report for von Ribbentrop, which was on 26 June 1937. The Haushofer papers imply that in fact they met again, in Berlin on 28 November 1938, although it is possible that this meeting was with Clydesdale's younger brother.*

Rudolf Hess of course always maintained that he had not met Clydesdale before at the Olympic Committee dinner, but it would have rung truer – and would explain Hess's message for Hamilton on his arrival – if Hess had in fact met the then Lord Clydesdale during that November visit. Is this why historian John Costello was refused access to the later correspondence between these inter-war friends? It is possible that the 'Hamilton' who visited Berlin in November was Clydesdale's younger brother David, killed on active service with the RAF in 1944, who had actually introduced Haushofer to Clydesdale in the first place. In a sense, it does not matter which Hamilton went to Berlin. The fact remains that a possible meeting with Hess and certainly a direct link to him – Haushofer – was made only ten months before war broke out; and not the two years suggested by James Douglas-Hamilton.

John Costello has gone further in suggesting that the Clydesdale-Hamilton relationship was a homosexual one, which perhaps explains the Hamilton family's reticence to release papers. Costello however had a reputation as a conspiracy theorist and perhaps something of a muck-raker and this may also explain the refusal. There is no evidence for such a relationship and it is one of the irrelevancies with which the Hess case is littered. What is certain is that Albrecht Haushofer was already

---

* There were four Douglas-Hamilton brothers, all serving in wartime with the RAF. Specifically, the Berlin meeting may have involved David.

known to British Intelligence long before the war began. A report on him, originally dated May 1937, but updated and included in a brief written in May 1941, reads:

Albrecht Haushofer is the son of Professor Karl Haushofer, editor of the German periodical 'Geopolitik' and is secretary of the German Geographical Society. He paid frequent visits to this country during 1935 to 1937 ... Haushofer has many intimate connections among whom is the Duke of Hamilton (then Lord Clydesdale). He is a close associate of Hitler and is on personal terms with most of the Nazi hierarchy and from his remarks to the informant it seems fairly certain that he was engaged on some work as secretary to the German Geographical Society. He is not a man of any means and it is believed that his frequent visits to this country were paid for by some government department. He was at that time a man of 34 years of age and had not been called to serve in the German army. His reason for not being called up was that his class had not been called upon to do their military service except as volunteers. This statement is not in accordance with the facts at that time and this enhances the possibility that he was engaged in some special type of work. (According to the War Office the fact that Albrecht Haushofer had not been called up in the German army was not regarded as being of any particular significance.) The source who reported this considered that Haushofer was probably engaged in the collection of intelligence in the United Kingdom.

At that time the 'Geopolitik' was of particular interest to Rudolf Hess, who was in close collaboration with Professor Karl Haushofer.

As regards Albrecht Haushofer's father, the German 'Wer Ist's' ('Who's Who') states that Karl Haushofer is professor at the University of Munich and was formerly in the Kriegs Akademie and was on the General Staff. He has written a large number of works dealing with geography, anthropology and geopolitics. His work on 'Geopolitik' is said to have received a great deal of attention from Hitler himself and from the Deputy Leader, Hess. It is even suggested that it influences Hitler's views on Foreign Policy and also on military questions. It was also suggested that Albrecht Haushofer visited this country in connection with the scientific and strategical questions on the lines of his father's work rather than to concern himself with intelligence matters in the ordinary sense. It is also believed that Karl Haushofer's strategic view found a place in *Mein Kampf*.

Somewhere around 1937 a book was written by two Germans, Hans Hummel and Wulf Siwert, entitled 'Der Mittlemeerraum'. These two were said to be among the leading exponents of the teachings of Karl Haushofer's principles and it was thought that this book which contained a strategical study of the Mediterranean might approximate closely to the views of the General Staff and was therefore worthy of consideration.

In June 1937 the use of the word 'Geopolitik' appeared in a questionnaire which was supplied to members of the Hitler Jugend [Hitler Youth] and similar organizations when touring in this and other countries. This fact was corroborated by a statement in the Press which contained instructions given to parties of Nazis cycling in various countries. These instructions impressed on all cyclists the necessity of paying attention to and memorizing the country through which they passed and noting all landmarks and acquainting themselves in such a way that they would be able to recognize them by night. It ended by saying 'the time has come when you will be able to serve your country by this knowledge'. It was also known at that time that the Hitler Jugend Party were instructed to obtain 'not only a knowledge of the landscape but also to see the true face of England and its people.' These instructions seem to come within the meaning of the word 'Geopolitik' and it was thought possible that they might in fact have been put out to the Party members under Haushofer's instructions.

In January 1938 it was reported from a source in Germany that Dr Albrecht Haushofer was said to be one of the coming men in Germany and the greatest expert in Germany on the British Empire.[26]

With the exception of Haushofer's briefing squadrons of young Nazi cyclists (for which there is no evidence) everything else is extremely accurate. Since the report goes on to include details of intercepted correspondence between Haushofer and Hamilton, it would seem possible that the anonymous provider of such extraordinarily accurate information was Hamilton himself and points to his close co-operation with the secret service, something that his son has always denied.

It is of course possible that Hamilton was unaware that he was in fact reporting to MI5 but if he is the source, this pins him to an element in the Hess story four years before the accepted view and at least three years before his subsequent involvement when Hess landed. In the accepted version of events, Hamilton's name first appears out of the blue, when 'Hauptmann Horn' landed in Scotland and demanded to see him. This is incomprehensible unless some sort of link existed prior to May 1941. Now we have the answer – the link was Albrecht Haushofer.

By July 1939, Albrecht Haushofer knew that all his hopes to modify or even control the aggressive German foreign policy were dashed. Ribbentrop, the man who had left Britain under what he imagined was a cloud of insult, was now running the Foreign Office in Berlin and scrawling his blue pencil across thousands of square miles of somebody else's territory to fulfil Hitler's desire for *lebensraum*. Haushofer was on a field trip to the Norwegian fjords with his students when he wrote the famous letter to Clydesdale which James Douglas-Hamilton quotes in full.

The half-Jewish intellectual whose own father had given Hitler, via Rudolf Hess, the idea of Eastern European domination, wrestled with his conscience on paper, as he had countless times at home to his friends and to Clydesdale in person: 'I just want to give you a sign of personal friendship – I do hope that you will survive whatever may happen in Europe – and I want to send you a word of warning.'[27]

Haushofer predicted war would break out at any time from the middle of August. Hitler was counting, he said, on British inactivity, fence-sitting, even more appeasement; and Hitler, with his strange fatalism, felt that he did not have much time left to him. Haushofer's assessment was that nothing could be done from inside Germany. The British however might still avert the crisis. The answer was to put pressure on Mussolini – 'the big man in Rome' – and broker a deal with Germany which would give her fair territorial rights.

He could not, in a letter, go into detail, but the tone was not far removed from what Hitler and Hess would ask for between 1940 and 1941. Ironically, it was probably far more achievable under Chamberlain and before actual war was declared than ever it would be under Churchill once the bombs began to fall. Haushofer was running the risk of execution in contacting Clydesdale in this way and he asked that the peer destroy the letter after he had shown it, if Clydesdale saw fit, to Halifax or Rab Butler. He asked for a bland postcard by return as acknowledgement that Clydesdale had received the correspondence.

With a great prescience, Clydesdale showed the letter to Churchill, still in the wilderness in the summer of 1939 and the soon-to-be-great man's cigar went out as he read its pessimistic forebodings. 'There is going to be war very soon,' he said. 'In that case,' said Clydesdale, 'I very much hope that you will be Prime Minister.' 'What a hell of a time,' came the reply, 'to become Prime Minister.'[28]

Halifax and Chamberlain saw the letter in due course and, according to James Douglas-Hamilton, Clydesdale sent his postcard to Haushofer, as arranged.

There is another letter in the Hess affair which in a sense began the chain reaction of events leading to Hess's arrival. On 31 August 1940, Rudolf Hess visited Karl Haushofer at his Bavarian Alpine lodge – the professor and his student talked until two in the morning. A subsequent letter written by the professor to Albrecht between 3 and 9 September chronicles their discussion and has never been quoted in full before.

Dearest Albrecht,

Warm thanks for your letter of the 29th from the Imperial Hotel in Vienna where I somehow guessed you might be.

You know that you wrote your birthday letter to me in the air-raid shelter? Well, I could have reciprocated the labour of love to you on the night of the 1st and 2nd because I promised your mother when she left the Alm to go down when the alarm sounded and so I spent 1½ hours doing somersaults and gymnastics!

As with you everything's really changed here. Lisa's sudden departure, which you witnessed, made mother's trip to Hart pointless. She stayed at Alm because her stomach and knee have got much worse at the same time and due to circumstances let me go to Tal alone from 31st to 3rd. It was well worth it since it allowed me to be together with Tomo [Hess] from 5 o'clock in the afternoon until 2 o'clock in the morning. During this time we went for a three-hour walk in the Grunwald Forest and talked a great deal about serious matters. I must tell you about some of this.

As you know, a hard and brutal procedure has been set in place for the island in question [Britain] that the man in charge only has to press a button for everything to go up in smoke.

But before this possibly unavoidable decision is taken, we should really set our minds to thinking whether there is some way of delaying the terrible consequences. In connection with this I have an idea which I must convey to you because it was clearly passed on to me with that aim in mind. Can you see any way of arranging talks about such possibilities at some neutral venue with a mediator, perhaps old Ian Hamilton or the other Hamilton? To these suggestions I replied that an excellent opportunity may have arisen in Lisbon during the centenary celebrations if it had been possible to send well-camouflaged political figures there rather than harmless puppets. In connection with this, it seems to me that it is the arm of fate which allowed our old friend Miss VR to find a way, even after a long delay, of sending a note bearing hearty greetings not only to your mother, but also to Heinz and me and showing the address. Address your reply to Miss V. Roberts, c/o Postbox 506, Lisbon, Portugal. I have the feeling that we should use every opportunity to think about this. I am not surprised that you were suddenly drawn into the great theatre; Tomo had almost the same feeling on Saturday and Sunday and his sincerity is charming.

I was as reluctant as you to take responsibility for decisions which are historically hard to bear. But on balance, there has been no time wasted if you consider that in return you had a wonderful flight over the Salzkammer land directly over Traunstein, right past the Schafberg and saw the Butzelware again – something for which you could not have hoped. As the writer of three Roman dramas, the political content of this conference – I don't wish to say like two years ago – must have moved you by its great humanity. But like one year ago, you must have been interested in the strange play, the remarkable delivery as 'Gebharen' (which I still spell with an 'h' like an old fashioned person) and in your position I should also have gone along to the hall more frequently this year. I know you and Bristol and I know what it means to you and to me that Larich, poor Camilla and Hedebum have retreated into the shadows and that Moretto's picture has been packed away somewhere in the cellar amongst sacks of sand.

You didn't need to hold anxious conversations with ambassadors and envoys; you should have ignored superior and nosy journalists and marionettes from the history of the world like Sulla's military or Augustus's diplomatic entourage or the hellenistic private secretary to the younger Scipio.

In any case, I thank you kindly collecting together the greetings for Polybius and others like her and think it's a pity you missed the satirical play in your beautiful big room. But it enabled me to receive a lovely long, letter which I shall take back to the Alm on Thursday so that I can enjoy the memories it brings to me of you and which, personally, I treasure as much as your mother does.

One final request. As a result of some mistake, your friend Wolfgang Hoffman seems to have drifted off into the upper echelons of the military. But I am returning the card to you as a sign of goodwill and because the picture shows a beautiful and dear piece of land which invokes pleasant memories.

Another piece of news: Oberleutnant Dr Steinacher, who has already written me three nice letters, can be contacted by No. 30761L. Not only Major Stolze in the OKV but also a relative of Dr Bausback (brother-in-law, commander of the army's non-commissioned officers in Grucher's 7th Army Corps) who claims to have access to influential references for him, are campaigning for his promotion to Oberstleutnant. Now that, as company boss, he is ready to be promoted to the top level, it must be about time that he is given the ring which he should have for his Austrian commission and medals, even if he did nothing between 1919 and 1939 other than sitting in coffee shops.

I replied to the Japanese ambassador's secretary as you suggested. Because of the American from Wisconsin, I hope I shall still be able to bring together Dai Nihon, the Japanese national representative, the pacific 'Geopolitik', the 'Weltpolitik', the borders and the various other special pressure groups. It will only be difficult because the 'mother' is out of action at the moment.

Tomo seems to be staying here until Wednesday and would very much like to see me again. I had to tell him about the affairs of our friends in Hamburg and the life history of their son and nephew on a Mark note and he promised me that he would sort out problems relating to the police and revenue office with the help of the most senior SS officials. Here too is a ray of hope and with that I send you my greetings and thank you sincerely in all the mad chaos.

Yours
 at present, Gallspach, 10.9.1940[29]

This letter, with its mix of family news, felicitations and classical allusion is so cryptic that some authorities have seen it as a code. 'Tomo' was the Haushofer family nickname for Hess. (Tomodachi was a Japanese military dictator, deified since the sixteenth century.) The 'hard and brutal procedure' to which Haushofer refers is clearly the switch to Britain's cities. Having failed to knock out the RAF with his attacks on airfields, Goering turned on civilians. Three weeks after this letter, death rained down on London in the first of countless air raids which the city had been expecting for a year. 'Old Ian Hamilton' was of course well known to Hess from his visit to Hitler at the Berghof. The 'other Hamilton' could be either Clydesdale or his brother, David, both of whom knew the Haushofers.

The Roman references are fascinating. Is this merely the banter of one intellectual to another or is it altogether deeper? Lucius Cornelius Sulla was a Roman general and statesman who saved Rome from attack by Mithridates and retired in 79 BC to lead a life of debauchery which finally killed him. Augustus was originally Octavius, the nephew of Julius Caesar, and perhaps the most successful of the Roman Emperors. Scipio could be any one of five generals and statesmen of the time of the wars against Carthage, but the *younger* Scipio and the Greek connection implies that Haushofer was probably referring to Publius Cornelius, known as Scipio Africanus Minor, himself no stranger to Intelligence gathering and subterfuge. Ronald Seth in *The Truth Benders* refers at length to the campaign in which Scipio sent his military experts to assess an enemy's strength while negotiating a feigned armistice with him. Polybius was a Greek historian, friend and chronicler of the younger Scipio. In view of Nazi doctrine, this is an interesting choice by Haushofer. Polybius believed that it was inevitable that all races should fall before the Romans because of their natural superiority. What gives the game away is the careless slip of pronoun – 'I thank you kindly collecting together the greetings for

Polybius and others like *her*' – when clearly the Greek historian was a man.

Just as Hess was Tomo, it seems likely that those names were veiled references to friends and enemies whose real names could not be used. Such mythological allusions are not unique to the Haushofers. In *Secret War* R.V. Jones reveals that the German radar systems were named after the Norse/Teutonic gods Freya and Wotan. Freya was fond of her fabulous necklace and Wotan had only one eye. From that Jones was able to deduce that the Freya system was a chain of radar stations and Wotan a single beam used for aircraft navigation.

The Haushofers, especially Albrecht, knew very well how dangerous their position was becoming. The son in particular was already dealing with those fragmented groups who were attempting to plot the overthrow of the Führer. Mail was intercepted, telephones were tapped. Walls, even of Bavarian hunting lodges, had ears. Is that why Hess and his professor had gone for a walk in the woods? Does that explain the cryptic references to other people? The phrase 'arm of fate' in particular is very telling. None of this was luck. It was part of a deliberate, purposeful and co-ordinated plan. The Haushofers, should this letter fall into the wrong hands, would need to protect their friends. Haushofer knew perfectly well that Hess's flight was not likely to succeed. He was a careful man and proceeded accordingly.

The references in fact relate to a meeting in Vienna on 27 August 1940 that Albrecht had attended. The principal delegates were von Ribbentrop and Ciano, his Italian opposite number, who took the opportunity to bully the Foreign Ministers of Romania and Hungary. The centenary celebrations in Lisbon marked the 700th anniversary of the city's existence. The British were represented by the Duke of Kent (who would die mysteriously in an air crash in 1942) and the British Press were humming with speculation that the Duke would or would not meet the Windsors, who had gravitated to Lisbon after the fall of France. Certainly these were the months of increasingly outspoken comments from the Duke of Windsor which some have interpreted as barely disguised Nazism. The 'harmless marionettes' reference may well be a gibe against those Germans who sought to win Windsor openly to their camp.

The most intriguing paragraph in the letter – one which James Douglas–Hamilton omits entirely – is of course the reference to the 'hearty greetings' sent by the Haushofers' old friend, Miss V.R. The 'long delay' mentioned by the professor surely refers to the fact that the widow Mary Violet Roberts had suddenly written to the Haushofers out of the blue. We will see that she had very good reasons to break the long silence. But why was she in Portugal?

The fact is that, contrary to the established school of thought, Mrs Roberts never left Cambridge, unless it was to go back to London occasionally. The executor of her estate is her cousin Edward Playfair, who was close to the lady throughout the war. He used to go on holiday with the Roberts family. His reply to my question 'Did Mrs Roberts ever go to Lisbon?' was a simple 'No.' So what about the Lisbon address, where all other authorities on the Hess flight have assumed Violet Roberts lived?

During modern wars, it is not possible merely to use the conventional postal system that operates in peacetime. The solution was to use a third neutral state as a go-between, a sort of international poste restante. Switzerland, the most persistent of the European neutrals, offered such a service – the International Freedom Bureau – and in 1917, with the First World War at its height, the travel agency Thomas Cook provided, with Government approval, a similar service operating out of Geneva and Berne. The letters were checked by censors, restamped with Swiss stamps and sent on their way.

At the outbreak of Hitler's war, Thomas Cook had used their Amsterdam office, but the fall of Holland in May 1940

Left: Hess at the Führer's side, during a pre-war Nazi Parade, Weimar.
© HULTON GETTY.

Below: Denis Sefton Delmer, Paris 1939. The man who lured Hess to Britain in 1941?
© EXPRESS

Right: This extract from the Hartschimmelhof visitor book clearly shows the Roberts' pre-war visit to Bavaria.

Hartschimmel Gäste 1916-1940

Renata von Dall' Armi 3. IX. 16
Hannah von Westernhagen
Ida Gräfin Spreti 6. X.16
Gisi "   "
Henny "   "
Sophia Goudstikker
Albert u Frau 17. IX.18
Bertha Gräfin Litzarag
Georg von Dall' Armi 27. V. 17
Gertrand Wolff 20. VI. 17
Helene von Dall' Armi 9. IX.17
Eduard Max Hofweber 7. VII.17
Paul Fohr 8. IX.18
Theobald Weiss
Alfred Haushofer 26. VI.18
Konrad von Dall' Armi 28. X.17
Flore Rickmers 21. VIII.17
Leo Hausleiter 6. X. 18
Ernst Heinrich Romberg 11. X. 18
Margret Hofweber 22. VI. 19
Wöbe und Ursula Kofler 19. IX.19
Karl Schneider 29. IX.19
Moritz Büttner IX.19
Rudolf Hess 4. X. 20
           4. VII.20

Violet Roberts 13. VIII.25 6/7 IX. 26
Patrick "
Richard Kiliani "
Elise Jung 15. VIII. 25
Paul Wentzke 15. VIII. 25
Camilla Meyer 27. VIII. 25
Gabrielle Gräfin Spreti 7. IX.25
Nina Baronin Hess 25. IX. 25
Christa Gräfin Drym 25. IX. 25
Hermann von Wissmann 25. IX. 25
Bruno Schweizer 4/5. X. 25
Elisabeth Michel 21. VIII.26
Hermann Heimpel 24. VIII.26
Eugenie Knorr 24. VIII.26
Adrienne " 25. VIII.26
Elly Seiglmayr 25. VIII.26
Patel 29. VIII.26
Wilhelm von Kloeber 29. VIII.26
Agnes Smedley 30. VIII.26
Ebba Gillmann 31. VIII.26
Carl 4. IX.26
Paul Rickpel "
Fritz Hesse "
K. Frey 10.IX.25
                    4. IX.26

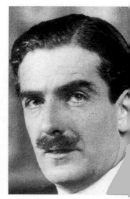

Top left: Leonard Ingrams, the brilliant former banker who recruited Sefton Delmer to PWE.

Top centre: Hugh Dalton, the abrasive head of SO1/PWE, 1947.
© POPPERFOTO

Top right: Anthony Eden. Why were both Eden and Hugh Dalton at Woburn on 10 May 1941?
© POPPERFOTO

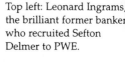

Left: Woburn Abbey. A pre-war picture showing the stable blocks which housed the PWE during the war.
© AEROFILMS

Left: Ian Hamilton and Hitler at Berchtesgaden 1938, from the front cover of the *Anglo-German Review*.
© LIDDELL HART CENTRE FOR MILITARY ARCHIVES

Right: 48 Storey Way, Cambridge, the home of Violet Roberts, the key to the understanding of the Hess conspiracy.
© JOHN HARRIS

Right: Lennoxlove House. Was this Hess's target?
© JOHN HARRIS

Right: Dungavel. The Duke of Hamilton's residence in 1941, now a high security prison.
© JOHN HARRIS

Left: The Rookery, Apsley Guise. Sefton Delmer's residence/office when not at Woburn. Was this where the plot was hatched?
© JOHN HARRIS

Above: His Royal Highness, the Duke of Kent, with General Sikorski, the Polish Prime Minister, who is presenting decorations to fighting heroes of Poland, at a port in Scotland (1939).
© HULTON GETTY

Left: Lennoxlove airstrip, looking towards Trapain Law.
© JOHN HARRIS

Top: The Duke of Hamilton's old airfield at Dungavel House. © JOHN HARRIS

Centre: The Messerschmitt BF110, which combined range with performance. © AEROSPACE

Below: Floors Farm, Eaglesham. It was here that Hess crashed at 23:09, 10 May 1941.
© JOHN HARRIS

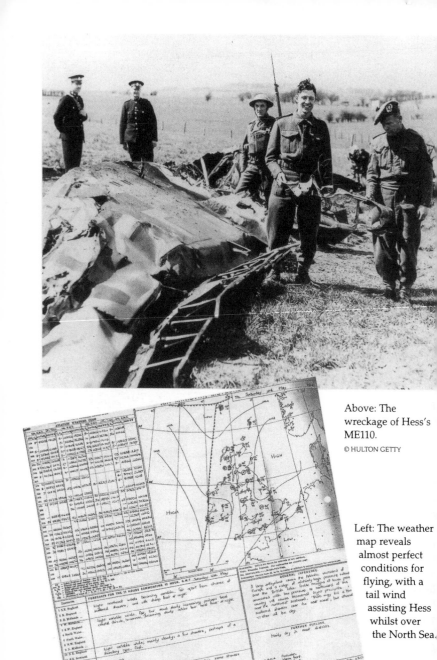

Above: The wreckage of Hess's ME110.

© HULTON GETTY

Left: The weather map reveals almost perfect conditions for flying, with a tail wind assisting Hess whilst over the North Sea.

	39	49				Nº300 ObserverCentre		
	38	48	58	68	78			
	37	47	57	67	77	87	97	07
	36	46	56	66	76	86	96	06
	35	45	55	65	75	85	95	05
	34	44	54	64	74	84	94	04
23	33	43	53	63	73	83	93	03
22	32	42	52	62	72	82	92	02
21	31	41	51	61	71	81	91	01
20	30	40	50	60	70	80	90	00
29	39	49	59	69	79	89	99	09
28	38	48	58	68	78	88	98	08
27	37	47	57	67	77	87	97	07
26	36	46	56	66	76	86	96	06
	35	45	55	65	75	85	95	05
	34	44	54	64	74	84	94	04
	33	43	53	63	73	83	93	03
	32	42	52	62	72	82	92	02
	31	41	51	61	71	81	9	

Left: This important document, the Observer Map of the night of Hess's flight, shows the Hess plane (Raid 42), a second enemy plane (Raid 42J) and a third plot (GU). None of the Operational Record Books (ORB's) mention the other two planes. So, where did plot GU take off or land? Why does Hamilton make no mention of plot GU?

Below: Rokeby, the Duke of Bedford's Priest, whilst at Cairnsmore. He was placed under house arrest with the Duke, after the Hess flight.

Right: The international, sceptical reaction to Hess's flight and the Nazi cries of madness,
Picture Post, May 31 1941.

THE NAZI RADIO: 'He knew nothing of matters of high policy.'

THE TRUTH: He has met every important minister to Germany for eight years.

THE NAZI RADIO: 'His limitations were recognised by Hitler.'

THE TRUTH: He was Hitler's oldest and only trusted friend.

THE TRUTH: He Has Met Every Important Visitor to Germany for Eight Years
In Munich, September, 1938. Hess drives with Mussolini, who calls him "my comrade." Five months before, Hess went with Hitler to Rome. They listen to call him in Germany "Father of the Axis." To understand other countries his manners are used as a prime tool of Nazi policy.

THE NAZI RADIO: "His Limitations were recognised by Hitler."

THE TRUTH: He was Hitler's oldest and only Trusted Friend
June, 1924. Hitler and Hess with their fellow prisoners in the fortress of Landsberg, Bavaria. In November, 1923, Hitler has tried to seize power in Bavaria, two members of the Government have arrested and it is Hess who kidnapped them on Hitler's orders. In the fortress "Mein Kampf" is written.

HESS: A

The arrival of Hess in Glasgow machine out of gear. Its announce—

WITH the flight of Rudolf Hess to Scotland on May 11, 1941, part of Hitler's own personality fell off, like the skin which is sloughed from some labouring monster. It is worth seeing that, shortly before the protective covering of Hess was removed from the figure of Hitler, possibly the most potent account in Russia, where Stalin, by assuming the Premiership, at last took the side responsibility for his own behaviour. In Russia, Molotov, who had behaved as such a faithful, pliable, trickling skin for so many years, was content to be left lying on a shelf as gct comfortably dusty, and his master was willing to leave him there. But in Germany these natural processes occur in a more extravagantly melodramatic way, which gives them the appearance of being highly unnatural. Melodrama, in fact, serves a useful purpose as the Nazis in hiding what is really happening.

Something more needs to be said on the relationship between Hess and Hitler. Stephen H. Roberts in his well-known book, "The House That Hitler Built," wrote:

"Hess is not very impressive personally. He would not stand out in a crowd. For the most part, he repeats Hitler's statements and makes

Hess in the dock at the Nuremberg War Trials, 21 September 1946. © HULTON GETTY

Spandau. The old Prussian prison which held Hess for forty years currently plays host to a supermarket. © JOHN HARRIS

made this impossible and they moved south to Lisbon, using PO Box 506 from June of the same year. If, as seems obvious from the 'hearty greetings' referred to in Karl Haushofer's letter to Albrecht, Mrs Roberts wanted to send a letter to her old friends in Bavaria, she would post it to the Thomas Cook office in London, together with a two-shilling postal order. The letter would then travel to Lisbon for redirection. The Germans were fully aware of this system and of the other undercover addresses used for the purpose.[30]

The question remains – why should Violet Roberts go to such lengths to write to the Haushofers? Whatever the private feelings of the two families, Britain and Germany were at war. Whatever double, treble and highly dangerous game the younger Haushofer was playing, he and Violet Roberts were technically enemies. I believe – and this is the kernel of the truth behind the Hess flight – that Mrs Roberts's 'hearty greeting', so unexpected and so timely, was actually the work of SO1 at Woburn.

At Woburn, the Director of Finance was Walter Roberts, the old lady's nephew. At Leonard Ingrams' instigation, did he ask his aunt to write to Karl Haushofer? Did he tell her what to say? Or did he merely provide a sample of her handwriting so that a master-forger like Ellic Howe could do the rest? The secretarial staff at Woburn was provided by Thomas Cook and Co. Walter Roberts would have been made fully conversant with the posting system. For Professor Haushofer to be referring to a letter he had already received by 3 September, the Mrs Roberts letter (which unfortunately has not survived) was probably composed and written in June or July, to allow for the inevitable delay in the system. This coincides with the date of formation of SO1 and SO2, when the most maverick and unaccountable plots of black propaganda were being hatched.[31]

What evidence is there to suggest that the Roberts letter came not from her but from Woburn? It is unlikely that the old lady had seen the Haushofers for at least nine years. Their documented meetings can be definitely traced to c.1899, 1926 and perhaps 1932. The letter from Karl Haushofer to Albrecht notes the arrival of the letter 'after a long delay'. Neither of them could be surprised at postal delays in wartime; the reference is clearly to the fact that Mrs Roberts's communication came out of the blue, and at such an auspicious time for a possible Anglo-German rapprochement. The fact that the actual letter has not survived is very telling. It is an example of the missing 'paper trail' which has so bedevilled research into this work.

The position of Walter Stewart Roberts at Woburn is just too much of a coincidence. For all Ellic Howe refers to him as the 'firm's accountant', I find this very hard to believe. Why should such a secret organization as SO1 recruit a high-flying City stockbroker to handle Woburn's petty cash? And why should that same stockbroker be given a CBE for his services, unless those services were actually far more important? And why have officials accepted Heinz Haushofer's statement that Mrs Roberts was the daughter-in-law of 'Bobs', unless it is in someone's interest to send researchers up the wrong garden path?

We do not know what else, besides 'hearty greetings' was in the Roberts letter of June/July 1940. But only one supposition satisfactorily explains the chain of events that now began: it offered the old lady's services as an intermediary between Hess and a potential British peace party.

On 10 September, Hess wrote to Karl Haushofer, continuing their discussion of a projected peace with Britain:

> 'It would be best to have the letter to the old lady with whom you are acquainted, delivered through a confidential agent of the A.O. [Ausland Organization] to the address that is known to you . . . Meanwhile, let's both

keep our fingers crossed. Should success be the fate of
the enterprise, the oracle given to you with regard to
the month of August would yet be fulfilled, since the
name of the young friend [Hamilton] and the old lady
friend of your family [Mrs Roberts] occurred to you
during our quiet walk on the last day of that month.'[32]

Nine days later, Albrecht Haushofer wrote to Hess pointing
out the difficulties of making direct contact with the Duke of
Hamilton, whose name must have been well known to SO1 –
he had a number of German friends, was part of that international aviation set whose friendship had crossed national
boundaries before the war and he fitted the pattern of a potential leader of the disquieted Scottish lords, ostensibly unhappy
with Churchill. Interestingly, Haushofer reversed the situation, imagining himself in Hamilton's shoes and he gave Hess
the vital suggestion which I believe the Stellvertreter acted
upon: 'I would then,' wrote Haushofer, 'be anxious to get my
instructions, if not from the Führer himself . . .'[33]

I believe that is precisely where Hess got his instructions
from. We know that it was in Hitler's interests to broker some
sort of deal with the British. We know that there was still a
vague trace of an anti-Churchill party to be found, largely
among the crankier elements of the aristocracy. We know that
Hess, the conscience of the party, the devoted lieutenant of
Hitler, the dreamer of dreams, was the perfect choice to act as
go-between.

Even while Professor Haushofer was writing to his son
from Gallspach, Hess sent for Albrecht and the essence of
their discussion was minuted by the younger Haushofer from
Berlin on 15 September, when the war was a year and two
weeks old:

'On 8 September, I was summoned to Bad G[odesberg]
to report to the Deputy of the Führer on the subject

155

discussed in this memorandum. The conversation which the two of us had alone lasted two hours. I had the opportunity to speak in all frankness.

I was immediately asked about the possibilities of making known to persons of importance in England Hitler's serious desire for peace. It was quite clear that the continuance of the war was suicidal for the white race. Even with complete peace in Europe, Germany was not in a position to take over the inheritance of the Empire. The Führer had not wanted to see the Empire destroyed and did not want it even today. Was there not somebody in England who was ready for peace?

First I asked for permission to discuss fundamental things. It was necessary to realize that not only Jews and Freemasons, but practically all Englishmen who mattered, regarded a treaty signed by the Führer as a worthless scrap of paper. To the question as to why this should be so, I referred to the ten-year term of our Polish treaty, to the non-aggression pact with Denmark signed only one year ago, to the final frontier demarcation of Munich. What guarantee did England have that the new treaty would not be broken again at once if it suited us? It must be realized that, even in the Anglo Saxon world, the Führer was regarded as Satan's representative on earth and had to be fought.

If the worst came to the worst, the English would rather transfer their whole Empire bit by bit to the Americans than sign a peace that left to National Socialist Germany the mastery of Europe. The present war, I was convinced, shows that Europe has become too small for its previous anarchic form of existence; it is only through close German–English co-operation that it can achieve a true federative order (based by no means merely on the police rule of a single power) while maintaining a part of its world position and having security against Soviet Russian Eurasia. France was smashed, probably for a long time to come, and we had opportunity currently to observe what Italy is capable of accomplishing. As long, however, as German–English rivalry existed and in so far as both sides thought in terms of security, the lesson of the war was this: every German had to tell himself: we have no security as long as provision is not made that the Atlantic gateways of Europe from Gibraltar to Narvik are free of any possible blockade. That is, there must be no English fleet. Every Englishman must, however, under the same conditions argue: we have no security as long as anywhere within a radius of 2,000 kilometres from London there is a place that we do not control. That is, there must be no German Air Force.

There is only one way out of this dilemma: friendship intensified to fusion, with a joint fleet, a joint air force and joint defence of possessions in the world – just what the English are now about to conclude with the United States.

Here I was interrupted and asked why, indeed, the English were prepared to seek such a relationship with America and not with us. My reply was: because Roosevelt is a man who represents a Weltanschauung [world outlook] and a way of life that the Englishman thinks he understands, to which he can become accustomed, even where it does not seem to be to his liking. Perhaps he can fool himself, but at any rate that is what he believes.

A man like Churchill – himself half American – is convinced of this. Hitler, however, seems to the Englishman the incarnation of what he hates, that he has fought against for centuries – this feeling grips the workers no less than the plutocrats. In fact, I am of the opinion that those Englishmen who have property to lose, that is, precisely the portions of the so-called plutocracy that count, are those who would be readiest to talk peace. But even they regard peace as an armistice.

I was compelled to express these things so strongly because I ought not – precisely because of my long experience in attempting to effect a settlement with England in the past and my numerous English friendships – to make it appear that I seriously believed in the possibility of a settlement between Adolf Hitler and England in the present stage of development.

I was thereupon asked whether I was not of the opinion that feelers had perhaps not been successful because the right language had not been used. I replied that, to be sure – if certain persons, whom we both knew well [Ribbentrop] were meant by this statement – then certainly the wrong language had been used. But at the present stage this had little significance.

I was then asked directly why all Englishmen were so opposed to Herr von Ribbentrop. I suggested that in the eyes of the English, Herr von Ribbentrop, like some other personages, played the same role as did Duff Cooper, Eden and Churchill in the eyes of the Germans. In the case of Herr von Ribbentrop, there was also the conviction, precisely in the view of Englishmen who were formerly friendly with Germany, that – from completely biased motives – he had informed the Führer wrongly about England and that he personally bore an unusually large share of responsibility for the outbreak of the war.

But I again stressed the fact that the rejection of peace feelers by England was today due not so much to persons as to the fundamental outlook above.

Nevertheless, I was asked to name those whom I thought might be reached as possible contacts.

I mentioned among diplomats, Minister O'Malley in

Budapest, the former head of the South Eastern Department of the Foreign Office, a clever person in the highest echelons of officialdom, but perhaps without influence precisely because of his former friendliness towards Germany; Sir Samuel Hoare, who is half-shelved and half on the watch in Madrid, whom I do not know well personally, but to whom I can at any time open a personal path; as the most promising, the Washington Ambassador, Lothian, with whom I have had close personal connections for years, who as a member of the highest aristocracy and at the same time as a person of very independent mind, is perhaps best in a position to undertake a bold step – provided that he could be convinced that even a bad or uncertain peace would be better than the continuance of the war – a conviction at which he will only arrive if he convinces himself in Washington that English hopes of America are not realisable. Whether or not this is so could only be judged in Washington itself; from Germany not at all.

As the final possibility I then mentioned that of a personal meeting on a neutral soil with the closest of my English [*sic*] friends; the young Duke of Hamilton who has access at all times to all important persons in London, even to Churchill and the King. I stressed in this case the inevitable difficulty of making a contact and again repeated my conviction of the improbability of its succeeding – whatever approach we took.

The upshot of the conversation was Hess's statement that he would consider the whole matter once more and send me word in case I was to take steps. For this extremely ticklish case, and in the event that I might possibly have to make a trip alone – I asked for very precise directions from the highest authority.

From the whole conversation I had the strong

impression that it was not conducted without the prior knowledge of the Führer, and that I probably would not hear any more about the matter unless a new understanding had been reached between him and his deputy.

On the personal side of the conversation I must say that – despite the fact that I felt bound to say unusually hard things – it ended in great friendliness, even cordiality.[34]

Albrecht Haushofer was between a rock and a hard place. It seems from his response to Hess that the Stellvertreter and Hitler were still keen to establish peace with Britain, having had official public overtures rejected in July by Sefton Delmer over the BBC airwaves. Why else would Hess ask for names of approachable contacts? Hess and Haushofer went back a long way and there is between the lines the air of a man who does not want to let an old friend down. But matters were too serious for niceties, hence Haushofer's 'unusually hard things'. He was bound to report the truth as he saw it – and he was right – that there wasn't a peace party in Britain worthy of the name. He wanted peace too – though his motives were more humane than Hess's or Hitler's – but he couldn't see how to achieve it, given the defiant mood of the British. Even his possible list of contacts was low key. Nearly all of them – O'Malley, Hoare and Lothian – were physically a long way from Britain and they were discredited in the eyes of British authorities because of their pacifist or Appeasement stance. Only Hamilton was on British soil, but even here, Haushofer knew the improbability of any support from that quarter. He knew perfectly well that Hamilton was a patriot and a serving officer in the RAF.

But Hess would not be deterred. The 10 September letter he wrote to Karl Haushofer needs to be quoted in full:

Highly esteemed and dear friend!

Albrecht has brought me your letter which, together

with the introductory remarks about service matters, reminded me of the combined walking tour on the last day of August, of which I too have such happy memories.

Albrecht will have informed you about our conversation, which, apart from Volksdeutschen Dingen, dealt alone with the other matter which we both hold most dear. I have once again given this matter most careful thought and have come up with the following conclusion:–

On no account must we overlook the connection or let it go cold. I think it would be best if you or Albrecht wrote to the old lady befriended by your family asking her if she would try to find out from Albrecht's friend [Hamilton] if he would be prepared, if need be, to come to the neutral country [Lisbon] where she lives or at any rate had her forwarding address, in order to talk to Albrecht. If he were not able to do this immediately perhaps he would at all events let it be known, through her, which place he intends to stay at in the immediate future. A neutral acquaintance who just happened to be active in that area would possibly look him up and pass on to him information concerning you or Albrecht. The same neutral would not wish to ask about his place of residence or to make fruitless journeys. You might both (you and Albrecht) think that knowing his place of residence has no military significance at all: you would also, if need be, pledge yourselves to make no use of this with regard to my post for which this [knowledge] could be of use. The information which the neutral (agent) might pass on would be of such significance that, in comparison, the disclosure of his place of residence would be of no account.

It is of course assumed that the relevant request and reply would not be sent by the official channels, for upon

161

no account would you wish to put your friend over there to any inconvenience.

It would probably be best if the letter to your friend the old lady was delivered by an intermediary agent at the AO [Ausland Organization] at the address known to you. For this purpose Albrecht would have to talk to Bohle [Hess's head man at the AO in Berlin] or my brother [who ran an AO department]. At the same time the agent's address in L[isbon] or another AO agent permanently residing there would have to be transmitted to the lady, who in turn would send the reply to the agent's address.

I would like to discuss with you sometime in person the kind of neutral envisaged for all this. This would not be enough in itself as I would need to have had a reply from the agent in the first place . . .[35]

Albrecht Haushofer wrote to his parents in response to Hess's tortuous scheme:

In the middle of some rather hectic activity just these few words for today to let you know that I have received that certain letter. I am going to think about the whole case for 24 hours and then will write immediately to T [Hess].

It won't really go the way he thinks it will. However I could formulate a letter to D.H. [either David or Duke of Hamilton] in such a way that the transmission of it will in no way endanger our lady friend; above all, I must make it clear to T. once again that my ducal friend of course can't write to me without the permission of his highest authority . . .[36]

It did not, indeed, go the way Hess thought it would. Whether he ever travelled to Lisbon with a view to setting out on some sort of peace mission has not been proven. Wolf Hess has no personal information from his father's papers or family reminiscences. Likewise, although Hamilton was approached on this matter, he never actually went. Believing that real prospects of peace awaited him, the Stellvertreter had taken the bait. But both Hess and Haushofer now seemed keen to let Mrs Roberts off the hook – she was not to be endangered. On 19 September, Haushofer wrote to his parents that he feared the whole thing was 'a fool's errand'.

Albrecht's letter to Hamilton was posted on 23 September, addressed to the PO Box 506 in Lisbon. It is odd that neither Hess nor Haushofer seemed to know that this was merely a posting convenience, not the likely address of Mrs Roberts, although Haushofer implies it might be a forwarding address in his letter of 10 September. How the old lady was supposed to forward the letter to Hamilton is another unsolved mystery. The 'hearty greetings' letter and/or other correspondence now missing may have explained how this last leg of the letter's journey was to be accomplished. It was clearly intended as an alternative route to official channels in order to avoid the censor.

In the event, the letter reached Hamilton in March 1941, having been intercepted by the censor's department at the Ministry of Information. I believe that this interception was nothing of the sort. There was no Mrs Roberts at PO Box 506 in Lisbon, but there was an agent of the Political Warfare Executive. Why it was bounced around in various corridors of power for the next five months has never satisfactorily been explained but the depth of the subterfuge is illustrated by the response of Sir Alexander Cadogan's Foreign Office memo of 22 November 1940:

A letter dated 23 September 1940 written by somebody named 'Dr A.H', obviously a German, to the Duke of Hamilton was intercepted by the censor and copies sent to M15, the Foreign Office and IRB.

'We don't seem to come into this very much . . .' a Foreign Office official noted, '. . . perhaps M15 does not step in that direction.'[37] The Secret Services, in the form of the black propagandists of SO1, stepped in a direction utterly secret from other branches of the service, and is a reminder that, despite the creation of liaison posts like that held by Dallas Brooks, the various branches were often less than co-operative with each other and could be petty in the extreme.

There was at least one more letter sent by Mrs Roberts to Karl Haushofer. Unfortunately, like much else in the Hess deception, it has not survived. Luckily, the envelope has. It is in the Bundesarchiv and is dated 10 May 1941, the very day of the Hess flight. The fact that Mrs Roberts was not in Lisbon (which Hess himself may not have known), and the fact that in his subsequent report to Hitler after Hess's flight, Albrecht Haushofer makes no mention of any later correspondence with her, would indicate that the Roberts/Haushofer/Hamilton route probably came to an end or at least was not carried on in isolation.

That Hess decided to try the personal approach on British soil rather than the safe ground of neutral Lisbon can be attributed to the black propaganda of SO1 which was now clicking into place, via the good offices of two further go-betweens, Carl Burkhardt and Tancred Borenius.

On 28 April, Albrecht Haushofer was sent to neutral Geneva to meet with Carl Burkhardt, a prominent member of the International Committee of the Red Cross. Burkhardt later told llse von Hassel that Haushofer had come with 'a double face' – in other words as a double agent for Hitler and Hess *and* the conservative Nazi opposition group known as the Wednesday Society.[38] Burkhardt's involvement in the Hess affair is outlined below, but the Red Cross man had already been visited three weeks previously by 'someone well known in City circles'. The identity of this someone has attracted much speculation, because it was possibly in this April meeting that the nitty-gritty details of the flight would have been worked out – dates, times, rendezvous, the names of the welcoming committee and so on. Alternatively, such information could have been relayed by post. The important point was to persuade Hess to make the flight.

Wolf Hess believes the 'someone' was Montagu Norman, Governor of the Bank of England. When I met the younger Hess and asked him how his father became aware of a desire for peace in this country, he gave the banker's name immediately. Norman had been a close friend of Hjalmar Schacht, financial genius of the Third Reich who got off lightly at Nuremberg and was one of those Nazis who bounced back into a second successful career (and fortune) after the war. The two men met on a monthly basis in the Thirties and Schacht's son was christened Montagu in honour of his friend. Norman had some interesting contacts. Between January and March 1941 he met regularly with Red Cross representatives, no doubt with an innocent financial purpose. Less easy to explain is his meeting with Sir Campbell Stuart, the former head of the Political Warfare Executive.

One biography of Norman makes mention of the fact that he ran some sort of unofficial Intelligence agency and delighted in the bizarre, often signing letters with false names. His dislike of Churchill was mutual and this may have put him in the camp of a possible peace party. The activities of the international banking community in wartime bear some scrutiny and revelations abound nearly sixty years on. A BBC *Timewatch* programme, *Banking With Hitler*, was broadcast in October 1998 and dealt with the diaries of Henry Morgenthau Jnr, Roosevelt's banking supremo.

The Bank for International Settlement (BIS), originally created to handle Germany's enormous reparations bill, became something of an international club for bankers whose countries were actually at war with each other. In theory, Montagu Norman could have met at the bank's headquarters in Basle, Switzerland, with his old friend Hjalmar Schacht. Norman's behaviour, in calmly passing over to the Germans £6 million in gold from the conquered Czech state, was criticized heavily in the Commons.

Moreover in 1942, although he vigorously denied it to Anthony Eden, Norman was said to be attempting to broker a German peace with Schacht via neutral Madrid. The BIS team had special travel permits which allowed them international travel all over western Europe. And Edward Playfair, executor of Mrs Roberts, was quoted in the programme as being perfectly happy for the Bank of England to go on collecting interest on pre-war German loans. What the *Timewatch* programme made no comment on were the delicious opportunities for espionage that this international community offered.

However, I believe that the City gent who met Burkhardt in the early spring of 1941 was not Montagu Norman. There are two possible contenders. One is Leonard Ingrams, the 'flying banker', a contender for the whole plot's instigation. What more natural than that the mastermind behind the whole thing should want to be 'hands-on' at this stage to make sure that Hess was soundly hooked? The other is Bernard Rickatson Hatt who was appointed Norman's press secretary early in 1941. Rickatson Hatt certainly visited Europe that spring, but precisely where is not recorded. What is odd is the elevated status he enjoyed, out of all proportion to his actual role. On 8 April, Norman's diary records, 'Clearance from Morton [Churchill's Intelligence adviser] re Hatt. Good with FO, Monckton and M15.'[39]

Why should a press secretary to a banker need to be on good terms with the Foreign Office, a secret service organization and the man who ran the Ministry of Information? And why should he need to be 'cleared' at such a high level?

*

The role of Burkhardt and Borenius was essentially the same. They had to persuade Hess not only that Haushofer was wrong and that there was an active anti-Churchill peace party in Britain, but also that it would welcome him with open arms if only the Stellvertreter could somehow reach British soil.

Carl J. Burkhardt became a member of the International Committee of the Red Cross in the year Hitler came to power. Tireless in his work there, Burkhardt was also High Commissioner to the Port of Danzig between 1937 and 1939. This gave him a more direct involvement with leading figures in the Third Reich, especially given Danzig's importance to Hitler.

The port was designated 'free' – in effect under the control of the League of Nations – in 1919 as part of the Versailles settlement. Its geographical position on the southern coast of the Baltic acquired great strategic importance – not one that should be entrusted to the new Polish state alone. As Hitler began to implement his *lebensraum* policy in the late 1930s, so the absorption of German East Prussia could only be accomplished by invasion of the Polish corridor – with Danzig at its sea end. Burkhardt was therefore well acquainted with German ambitions and knew various leading Nazis well, including Rudolf Hess. Burkhardt's name features in almost all books on the peace feelers of 1939–41, yet his own records in the University of Basle are silent on the matter of his intermediary activities. Fortunately for us, Ulrich von Hassell, a diplomat and later opponent of the Nazi regime who would be sentenced to death for his opposition, is rather more forthcoming.

In his diaries, von Hassell tells us that he was approached by Burkhardt on 30 January 1941 with the idea that a peace proposal was still very much on the cards, some six months after Sefton Delmer, apparently off his own bat, had publicly denounced such a possibility. Burkhardt was in a perfect position to act as a mediator. He was undoubtedly pro-German in the Thirties and his position in the Red Cross gave him an international freedom and status which was invaluable. Closer to the point, it was Rudolf Hess who had overseen the appointment of Burkhardt at Danzig, through his authority in the Ausland Organization. This gave him impeccable credentials as far as Hess and Hitler were concerned – the man was already tried and tested. On the British side, Burkhardt was acceptable simply because, like Mrs Roberts, he was outside official channels and all knowledge could be denied at a moment's notice. Churchill persisted with such denials for the rest of his life.

It has also recently come to light that a delegation from the International Red Cross in Geneva visited London in April 1941, a month before the flight. Marcel Junod and Mlle Odier came to the capital to discuss prisoner of war camps and, according to the records, they visited the British Red Cross and various government departments. They also brought with them a letter of commendation from Burkhardt, addressed to R. A. Butler, which is on file in the Public Record Office.

Of course, there is no evidence that they brought any form of instruction concerning Hess, nor that they delivered any form of plan back to Berlin. However, when Burkhardt expressed the desire to visit Britain in the autumn of 1941, Anthony Eden stated that he held 'considerable misgivings …　in view of his political ambitions and the possibility that he might put out peace feelers on behalf of the Germans…' What had happened to give Eden this impression of Burkhardt? In the event, Burkhardt did make the visit and was wined and dined by R. A. Butler, who appears to have been the 'Minister for Peace feelers'!

Complementary to the use of Burkhardt as an intermediary between SO1 and Hess was the Finnish art historian, Dr Tancred Borenius. The multilingual and cosmospolitan

Borenius was an Anglophile, holding a chair of Art History at University College, London between 1922 and 1947. From time to time he acted as a diplomat on behalf of Finland, notably in the high-level economic talks held in London in 1933. He edited the high-brow Arts review *The Burlington Magazine* from 1940 and personally directed the excavation of Clarendon Palace, near Salisbury.

The von Hassell diaries make it clear that Burkhardt's peace party information came directly from Borenius, who had friends in high places. Despite Halifax's recent replacement by Eden, it was nevertheless the mood of most of the Cabinet that peace was vital. When I spoke to Borenius's son during the writing of this book, he made it clear that his father had indeed pursued a peace initiative, and that initiative had official backing. He had been given a suicide pill in the shape of a golf ball and it was a standing joke in the Borenius family that he'd choke to death on something like that long before the poison took effect!

At some point, the art historian-cum-agent (it seems that that was exactly what he was) worked for the BBC, transmitting to Finland. It is also likely, although none of the files *currently* available confirm it, that he was there at the same time as Sefton Delmer. Borenius's son believes that his father's role was to travel to Italy in 1941 to sow discord between Mussolini and Hitler, to grind down the Pact of Steel. This failed as the Italians were suspicious of the Anglophile Borenius and refused him entry to the country.

Be that as it may, Borenius did broadcast to Finland via the BBC in 1941 to persuade the Finns to abandon their alliance with Germany. More importantly, we know that Borenius had Intelligence connections. He was asked by British Intelligence to deliver a detective novel to the British consulate in Geneva (possibly on the same trip as his meeting with Burkhardt). When he handed it over, the reponse was 'Thank God!' The novel was in fact a new secret code book.

I have it on good authority that the agent who briefed Borenius prior to the Swiss trip in the winter of 1940 was Claude Dansey, the maverick who had set up M16's 'Z system' in Europe in the Thirties. Borenius's son is in no doubt that his father was effectively working for the British Government.

Von Hassell quizzed Burkhardt on the exact nature of the British peace proposals in January 1941. Holland and Belgium, Borenius had told the Red Cross man, must be restored to their own governments. Denmark could remain under German influence, but areas of Poland at least had to be resurrected 'because the Poles fought so bravely for England'. There was no other mention of eastern Europe. The former German colonies were to be restored. France was left to its own devices. The sticking point was Hitler. Just as the Germans would not negotiate with Churchill, so the average Englishman 'can't believe a word [Hitler] says'.[40]

Wolf Hess, John Costello, James Douglas-Hamilton – they all mention the von Hassell diaries, but have ignored Borenius as unofficial envoy. The mechanics of the whole thing lie buried perhaps in a dusty vault at the Foreign Office in Whitehall or perhaps long ago disappeared in a Civil Service incinerator. In short, we do not know exactly how Hess was contacted and what instructions he received. It is likely that the instructions came via Haushofer, who had met Burkhardt, who had in turn met Borenius. Historian John Costello is of the opinion that Hitler too knew of the Burkhardt meeting and we also know from a letter to his mother in the family papers that Haushofer was pleased with its outcome.

It was this meeting which was crucial, because it gave the final kick-start to Hess's flight.

CHAPTER 7

Zero Base

In the honourable profession of accountancy, there is a discipline called zero base budgeting. In this, all preconceived ideas of cost-structure are disregarded and a complete financial review is conducted with total disregard for any earlier formats. In other words, back to basics, begin at the beginning.

Not least in the strata of assumptions, fabrications and outright nonsense in the Hess affair is the legend of the flight itself. Theories range from James Douglas-Hamilton's lone flyer overshooting Dungavel (his father's country house in Lanarkshire) in the dark, to Peter Padfield's escort by the dashing 'blond beast' Reinhard Heydrich, to Hugh Thomas's *doppelgänger* hovering somewhere in the blackness over the North Sea while the real Hess plunged into the water, shot down by his own Luftwaffe.

1) *Time*

So ... zero base. Let us start with the all-important time factor. World time is measured by reference to Greenwich Mean Time, fixed to the Meridian that passes through Greenwich. However, because of wartime blackouts, road deaths almost doubled in the first month of the war and the Chamberlain Government introduced 'Double Summer Time' to combat the problem.

This was first made operative on 4 May 1941 and continued until 10 August. What this means is that when Hess's plane crashed at Floors Farm, Eaglesham at 23.09 on Saturday 10 May (almost the only undisputed fact of the entire journey) the light conditions were those of 21.09 GMT. Sunset on that day was at 21.36 British Double Summer Time in London and approximately 22.00 in Glasgow, three hundred miles to the north. The moon rose at 20.43 BDST and the blackout in London started at 22.21. There are stories of Hess landing by parachute in daylight, but a careful calculation of the time factor makes this impossible.

To calculate the length of the flight itself, however, we need to realize that German time was based on *Mitteleuropaische Zeit*, which is GMT plus one hour and is determined by reference to Germany's longitudinal position in relation to Greenwich. The Germans had advanced their time scale too and for the same reason that we had. But, *Mitteleuropaische Sommerzeit* was only one hour ahead, so that it corresponded exactly to the situation in this country. This German time system operated from 1 January 1941 to 2 November. In other words, all the times for the Hess flight in Germany were identical with those in Scotland. When the Messerschmitt hit the ground on Eaglesham Moor at 23.09, it was also 23.09 at the Berghof, where the Führer waited for news.

All the leading works on the flight agree that the time of take-off from Augsburg was 17.45. Wolf Hess, ever anxious to vindicate his father, says, '. . . the great plane accelerated and took off. It was just 17.45 Middle European Time'. Hugh Thomas, convinced the man to end his days in Spandau was an impostor, wrote 'The real Rudolf Hess took off from Augsburg . . . at 5.45 pm.' A simple mathematical calculation gives us Hess's journey time, from Augsburg to Eaglesham, as 5 hours 24 minutes.

2) *Range*

One of Goering's contemptuous comments in the days that followed 10 May (and one clearly for public consumption) was that Hess could not possibly have reached Scotland because an Me 110 did not have the range for that. The plane that Hess had chosen was a Messerschmitt 110 Bf, type D or E (a variety of designs from A had been devised in the late Thirties), and was a twin engine fighter-bomber, designed for optimum versatility. Fighters on their own were fast and manouevrable but carried no bomb load, and unescorted bombers, though capable of inflicting devastation on the ground, were at the mercy of the hornet enemy fighters buzzing round them. The Me 110 was a good compromise, but of course it was neither as a fighter nor a bomber that Hess needed VJ+OQ that Saturday in May 1941.

The plane he chose was perfect for his purposes, combining as it did range, speed and its capability of being flown by a single pilot. The average cruising speed of all the Me 110s, irrespective of type, was 220 miles an hour, a figure calculated to optimize flight speed with fuel consumption. Taking the flight time as 5 hours 24 minutes, at normal cruising speed, Hess's plane could have travelled around 1,188 miles. Travelling faster, as reports of the Royal Observer Corps maintained that Hess did over Northumbria and Scotland, it could cover a greater distance but only at the cost of more fuel. If Hess's speed was around the reported 300 mph over Scotland, he could have travelled a further 80 miles, bringing his total mileage up to around 1,260.

Early in the war, an Me 110 was shot down and acquired by the RAF for test flying. Though the aircraft had crash-landed, its technology was in good enough condition to study. The official report, dated September 1940, specifies that the craft was fitted with Daimler Benz 601A engines, which made it a C-type or later. The plane was patched up and flown at Farnborough, the country's top aircraft research establishment in Hampshire. The report tells us that the total fuel capacity of the crashed Me 110 was 278 gallons. The dilemma over Hess's plane was whether it was fitted with drop tanks or not. James Leasor, hearing the story from Pintsch, Hess's adjutant, is in no doubt:

'To Messerschmitt's displeasure [Hess] criticized [the Me 110's] range and persuaded the engineers at . . . Augsburg to construct extra fuel tanks of a weight equal to the second man who would normally have accompanied the pilot. Messerschmitt fitted two tanks, each of 700 litres (187 gallons) into the wings.'[1]

The photographs in Leasor's book, *The Uninvited Envoy*, which were presumably provided by Pintsch, are unhelpful. They show Hess, in flying suit with fur collar, being buckled into his helmet by his trenchcoated staff. There is a perplexing still of Hess at the controls of an Me 110, this time with goggles but no helmet, apparently trying to work out why the plane would not start. Four equally bemused technicians look on. In the fourth photograph, bravely captioned 'Hess takes off', an Me 110 is taxiing along the runway towards the camera. Because of the angle of the shot, no pilot is visible. And there are certainly no drop tanks visible on the wings.

According to Hess himself, he had practised for this flight several times, ever since Hitler lifted the command ban on all Nazi leaders from flying. He had also attempted take-off on four previous occasions but had been beaten by the weather. We only have Pintsch's word, which is known to be unreliable, that these photographs were taken on the same day and at Augsburg. Not a single photograph is conclusive and nowhere in his text does Leasor mention Hess having engine trouble on 10 May. If the photographs were taken on that day, of course, it strengthens the view that Hess was flying under Hitler's orders. If this was the lone mission beloved of James Douglas-Hamilton and James Leasor, then surely Hess would not want it recorded on film as that would give the whole venture a permanence and public face that he could not risk.

Other commentators have not been so sure about the fitting of drop tanks. Some contend tanks of 66-gallon capacity were fitted, others 198, still others none at all. Drop tanks could be fitted to all types after the D1. The D1/R1 was a further variant with an enormous 264-gallon tank incorporated into the fuselage of the plane, which, like the smaller ones in the wings, could be jettisoned. Such a craft, however, was sluggish because of its extra weight and Hess, an experienced pilot, knew that he might have to try to outrun any number of faster fighters over British airspace. None of the alleged photographs of Hess's plane show such a tank fitted.

The surviving tangle of wreckage of the Hess plane preserved at the Imperial War Museum and at East Fortune airfield is no help, because the wings are not present and again, various photographs of the wreck, *in situ* on Eaglesham Moor are taken at the wrong angle to be useful. There are some accounts of drop tanks being found in the mud of the Firth of Clyde, where Hess banked, realizing he had overshot his target, but these have not been confirmed. There are even reports that Hess's plane was reconstructed in Carlisle late in May 1941 to discover more about its specifications.

The fuel capacity possibilities for Hess's plane are any of four combinations. A standard Me 110 without drop tanks would carry 278 gallons. A standard plane with 66-gallon drop tanks would carry 410 gallons; or the larger 198-gallon version, 674 gallons. The D1-Rl type with the 264 gallon belly tank could not have been fitted with drop tanks as the weight would have exceeded the maximum take-off weight.

The range of the aircrafts can also be calculated. The standard plane without drop tanks could make 482 miles; the 66-gallon drop tank version 710 miles; the 198 gallon version 1,168 and the D1-Rl 264-gallon belly tank type 939 miles. In practice, the ranges could be slightly less as the higher take-off weights created by the addition of tanks would require more power to take off and climb. The maximum range of Hess's plane was probably around 1,150 miles. The unmistakeable conclusion is that Hess could only reach Scotland either if his plane was fitted with twin 198 gallon drop tanks or if he refuelled somewhere on the way.

3) *Destination*

Why is all this important? It is important because I believe that, contrary to what he told his captors in Scotland and at Mytchett Place, Hess was actually intending to fly somewhere other than Dungavel, near to where we know he crashed. The first alleged flight plan appeared in *The Case of Rudolf Hess* by Dr John Rees, in 1947, and vitally all this tells us is where Hess actually went, not where he was intending to go. Using Rees's version of the flight plan, we can calculate 1,284 miles. Even using Hugh Thomas's more conservative estimate of 1,260 miles, it would not have been possible for Hess to have had that much fuel. Given the known flight time of 5 hours, 24 minutes, on the 1,284 miles reckoning that would give an average speed of 237 mph. This was above normal cruising speed and would have resulted in increased fuel consumption.

Taking Hess's version of his deviations at the end of his flight ('overshooting' to the Firth of Clyde, then turning back to skirt Glasgow) he would have had to have flown in almost a straight line to Scotland, avoiding the Home Chain Radar, to ensure that he had enough fuel. This would have represented a distance of about 905 miles. That gives, calculating by the known flight time, an average speed of 167 mph which seems too low. So, the flight route that Hess himself sketched is either wrong or he landed somewhere en route, in Germany or the Low Countries, to refuel.

The 1947 Rees flight plan gives the impression that Hess was attempting to rendezvous over the North Sea. If so, with whom? Was this some sort of ritual 'farewell' with Heydrich in escort, looping the loop in a romantic Wagnerian victory roll in the dying sun? Hardly. It does of course give Hugh Thomas the loophole he needs for the *doppelgänger* to soar in and for the real Stellvertreter to fall victim to one of the intercepting fighters ordered by Goering. What is wrong with this flight plan is its extraordinary precision of time. Hess was flying alone, in fading light, with the risk of enemy interception growing with every mile. Yet, in captivity, with all the uncertainties that that posed, he was able to draw calmly and accurately a flight plan based on his memory alone?

Hess's explanation is a rational one: he was waiting over the North Sea, idling until darkness could cover his approach. But darkness, while it might save him from the Turnhouse Spitfires and the Ayr Defiants, made his finding and landing at Dungavel highly problematic. Dungavel is currently a maximum security prison, and is, as then, surrounded by fir trees and very remote – a pinprick on the most detailed map. Its runway was intended for Hamilton's private biplanes and would have been woefully short for a Messerschmitt Bf 110. Had he ever found Dungavel and landed, Hess would have ploughed, with his plane, into a stand of Scots pines.

Assuming, as we must in the lack of contradictory evidence, that Hess left Augsburg at 5.45, he could have landed at Köln or at an airfield nearby to refuel. That distance is approximately 220 miles and would have taken about an hour. He would then have used just under half the normal fuel tank capacity of 278 gallons. If drop tanks were fitted then (which would explain the absence of them in Pintsch's photographs *if* they are genuine), he would have had enough fuel for a further 1168 miles from Köln. Allowing for half an hour's landing procedure, the total flight time in the air now becomes 4 hours, 54 mins from Augsburg. The distance remaining from Köln was actually 1040 miles, using Hess's plan. The route would now fit closely with Hess's own account and would give a more realistic speed of 212 mph.* The conclusion is that Hess could have landed to refuel and still have followed a similar route to that described in 1947. If true this destroys the 'lone flyer' theory.

* For a fuller illustration of the complexities of Hess's flight, see Appendix 3.

Why did Hess choose a Messerschmitt 110? By the summer of 1939 the Luftwaffe had 195 Me Bf 110s of the C-type. They did brilliant service in the Polish campaign, as part of the initial thrust of blitzkrieg and 350 of them snarled over the skies of Holland and France. Only in the Battle of Britain did their weakness show. They were not as fast or as manouevrable as Fighter Command's Spitfires and Hurricanes and the 110s had to be escorted by the genuine Messerschmitt fighters, the Bf 109s.

The true fighters lacked range. The Me 109 E-7 could reach 680 miles; the Me 110 C-4 482; and the Focke-Wulf 190A-8 500 miles. The bombers' range was of course greater – for example, a Dornier Do 217 could manage about 1,300 miles fully laden – but for conventional missions, it was not realistic for these to be flown solo. The range of the Me 110 was extended with the use of drop tanks from the D-type onwards and this could be operated by a single pilot at speed.

The fact that Willi Messerschmitt was a personal friend of Hess and lived near him meant that all kinds of 'customizing' was possible on VJ+OQ to enable the Stellvertreter to make his flight. Hess was familiar with Messerschmitts – he had flown the earlier 108 type and, with modified specifications, it was ideal for his purposes. The bomb load and guns were in a sense irrelevant. We know from the crashed aircraft that its guns were still greased and carried no cartridge belts and there were no bombs on board, otherwise the plane would have exploded on impact with the ground. The Me 110 was virtually the only plane which combined range with single pilot performance. A single pilot would be essential to corroborate the 'simply say I am mad' excuse, should things not go according to plan.

How did Hess, experienced pilot though he was, manage the navigation? In 1941 there were three types of German navigational aid used by the Luftwaffe, all based on radio waves. If Hess relied on any of these devices, then the 'lone flyer' theory can be discounted, because they all depended on assistance from the

Luftwaffe. Such assistance would only be given if operators were comfortable that the journey was officially sanctioned, implying the direct approval of Goering; in turn implied the direct approval of Hitler. Hess's VJ+OQ cockpit is not available for study, so we are unable to say unequivocally what sort of technical modifications were fitted. The radar instrumentation for example was usually operated by the navigator, seated behind the pilot. Any modifications to the cockpit would have required the assistance of ground crew, yet no action was taken against the Augsburg team. How odd that necromancers and occultists were rounded up in a flurry of righteous indignation by the Führer, but the men who fitted up Hess's plane were left alone.

It would have been possible for Hess to have flown from Augsburg to Scotland without radio aid. A compass was a standard fitment in the Me 110 and as long as Hess had correct bearings on take-off, he could have found his way via natural landmarks – coastlines and estuaries. This however called for a great deal of skill and not a little luck. In conventional bombing raids, with a full bomb load, the Me 110 carried a crew of three. On his own, Hess would have had to navigate, monitor the plane's performance and actually fly the thing. And the Me 110 was something of a monster. The planes on which Hess had learned to fly in 1918 were the rough equivalent in terms of power of a modern Cessna 150, the cruising speed of which is 95 mph. The Me 110's cruising speed was 220 mph and its best performance 349 mph. The ground crews of the Royal Observer Corps who saw Hess hurtling over Northumbria and Lowland Scotland reported speeds of over 300 mph.

The greatest problem for a lone pilot would be knowing how far he had flown. Over land, there were visible aids. In daylight as he still was over Germany and the Low Countries, this was easy. He would recognize Düsseldorf and Köln for example. But over the sea in the gathering gloom there would be problems. Wind speed, wind direction, air speed and time travelled would all need to be calculated, a knotty enough problem at leisure with a modern calculator, but a major problem flying at night over enemy territory. Hess was rightly proud of his flight. He drew little pictures for his son 'Buz' of himself baling out and kept his flying suit with him until it was stolen from Spandau.[2]

The difficulties Hess would have encountered in the flight are covered in the Butt report, presented to the Air Marshals of the RAF in 1941, which was concerned with the problems and shortcomings of the bomber missions over Germany. Its findings showed that only one tenth of the new Lancasters and slightly older Hampdens dropped their loads within five miles of their targets on the Ruhr. The bomber crews used astronavigation and dead reckoning as their means of navigation, and the results were poor, even with specialist navigators aboard. The Butt report led to the RAF facing its shortcomings head on and the brass hats began to look into radio navigational techniques which ultimately led to the 'Gee' and 'Oboe' systems.

In the year that Hitler became Chancellor, the German Lorenz company had developed a blind landing system which used a radio beam directed along the middle of a landing strip. The aircraft coming into land followed the beam by means of a receiver in the cockpit, safe in the knowledge that it would lead to the runway. In Britain, the similar 'Radio Range' system was gaining popularity. Here, radio transmitters were established on a given route and the plane followed the route marked out by the transmitters. The pilot would hear a Morse 'A' signal when flying on one side of the centre line and a Morse 'N' on the other. This system of course depended very much on the peaceful co-existence of airforces. In wartime, these transmitters could not distinguish between friend and foe.

While the British concentrated on radar development – and crucially outstripped the Germans – Lorenz devised the beacon during the Thirties and by May 1941 was using two further variants on the radio beam – the X-Gerat and the Y system. Operating at different wavelengths, the beacon and the X-Gerat depended on intersecting beams, while the third relied on relaying radio waves back to the station to measure distance travelled. Using X-Gerat, one beam would be transmitted from one station, the second from another. The bomber crew flew along the first beam and when it met the converging second beam, it was over target. If the pilot flew off the beam, perhaps to avoid interceptor fighters, an audible Morse signal would steer him back on course.

Stations transmitting these '*knickbeins*' were available to Hess. One of them was at Kleves, on the Dutch border, forty-five miles north-north-west of Düsseldorf. Following the flight plan that Hess claimed he followed, it was possible for him to 'hook on' to the beam here. A second beam would be necessary to intersect the first. At this radio crossroads, he either met someone over the North Sea or turned due west, towards the British coast.

On the detailed flight plan reproduced by Hugh Thomas in *The Murder of Rudolf Hess*, a line is marked with the legend '02'. This surely represents *Orierungsfever* 2 (route beacon 2). There were also devices at Bredstedt and Stavanger near the flight path that were capable of providing such a beam. Many authors refer to Hess listening in, as did many Germans, to a radio station at Kalunborg in Denmark. But what if he was really tuning in to the Bredstedt transmitter or the beam station at Aalborg?

Equipment of this type was standard issue for many Luftwaffe aircraft, not specially prepared for Hess. It was the navigator who usually operated it and for Hess to cope at all, the necessary instrumentation would need to have been re-housed in the pilot's cockpit. What Hess did not seem to know, although the rumour existed in the Luftwaffe, was that by May 1941 the British could jam the beams because they could locate them. It is even conceivable that Hess turned inland too soon and missed his ultimate destination precisely because of this jamming, or more likely error.

4) *Wind/Weather* The final part of the navigation equation is wind speed. If an aircraft travelling at 220 mph flies into a 40

mph headwind, its actual relative ground speed is 180 mph. A following wind of 40 mph would conversely give a ground-speed of 260 mph. Crosswinds provide a ground speed between the two. We have no way of knowing what conditions Hess flew in on 10 May 1941, but it is relevant, as it creates an 18 per cent variance; 905 miles becomes either 1,068 or 742 depending on the direction and speed of the wind.

The weather report for Saturday 10 May reads: 'A large anti-cyclone covers the Atlantic and a ridge of high pressure extends over the British Isles. There may be a few scattered showers near the east coast, but otherwise weather will be dry.'[3] The winds were described as 'light variable to north-west' – in other words, behind Hess as he flew north over the sea. This would suggest that flying conditions were ideal and that he would need less fuel to reach his destination because of the tailwind.

The zero-base philosophy led me to investigate the RAF records in Lowland Scotland and Northumbria for the night of 10 May 1941 and in doing so I realized that both James Douglas–Hamilton and John Costello are wrong in their conclusions. As specified in *The Truth About Rudolf Hess*, 13 Group of the RAF was organized as follows. There was a Squadron 41 (Spitfires) at Catterick, 72 was at Acklington, the Polish 317 Squadron (Hurricanes) was at Ouston, 603 (Spitfires) were at Turnhouse, 43 (Hurricanes) at Drem and 602 (Spitfires) at Ayr. There was a further squadron of Hurricanes (245) stationed at Aldergrove in Northern Ireland and a Defiant Squadron (141) also at Ayr. Omitted from Douglas-Hamilton's list however are the Satellite Landing Grounds at Lennoxlove and MacMerry, being used by 614 Squadron.

The timings for the sightings of Hess's plane and the various interceptions are also crucial. According to the all-important Operational Record Books (kept by both base and squadron), two aircraft took off from the Ouston base, flown by the Polish pilots Martel and Sztranko at 12.40. They landed at 13.35. The Spitfires took off from Blue Section of 72 Squadron at

Acklington at 19.59, flown by Gregson and Biel. They landed at 21.10. It was at 22.08 that the first plots of an aircraft approaching the Northumberland coast at 12,000 feet were recorded. Twelve minutes later (rather a slow response from a Battle of Britain veteran) Maurice Pocock took off in his Spitfire from Acklington and patrolled the base at 15,000 feet. There is, incidentally, no mention of the word 'scramble' or 'intercept' in the report. Three minutes later, Hess crossed the coast, heading inland. At 22.35, Flying Officer Cuddie was scrambled in his Defiant from Ayr. Pocock landed at 22.55, fourteen minutes before Hess's plane hit the heather at Eaglesham.

Among the many references to Hess in the database in the National Archives in Chancery Lane is one concerning a map kept in the County Hall at Durham. This archive seems to have been overlooked by other researchers who have been happy to follow the version of Douglas-Hamilton and Conyers Nesbit. Interestingly, it reveals not one but two aircraft in the sky – something which no one has commented on to date. They are designated GU and 42J. The map is described in the Durham archives as D/X1064/1: 'The actual recording (Raid 42) made at the time of the flight at the Durham Operations Room of the Royal Observer Corps.'

The previously accepted version of the Observer Corps' tracking of the Hess flight is to be found in Derek Wood's *Attack Warning Red*, which of course reports the flight path of where the Me 110 actually went, not where it was supposed to go. The plane or planes on the Durham map are marked GU and appear by the plot to have been moving quickly. According to Wood, however, fighters were marked on maps with the code F followed by a second letter. Did these aircraft take off from MacMerry, which Douglas-Hamilton does not include in his account? And if they did not take off from MacMerry, where was their base? No other airfield was, on the face of it, operational (by reference to their Operational Record Book).

The whole question of the MacMerry base is a vexed one. 607 Squadron, flying Hurricanes, left the base, according to the records, on 16 April 1941. The base Operational Record Book for MacMerry does not start until June 1941 and it contains routine details of work done to bring it up to operational standard. 614 Squadron however was based at MacMerry earlier in the year and was certainly there on the night of the Hess flight, having moved from Inverness earlier in the month. 614 were mainly engaged, at this time, testing Lysander aircraft for fuel consumption and, oddly, the ORB does not specify flights or take-off times. Night flights did take place and a total of hours logged is included. Other ORBs are very specific, but this one is handwritten rather than typed and the usual meticulous details are missing.

Curiously again, the Hurricanes based at MacMerry until April were posted to Skitten in north Scotland and there is no ORB available at all for May. We do know, however, that two Hurricanes of 607 Squadron, flown by pilots Barnwell and McColpin, apparently took off from Skitten at 22.45 on the night 10 May.

What this contradictory evidence gives us is, at the very least, food for thought. What is the aircraft designated GU on the Durham map? Is it actually one plane or two and from where did it/they take off? Were they merely Lysanders on routine test flights or something altogether different? Alternatively, could the aircraft designated 42J on the map be, in Padfield's estimation, Heydrich's escort plane flying back from the British coast? And where did aircraft GU land? On the Durham map, the plotted line reaches to RAF Acklington, but there is no further mention of planes landing that night.

Irrespective of the Durham map, we now have definite evidence that, contrary to every established version, there were no aircraft in the sky between Newcastle and Edinburgh as Hess approached the north coast of England. Douglas-Hamilton's 'hunted by the Spitfires already on patrol' is inaccurate – Gregson and Biel had already landed nearby an hour earlier at 21.10. Pocock was scrambled twelve minutes after the Hess plane had been picked up by Radar off the coast. Contrary to Douglas-Hamilton's 'pursued by another Spitfire', Pocock had no hope of catching Hess and his own report makes no mention of trying to do so.

After the hardback edition of this book was published, fascinating new evidence came to light with regard to Czech aircrew from RAF Aldergrove in Northern Ireland who were on patrol on the night of 10 May 1941. According to a book recently published in Prague, the pilots, Bauman and Srom were scrambled and visually contacted a plane, which turned out to be the Hess plane. Upon closing in on the same they were told to disengage and return to base.

Aldergrove was also in 13 Group and was therefore subject to the same command structure as the Scottish bases. Needless to say the Aldergrove Operational Record Book makes no mention of the incident, it only being recorded in the pilots' log books.

There is no means of corroborating this new evidence 58 years after the event. Both men are dead. However, if true then it gives further weight to my allegation that the Hess plane was deliberately allowed to pass through British air space.

5) *Conclusions*

Every author on Hess has slavishly followed the notion that he was flying to Dungavel House because he asked, on capture, to see the Duke of Hamilton. We have seen how isolated Dungavel was – although Hess could not have asked for a better setting for a clandestine meeting to plot the overthrow of the Churchill Government. It remains to be answered how Hess knew that Hamilton would be in residence. The Duke had been in France in 1940 and was a serving RAF officer. The chance of his being at home, with pipe and dogs, as the Stellvertreter taxied along his airstrip, is the sort of thing not even Ian Fleming would conjure up for James Bond. But I contend that Hess was fed information by the black propagandists of SO1;

false information that there was an active anti-Churchill peace cell in Lowland Scotland and correct information that the Duke of Hamilton was back in Scotland.

Unfortunately, the less discerning writers on Hess have bought the Churchill-inspired and Hitler-inspired myth that the Stellvertreter was deranged.* So his turning up at a country house whose runway was too short to see a man who was not there was perfect ammunition for them. I have sought to prove that the actuality was nothing of the sort. Dungavel was dangerously close to Glasgow, heavily defended with a ring of anti-aircraft guns and barrage balloons. Would SO1 have been so rash as to offer Hess a tiny target he could not hope to find in the dark, suicidally near to air defences?

My contention is that Hess's situation over Eaglesham Moor was that he was either lost or following his second option. In April 1997 I travelled to Scotland to research for this book and visited the Museum of Flight at East Fortune airfield to see, for the second time, one of the DB601A engines retrieved from the wreck of Hess's plane. Near it was an exhibit from RAF Haddington, built in the grounds of Lennoxlove House. Haddington now is sown to wheat. Like Tangmere far to the south, there is little trace of its vital wartime usage. In 1941, it was a satellite landing ground, used as a storage area for planes parked under the sheltering arms of trees for safety and invisible to enemy aerial reconnaissance aircraft. The airfield was a mere 800 yards from Lennoxlove. (In the tangle of coincidences which surround the case of Rudolf Hess, the Hamiltons bought Lennoxlove shortly after the war and live there today. They bought it from the Baird family who had rented the house earlier to General Sir Ian Hamilton, who knew and admired Karl and Albrecht Haushofer. Ironically, General Hamilton had invited Hess to Lennoxlove in 1938, but the Stellvertreter had declined the invitation.)

* See Chapter 8.

It is ironic too that Hess's flight plan is now on display at Lennoxlove, for I believe that this, or the RAF base at Acklington further south, was his real destination. Close inspection reveals that the Lennoxlove version is not a proper flight plan but a school atlas map of Scotland. In no way can it be taken as an aeronautical map or chart. Dungavel House is certainly not circled as some authors contend. A red arrow points to its location, but red arrows also point to railways, which are emboldened, towns, lakes and rivers. Clearly what the map does show is visible landmarks which Hess could have used, at least in daylight, to find his way. There are no markings in the Haddington area, but there *are* two parallel blue lines, lightly drawn. In the margin next to them is the German word *'peilung'*, to take a bearing (which also translates as 'beam'). The more southerly of these lines runs through the coastal town of Bamburgh, then on through the Cheviots and Glenluce. Extend this line with a ruler out to the North Sea and it reaches Aalborg, the *knickebein* transmitter station. The more northerly line passes through Haddington.

This flight plan may well have been found on Hess himself or in the cockpit of his plane and it may have been used in Hess's planning with his flight co-ordinators; but it is not the flight plan itself. For the Air Ministry to have given the actual plan to the Duke of Hamilton a week after Hess arrived would seem to be highly unlikely and nearly fifty years later it has still to 'resurface'.

We know that on 24 April 1941, only two weeks before the Hess flight, a Bristol Beaufighter, greater in wing span, length and weight than the Me 110, landed at Lennoxlove. The airstrip could therefore easily accommodate Hess's plane. Later in the war, the much bigger Halifax and Wellington bombers were landed there. But what is most fascinating of all is the view from the wheatfields of Lennoxlove. To the east lies the massive 725-foot escarpment known as Traprain Law. Draw a straight line on a navigation chart from Lennoxlove to Traprain and straight on and it bisects the coast at Dunbar. Suddenly, it all falls into place.

Where possible, a pilot would prefer to use clearly visible landmarks rather than trusting to the *knickebein* system which, once he was over enemy territory, could only be an invisible guide. But what if – in the dark and in a hurry, flying a two- or three-man plane single-handed and realizing that enemy aircraft might already be up after him – Hess misjudged his approach? What if he mistook the coastline landmarks? In peacetime, Hess could have flown up and down Scotland's east coast until he recognized the land formations below, but he did not have that luxury. If the British radar chain picked him up and if he dithered too long, he might be shot down before he could even set foot on British soil, let alone begin his negotiations.

Hess was indeed circling over the North Sea to wait for dark, but also to get his bearings right. In essence, he'd have one hit, no more. His angle of approach was about 240 degrees, according to his flight plan. Copy the angle of bearing across Dunbar and the straight line emerges that runs from the coast, via the escarpment of Traprain Law to Lennoxlove House. It fits exactly.

And a close study of the surface geography of south-east Scotland reveals some fascinating parallels. Hess actually flew in over the coast near Bamburgh towards the Cheviot, a huge outcrop of rock 2,674 feet above sea level. This is at the same bearing as Traprain Law is to Dunbar and its relative height difference would be indistinguishable in the dark. Study the coastlines at Dunbar and at Bamburgh and they are remarkably similar. When the Royal Observer Corps at Chatto spotted Hess's plane twelve miles from the Cheviot, he was flying very low. This would make perfect sense: Hess thought he'd just flown over Traprain Law. He was low because he was coming in to land, as he thought, at Lennoxlove. Unfortunately for him, he was forty miles too far south. Realizing his error, he swung north-west, desperately trying to get back on track.

The other possibility is that Hess was ten miles too far north on his approach to the coast and that his actual target was the airfield at RAF Acklington, housing 72 Squadron, some four miles inland from Amble on the Northumbrian coast. Hess flew in over the castle at Bamburgh, near the Farne lighthouse, but again he may have mistaken these for the geographical parallels to the south. Two miles from Amble is the castle of Warkworth, and opposite the river mouth stands Coquet Island with its own lighthouse. He may well have confused the Farne lighthouse with that of Coquet Island.

We do not know if Hess used the *knickebein* system. If he did, he may have missed or misread it. The one instrument he would have relied on was his compass, fitted in the cockpit and linked to the master compass in the Me's tail-section. And the one figure that Hess would have recognized from his plans would be the zero-degree angle of approach to Scotland. Ironically, all that Hess got wrong was his position as he started to approach, but it was probably enough to cause panic.

There was no welcoming airstrip beyond the Cheviots, just the unrelenting blackness of the Scottish borders. Every minute that passed he was hurtling over the moors a further five miles and his fuel supply was becoming critical. He had no idea now of his latitude. His only hope was to fly west, reach the coast, get a visual bearing over the Firth of Clyde and double back. In prison he remembered the 'large rock' in the sea. This would have been either Cumbrae Island in the Firth of Clyde or Ailsa Craig, further south (by which point the Observer Corps had lost him). Even so, he realized he had insufficient fuel to reach Lennoxlove – and still less Acklington – and the longer he was in the air, the greater the chance of fighter intercept. The Duke of Hamilton's home was at Dungavel but it had an inadequate landing strip (Hamilton only flew small, light aircraft) and it would be unlikely that he could find it in the dark, even if he had enough fuel to do so. Time was running out, he would have to bale out and hope to make contact with the peace party somehow.

And if, my Führer, this project – which I admit has but very small chance of success – ends in failure and the fates decide against me, this can have no detrimental results either for you or for Germany: it will always be possible for you to deny any responsibility. Simply say I was mad.[4]

So ended the famous letter that Karl-Heinz Pintsch, Hess's adjutant, handed to Hitler at the Berghof on the morning of Sunday, 11 May 1941. Pintsch was carrying out Hess's instructions and was told that the Führer was busy with a full day's schedule and he would have to wait. Albert Bormann, the brother of the man who would succeed Hess in his administrative role in the Nazi hierarchy, simply closed the door on him. Waiting in the ante-room was Dr Fritz Todt, Minister of Armaments and Munitions, who had a morning appointment with Hitler. Pintsch asked permission to nip in to see the Führer first and in his vast study (probably the biggest in the world), with its red marble floor and huge landscape windows, he read the letter which Hess had left. He read it again, then sent an aide to find Goering, who was at Nuremberg and von Ribbentrop, at home in Fuschl.

The account, given by Pintsch many years later to writer James Leasor, does not square with what Albert Speer remembered. The architect was working on sketches in an adjoining room (curious how busy everybody was on a Sunday morning bearing in mind that the Berghof was a country retreat) 'suddenly heard an inarticulate, almost animal outcry'. 'Bormann, at once!' Hitler roared, 'Where is Bormann?' According to the Leasor-Pintsch version, Bormann sidled in quietly and, at a whisper, distanced himself from Hess's activities. Douglas-Hamilton has Hitler's anger building as the day progressed; Speer says there was an initial explosion – as the Führer's interpreter, Schmidt remembered 'as though a bomb had hit the Berghof' – and that Hitler calmed down later.

How are we to account for these discrepancies? Did memory gild their various lilies? The flight of Rudolf Hess was one of the most bizarre scenes they would ever witness. Would not every word, every gesture, stay in their minds? It would and it did. Except that like an eager, gullible audience at the theatre, they were all watching the dazzling show that Hitler was putting on for them. None of it was real. The sleepwalker was playing to the gallery as only he knew how. Because, as we shall see, the news that Pintsch brought to the Berghof came as no surprise to the Führer.

Seen in this context, the events of the days following Hess's flight become explicable as a complex exercise in what today we would call damage limitation. Every commentator from Albert Speer to James Douglas–Hamilton highlights Hitler's fury and bewilderment at Pintsch's news. 'Turmoil at the Dictator's Court' is Douglas-Hamilton's view; Leasor calls it 'Consternation at the Berghof'. But the turmoil and the consternation were not caused by the discovery of Hess's flight – they were caused by the growing realisation that the mission had failed. The Stellvertreter had been duped. The German nightmare – a war on two fronts – was now inevitable.

What was the nature of the turmoil? The Gestapo arrested Pintsch and Hess's other adjutant, Alfred Leitgen. Personnel at Augsburg airfield were rounded up for interrogation. Karl Haushofer was placed under house arrest. In the slightly longer term, astrologers and occultists were locked up and beyond that still, the Rudolf Steiner schools that Hess supported were closed. *If* the letter that Pintsch delivered to Hitler is genuine, then Hess gave his beloved Führer the necessary loophole – 'Simply say I was mad.' And that is precisely what Hitler did. He was, as we might say today, between a rock and a hard place. If he declared Hess mad and disowned him, it did not say much for the Führer's choice of deputy; if he admitted that the peace plan had been sent with his knowledge and blessing, and that it had been scorned, his whole credibility on the world stage would be called into question. It would also give a clue to the Russians that a German attack was imminent. Unsurprisingly, Hitler chose the former course.

In reality, Hess had failed in a mission which was impossible. In reality, he had been lured over to an enemy country where he was expecting – or at least hoping – to meet men with whom he could deal. Instead, he met a bewildered Duke of Hamilton and a dismissive Ivone Kirkpatrick and John Simon.* In the fiction- that Hitler created – and which his contemporaries and recent commentators have been happy to swallow – Hess became first deluded and then a traitor. As Speer reminds us, after the failed von Stauffenberg plot to kill Hitler in July 1944, the Führer decided that Hess must be hanged.

So General Wilhelm Keitel, Hitler's Chief of Staff, was at the Berghof on that hysterical Sunday, watching Hitler trying to compose a news bulletin that would not cause alarm and despondency. Albert Speer assumed that it was Martin Bormann's ambition that had driven Hess to the insane act he had carried out. A gardener, who had more guts than Goebbels who simply stayed at home out of the way, was heard to mutter, 'Didn't you already know we were governed by madmen?' The British cartoonist David Low concurred. In his 15 May cartoon, a bevy of highly placed and clearly deranged Nazis are standing in a bunch looking at a window, the iron bars of which have been forced. Pinned to the wall below it is a note which reads, 'Had enough – skipped out, Hess.'

Hitler, Goering and Ribbentrop, three of the four likely to have been privy to the flight plan, worked with the Führer's Press chief, Otto Dietrich, to draft a communiqué for Berlin radio. It was broadcast, on the evening of 12 May:

> The Party authorities state – Party leader Hess, who
> had been expressly forbidden by the Führer to use an

* See Chapter 8.

aeroplane because of a disease which had been becoming worse for years, was, in contradiction of this order, able to get hold of a plane recently. Hess started on Saturday 10 May, at about 1800 hours from Augsburg on a flight from which he has not yet returned. A letter which he left behind unfortunately showed traces of a mental disturbance which justifies the fear that Hess was the victim of hallucinations.

The Führer at once ordered the arrest of Hess's adjutants, who alone knew of his flights [Hess had, allegedly, attempted to reach Scotland earlier, but the weather had beaten him] and who in contradiction of the Führer's ban, of which they were aware, did not prevent nor report it at once.[6]

The mental instability of Hess was, of course, borne out by his subsequent behaviour before, during and after the Nuremberg Trials and many writers have pointed to this as merely a continuation of a long mental decline which had begun before 1941 and became clearly manifest on 10 May.

Here we see the seductiveness of hindsight. Hitler, Goering, Ribbentrop, Dietrich and Goebbels, who later perpetuated the myth, would no doubt be delighted that their propaganda was so effective. Is there any evidence that Hess's decline in influence – which has been suggested as the motive for his mission: to impress the Führer and regain his favour – has a basis in fact? Albert Speer maintains that Hess was still ambitious even after the war started. The problem was that Hess's role in the Nazi hierarchy had no precise military focus. In a wartime situation, it was inevitable that men like Goering, as head of the Luftwaffe, Keitel as Chief of Staff, Raeder as the naval overlord and Goebbels as propaganda chief, should be elevated by sheer necessity. It is also true that Hess's dietary habits annoyed Hitler and his absence from the Berghof dining-table has been misconstrued.

We have seen that the Hitler-Hess relationship was a close one – the Führer used the familiar '*Du*' rather than '*Sie*' to his Stellvertreter. They had shared the horrors of the trenches, the beer-hall haranguings and the street fights, the same jail at Landsberg, and in the writing of *Mein Kampf* it is sometimes difficult to see who is the leader and who the led. Whether the OSS was right or not in its belief that Hitler and Hess had been lovers, the fact remains that Hess was utterly devoted to Hitler and Hitler genuinely fond of his 'Rudi', his 'Hesserl'. The Führer was also known for his love of nostalgia – witness the veneration of the dead of the Beer-hall Putsch – and few went back further than Hess. Hitler was even the godfather of Wolf Rudiger Hess, christened in 1938.

Hess's position in the party hierarchy was actually very strong and remained so. When Hitler declared himself Führer, combining the offices of President and Chancellor in 1934, his day to day involvement with the Party came to an end. Hess, as acting leader, exercised far more control than did Hitler, but it was in foreign affairs that Hess could wield a unique power. It was through his control of the Verbindungsstab, which Donald McCormick has likened to a second secret service in Germany, that Hess found himself ideally placed to deal with the various peace-feelers of 1939–41. It was to this organization, with Hess at its head, that Anna Wolkoff sent her messages, rather than to Canaris's Abwehr, and it was because of his position here that S01's contacts with him were credible.

There was only ever circumstantial evidence to suggest that Hess's influence on Hitler was in decline, other than that Goering was now the Führer's official successor. Given the fact that a world war was underway, Hitler's elevation of the fighting man over the secretary and 'conscience of the party' was perhaps inevitable and certainly understandable. It was made public in a speech to the Reichstag on 1 September 1939. Goering had become the man of the moment, promising

Hitler the earth with the devastating effects of his Luftwaffe.

Neither is there any evidence to suggest that Hess was mad. Intelligent men confided in the safety of their diaries their doubts on the official line. Ernst Weiszäcker at the Foreign Office wrote, 'Yesterday [Hess] had been a demigod and today he was nothing but a pitiful idiot . . . I was sorry when his old friends attributed to his defects other than defects of intelligence.'[7] And Ulrich von Hassell, a diplomat of the old school whose allegiance to Hitler, never great, would waver to the point of open opposition: 'The background of Hess's flight is not yet clear. The official explanations are, to say the least, incomplete. Hess's sporting and technical performance alone showed that he could not be called crazy.'[8]

While the official line poured scorn on Hess and called him a 'lunatic', in whom eternal optimism and idealism were the hallmarks of insanity, and while Hitler worried about what Hess would tell his captors, especially about the imminent invasion of Russia, realists and cynics did not buy a word of it.

In Germany, after the initial furore and the unconvincing cover-up, Hess's identity vanished. His photograph was removed from public places. Streets named after him were renamed. Books on the Party and the Reich no longer carried his photograph; nor was his name in the index. Two weeks after the flight, Martin Bormann stepped delightedly into Hess's shoes as Party administrator and the office of Stellvertreter was abolished. Bormann said Hess was impotent; Goering accused him of conjuring up South American Indian ritual magic so that Ilse could conceive a son. Hitler barely spoke of him again. Goebbels, arguably the most intelligent of all the Nazi leadership, was at a loss to understand the silence of Churchill's Government over the Hess affair – 'What I would have made of the case!' And his frustration led Josef Goebbels into precisely the wrong conclusion, relating to British propagandists: 'We are dealing with dumb amateurs over there.'

Peter Padfield has an altogether different view of the Hess flight. He suggests that Alfred Rosenberg told Hitler of the Stellvertreter's intentions on the afternoon of 10 May. Rosenberg was head of the Party Foreign Affairs Department, and would have worked with Hess in the Ausland Organization. He was the fourth member of the Nazi high command to have been privy to the peace plan. Padfield also postulates that Pintsch, or another of Hess's aides, visited Hitler at the Berghof with details that Hess had taken off from Augsburg as planned. The period of imprisonment which all the relevant Hess team underwent was, of course, ideal for a cover story to be devised and no doubt it was then that the Party line was agreed on. So all the details that Pintsch provided to Leasor were *after* this debriefing and Pintsch (like Leitgen) stuck to the story for the rest of his life. To make it fully convincing, it is even likely that Pintsch really did arrive on the Sunday morning, as he had been ordered by Hess the day before. From then on, Hitler's tantrums took over. The Führer, notoriously prone to lie in bed until 11 o'clock, was up and in uniform by 7.30. The plan had gone wrong. Hess was not dining with the Duke of Hamilton, nor Lords Bedford, Brocket or Buccleuch, still less with the King. It was time for the Nazi establishment to dissociate itself from Hess. Padfield is probably right when he attributes Pintsch's and Leitgen's loyalty to Hess as the motive for their solidarity in later years. If it could be proved – as Stalin had suspected – that Hess flew officially with the full backing of Hitler, then his complicity in Barbarossa was complete and there would be no chance that Hess would ever be released.

An extraordinary piece of proof that Hitler knew of the Hess flight earlier than 11 May comes from Adolf Galland, who months later would succeed to the command of the Luftwaffe's fighter groups. According to his diary – and any motive he may have had for lying seems incomprehensible – Goering telephoned him on the evening of 10 May to order him to intercept the Stellvertreter who had gone mad and was flying to England. With only minutes of daylight left, this was a fatuous order for Goering to have given. Galland did what he could, but his fighters found nothing – largely because Hess was well over the North Sea by then. Doubtless this rumour lent fuel to Hugh Thomas's theory that Hess was shot down by intercepting Luftwaffe aircraft and a double substituted. Why should Goering have given Galland this peculiar order?

He was simply covering his back. Knowing that the mission had slim chance of success, he wanted it to be said in later years that he had done his best to stop it. On the other hand, just in case it succeeded, he did not want to be seen to be trying too hard. It may even have been that Goering's order, so timed that Galland could not possibly accomplish it, was a sop to the Russians – still technically Germany's allies and (in the case of Stalin at least) apparently unaware that Barbarossa was now only weeks away. It was typical of Goering to have his cake as well as eating it. The Fieldmarshal's outrage and scorn of Hess the following day over lunch at the Berghof was just another piece of play-acting.

In the rash of arrests that took place on Sunday 11 May, two were precipitate. Hess's driver Lippert and the body-guard who had accompanied him to the Augsburg airfield were both picked up at Gallspach, a little village across the Austrian border. But the time was 5.30 a.m. – nearly four hours before Pintsch arrived with the shock news of Hess's flight. Peter Padfield believes there was also a coded tele-phone message from Augsburg to the Berghof to the effect that Hess was in the air. And he goes even further in his belief that Reinhard Heydrich – the 'blond beast' who helped Himmler in the Final Solution – flew as escort to Hess over the North Sea and reported back, probably to Hitler, that that part of the journey had gone well. There is no solid evidence for this, but certainly Heydrich was a brilliant pilot and in the early weeks of the Russian invasion which was to follow

Hess's flight, flew operationally with the Luftwaffe. As we have seen on the Durham Map, the mysterious aircraft 42J may have been Heydrich breaking off his escort duty and turning for home.

At the Berghof, a heated discussion took place that Sunday night, twenty-four hours after the flight. Hitler, Goering, Ribbentrop and Bormann were all shouting the odds; but according to Walther Hewel, on Ribbentrop's staff, this took place in the hall and was again, no doubt, intended for public consumption. Albrecht Haushofer was summoned on 12 May and left in a room with paper and pencil to make a list of his English contacts. He cited Hamilton, Rab Butler, Lord Home and stressed Hamilton's links with other members of the aristocracy close to court – the Astors, Derbys and Stanleys. Samuel Hoare, the British Ambassador to the Court of St James at Madrid was also listed. Haushofer had of course been summoned not to explain his part in the Hess affair; from various papers the SS now had, after ransacking his father's house, it was clear that Haushofer had *not* known Hess's immediate plans. All the Führer was doing was checking the background in an attempt to understand the deafening silence from across the Channel.

But Haushofer's days were numbered. He was released four days later from the Berghof and re-questioned in July. The fact was that the Jewish connection was now laid bare. Without Hess to protect the family, there was a real and growing danger – a danger which would ultimately lead to Moabit prison and a bullet in the back of the head. There is evidence that Himmler wanted Haushofer alive as a pawn in any British-German peace initiative; especially since, as seemed likely by 1945, Hitler would not always be the man in power. It was not to be.

It was easy for Hitler to scream and rant in public, to issue disowning communiqués to the German people over the radio, to point to Hess's homoeopathic peculiarities and his dabbling with the occult. It was easy to round up a few personnel and lean on them to shut them up. But others involved he left surprisingly alone. Ilse Hess continued to live in her fine house and received a government pension for as long as the Reich lasted. Willi Messerschmitt and others at the Augsburg works were not touched. Why should they be, when they were, in the time-honoured tradition of good Nazis 'only obeying orders'? And when those orders came ultimately, not from Hess, but from the Führer himself.

Peter Padfield cites a throwaway but telling line from Hitler to Karl Wolff, Himmler's man in Italy in 1945. Wolff was trying to create a direct link between Hitler and the White House, as Berlin was collapsing into rubble under the Russian bombardment. 'Should you fail,' Hitler said to Wolff, 'I shall have to drop you exactly like Hess.'[9]

CHAPTER 8

In the Prison of His Days . . .

> In the deserts of the heart
> Let the healing fountain start,
> In the prison of his days
> Teach the free man how to praise.
>
> *In Memory of W.B. Yeats*
> W.H. Auden

At ten o'clock on that Sunday morning, 11 May 1941, the Duke of Hamilton and Flight Lieutenant Benson reached Maryhill Barracks. First the officer of the watch showed Hamilton 'Hauptmann Horn's' personal effects. Homoeopathic medicines, a photograph of Hess and a small boy (his three-year-old son, Wolf-Rudiger), a map, a Leica camera and two visiting cards. This was all Hamilton saw. He made no mention of the letter which Hess had with him the night before and was so adamant that Hamilton should receive. It is not known what happened to this letter or what exactly it contained.

Hess was in bed in a side room in the barracks and immediately asked Benson and the other officer to leave so that he could speak to Hamilton alone. The only account of the meeting that followed is Hamilton's. It was duly recorded in a report to Churchill:

The German opened by saying that he had seen me in Berlin at the Olympic Games in 1936 and that I had lunched in his house. He said 'I do not know if you recognize me, but I am Rudolf Hess'. He went on to say that he was on a mission of humanity and that the Führer did not want to defeat England and wished to stop fighting. His friend Albrecht Haushofer [whose visiting card Hess carried] told him that I was an Englishman who he thought would understand his (Hess's) point of view. He had consequently tried to arrange a meeting with me in Lisbon (see Haushofer's letter to me dated September 23rd 1940). Hess went on to say that he had tried to fly to Dungavel and this was the fourth time he had set out, the first time being in December. On the three previous occasions he had turned back owing to bad weather. He had not attempted to make this journey during the time when Britain was gaining victories in Libya, as he thought his mission then might be interpreted as weakness, but now that Germany had gained successes in North Africa and Greece, he was glad to come.

The fact that Reich Minister Hess had come to this country in person would, he stated, show his sincerity and Germany's willingness for peace. He then went on to say that the Führer was convinced that Germany would win the war, possibly soon but certainly in one, two or three years. He wanted to stop unnecessary slaughter that would otherwise inevitably take place. He asked me if I could get together leading members of my party to talk over things with a view to making peace proposals.[*] I replied that there was now only one party in this country.

* The fact that Hess refers to Hamilton's party (i.e. a peace party) shows how far he had ignored Haushofer's sound advice that no such group existed and how far he had accepted the bait of SO1.

He then said he could tell me what Hitler's peace terms would be. First he would insist on an arrangement whereby our two countries would never go to war again. I questioned him as to how that arrangement could be brought about and he replied that one of the conditions, of course, was that Britain would give up her traditional policy of always opposing the strongest power in Europe.

I then told him that if we made peace now, we would be at war again certainly within two years. He asked why, to which I replied that if a peace agreement was possible, the arrangement could have been made before the war started, but since Germany chose war in prefer-ence to peace at a time when we were most anxious to preserve peace, I could put forward no hope of a peace agreement now.

He requested me to ask the King to give him 'parole' as he had come unarmed and of his own free will.

He further asked if he could inform his family that he was safe by sending a telegram to Rothacker [Emma, one of Hess's elderly aunts] Herzog Str. 17, Zürich, stating that Alfred Horn was in good health. He also asked that his identity should not be disclosed to the Press ... Throughout the interview, Hess was able to express himself fairly clearly, but he did not properly understand what I was saying and I suggested that I should return with an interpreter and have further conversation with him ... From Press photographs and Albrecht Haushofer's description of Hess, I believed that this prisoner was indeed Hess himself. Until this interview I had not the slightest idea that the invitation in Haushofer's letter to meet him (Haushofer),in Lisbon had any connection with Hess.'[1]

The text of Hamilton's interview of 11 May, uncorroborated and without the benefit of a translator, begs a whole series of questions which will be addressed later.

On whose orders is uncertain, Rudolf Hess was moved by ambulance to the first of his many prisons – Drymen Military Hospital in Buchanan Castle near Loch Lomond, with its magical wooded islands rising from the peat-brown waters.

Hamilton was summoned to Northolt aerodrome and then to Ditchley Park to meet Churchill. The Prime Minister was convivial over dinner when the Duke arrived. Brandy in one hand and cigar in the other, his reception of the Scottish peer was, to say the least, cavalier – 'Now, tell us this funny story of yours.' After he had heard it he went with his guests into an adjoining room in the Hall to watch a Marx Brothers film.

On the Monday, while Munich Radio was at pains to distance Hess from all that was sane and right and German, the Prime Minister took the whole matter rather more seriously. In discussion with Anthony Eden, the Foreign Secretary and Stewart Menzies, Head of SIS, Churchill decided to send Ivone Kirkpatrick with the Duke of Hamilton to interrogate Hauptmann Horn. Kirkpatrick was head of the BBC European Section and had been First Secretary at the British Embassy in Berlin for five years before the war. If anyone could recognize and evaluate the Stellvertreter, Kirkpatrick was the man. Sefton Delmer disagreed. In *Black Boomerang* it is clear that SO1 was involved at a very early stage in the Hess case. Valentine Williams rang Delmer to tell him that they were to interrogate Hess. When that idea fell through, Delmer was sceptical of Kirkpatrick – 'not nearly exalted enough' to appeal to Hess's sense of his own importance.

Perhaps the early hours of Tuesday morning was not the best time for the Stellvertreter to be woken out of a deep sleep, but Kirkpatrick had to work hard to remind Hess of their earlier meetings in Germany. Hess himself had produced copious pages of notes explaining the reason for his flight and began to wax lyrical on the geopolitics expounded by his old professor and the Nazi view of developments in European history since the Anglo-French entente cordiale of 1904.* This was delivered in German and, before the Duke of Hamilton nodded off in mid-ramble, he had already written it off as 'one long eulogy of Hitler'. After well over two hours of rapid monologue, Hess explained why he had come:

> ... horrified at the prospect of the prolongation of the struggle, he had come here without the knowledge of Hitler to convince responsible persons that, since England could not win the war, the wisest course was to make peace now ... he could give his word of honour that the Führer had never entertained any designs against the British Empire, nor had he ever aspired to world domination. He believed that Germany's sphere of interest was Europe and that any dissipation of Germany's strength beyond Europe's frontiers would be a weakness and would carry with it the seeds of Germany's destruction ...[2]

Specifically, Hess proposed a free hand for Germany in Europe in exchange for an equally free hand for Britain in the Empire. Looking forward to his breakfast and having heard enough propaganda for one night, Kirkpatrick only made enquiries about Hitler's designs on Russia and what the position of Italy might be. More complex questions and challenges, Kirkpatrick thought, might have taken another two and a half hours. It was clear that Hess would not negotiate with Churchill, a dangerous warmonger who in Nazi opinion would have to go.

* The Anglo-French entente was merely one of a series of agreements and alliances during the late nineteenth and early twentieth centuries, which saw an edgy and suspicious Europe looking for friends in a sea of enemies. It was specifically these alliances that created the 'armed camps' of 1914 and made a European war ever more likely.

At least it had been established without doubt that the mysterious airman *was* Rudolf Hess, even if the Permanent Under-Secretary at the Foreign Office, Sir Alexander Cadogan, along with most others, continued to question his sanity – '. . . can't say why he's come,' he wrote in his diary, 'unless he's mad.'[3]

Churchill now decided on the gameplan. With hindsight it may have been the wrong one. Hess was to be kept strictly incommunicado 'in a convenient house not too far from London'. This house was to be bugged to monitor the Stellvertreter's every conversation. He was not to be allowed newspapers or access to a radio. He was to have food, books, writing materials and recreation. His 'health and comfort' were to be catered for, 'he should be treated with dignity as if he were an important general who had fallen into our hands'.

Before he left Buchanan Castle, Hess was interviewed twice more by Ivone Kirkpatrick, on Wednesday 14 and Thursday 15 May. Little more was learnt here. The Stellvertreter asked for three books to read: *Seapower* by Commander Russell Grenfell, *Dynamic Defence* by Basil Liddell-Hart and *Three Men in a Boat* by Jerome K. Jerome. Peter Padfield points out that the first two dealt with non-involvement in European affairs which may have echoed Hess's peace proposals.* The juxtaposition of the third has caused speculation among writers on Hess. As an Anglophile (which he undoubtedly was before the war) he may have actually enjoyed Jerome's Edwardian romp as a typical piece of English whimsy. On the other hand, few people understood Hess's sense of humour and *Three Men in a Boat* was certainly a little 'mainstream' for him. Did he simply request this book as a light-hearted antidote to the more serious

---

* Hess was not to know presumably that Liddell-Hart was one of those advising Churchill that the British were unlikely to win the war on military grounds.

volumes he had ordered? Or was this the start of some sort of game he was playing with his captors which would develop in the long years of confinement ahead?

Behind the scenes, there was confusion and disagreement about how to play the Hess affair. Churchill wanted to make obvious political capital out of it – the propaganda value of the 'defection' of Hitler's number two was immense. Others, like Duff Cooper, Minister of Information, dithered and wasted a golden opportunity.

It would also appear that there was a genuine sense of bewilderment, amongst members of the War Cabinet, as to what precisely had led to the flight. Certainly not all of them were 'in on the details' of the Intelligence scam, the success of which, by then, may have exceeded the dreams of the instigators.

In 1994, John Costello was kind enough to pass me a copy of the War Cabinet document, which clearly shows that Lord Thomas of Swinton, the Chairman of the Security Executive, had been asked to produce an explanation of the flight for Clement Attlee, who presumably, by reason of the request was unaware of the events leading up to the flight. Part of this document is reproduced on pages 142 and 143. This sense of 'not knowing' by a significant section of the War Cabinet, if true, must have distilled distrust and rumour within the coalition cabinet itself, a state of affairs that must surely have increased the uncertainty of approach when dealing with the matter publicly.

Under guard and accompanied by a Major J.J. Shepherd, Hess was taken to London. Shepherd reported:

> In the train he became very restive and objected to having any lighting in the compartment and wanted the guard officers withdrawn. These requests were naturally refused, whereupon he raised his voice in temper, saying he would not make any attempt to sleep if under

observation. Finding his demands very ineffective, he appeared to sulk for the greater part of the night.[4]

This sulking was to persist on and off for the next forty-six years.

Hess's temporary accommodation for the next four days was the Tower of London. More recently, the outer ward of the former royal castle and mint had been converted into a military hospital and the recessed windows set into the wall became cells. Peter Padfield paints a charming picture of Hess lodging in the Governor's House and watching the guards drill to pipes and drums under his window. Hess may have found the experience less pleasing had he known that two walls away was the small arms range where eleven spies had been executed in the First World War. The legend of the Tower as a place of death was not to end until the war Hess tried to stop. He was the last person ever to be held prisoner there.

During those four days, Mytchett Place, near Aldershot, was being wired up, inside and out, and the Scots and Coldstream Guards who were to be his jailers took Hess there on Tuesday, 20 May. Although in his reports, Major Shepherd refers to 'X', Hess was now officially 'Z' in all communiqués and Mytchett Place 'Camp Z'. He was watched carefully, by Shepherd and a team of officers, and the Major's report to Churchill hit the nail very exactly on the head: 'He is cunning, shrewd and self-centred . . . very temperamental and will need careful handling if he is to be outwitted.'[5]

Hess had been at 'Camp Z' for a day when his paranoia emerged. Feigned or real, he complained that his lunch was poisoned and would trust only Lieutenant-Colonel Gibson Graham, the doctor at Buchanan Castle who had accompanied him south. Hess described sensations of 'warmth', 'headache pains', 'extraordinary well-being', 'joie de vivre', followed by 'pessimism' and 'extraordinary fatigue of the brain'. His obsession with murder grew and in a presentiment of what might have been his death forty-six years later, he imagined a commando cutting an artery in the darkness of his room to resemble suicide.

Even by the end of the first week, Lieutenant W. Malone, one of the Guards officers, was writing a description that fitted the photographs later associated with Hess – 'shaggy eyebrows, deep animal sad eyes, a look of anguish and torture on his face'. The mood swings would not improve.

The night of 27–28 May was one of mixed fortunes for Britain. That day the invincible *Bismarck*, the most advanced and terrifying of all the German battle fleet, was sunk by torpedoes from the cruisers *Dorsetshire* and *Norfolk*. In Iraq the 20th Indian Brigade occupied the ancient city of Ur. But in North Africa, Erwin Rommel the 'Desert Fox', who was probably the ablest general of the war was massing his Panzers on the Egyptian border. And in Crete, following the airborne invasion of 22 May, the British were beginning to weaken and fall back.

On the Home Front, however, something extraordinary was happening. Unknown until 1979, when one of those involved went public, an unspecified number of German commandos were parachuted down near Luton during an air raid. The official record is silent on all this, but the speculation is that these parachutists were assassins looking for Hess before he did too much damage by talking to the enemy. In civilian clothes and probably with forged identities, the parachutists were caught and shot, miles away from Mytchett Place in the wrong county.

Dr Gibson Graham was replaced, in view of what was regarded as the Stellvertreter's deteriorating mental state, by a psychiatrist, Major Henry Dicks. Perhaps as a sign of his contempt for the new man, perhaps in a genuine state of despair, Hess sat on Wednesday, 4 June, 'in the most uncomfortable position, refused to speak to anyone, was morose and in a fit of the deepest depression.'[6] Then, another interrogator arrived.

Viscount Simon of Stackpole Elidor was an enormously experienced lawyer and politician whom Churchill had made his Lord Chancellor the previous year. As a former Foreign Secretary, Simon had done his best to steer a middle course through the notoriously treacherous political waters of 1930s Europe. As such, in the public mind, and probably in Hess's too, he had the reputation of an Appeaser. But if Hess hoped that Simon was the ambassador of any possible peace party reaching out to grasp the Stellvertreter's olive branch, he was mistaken. Simon had orders from Churchill to find out what the man knew. Once again, Sefton Delmer was unimpressed. Simon had status, but that was all. 'I cannot conceive a worse choice,' he wrote in *Black Boomerang*. Simon was 'frigid, inhibited. He was not the man to deal with Hess either'.

A little after two o'clock on Monday, 9 June, Simon, with a pass marked 'Dr Guthrie' and Ivone Kirkpatrick posing as 'Dr Mackenzie', interviewed Hess at Mytchett Place. It was of course the fourth time that Kirkpatrick had interviewed the prisoner and although everyone knew everyone else's real identity, in the proceedings Hess was called 'Jonathan'. He had eaten only glucose tablets that morning and was dressed in his Luftwaffe uniform. One of the regular companions appointed by the secret service to observe him, known by the alias of 'Captain Barnes', acted as interpreter. The recorded, translated conversation revolved around the need for Britain and Germany to co-operate to prevent the full horrors of blitzkrieg. Once again, as with Hamilton and Kirkpatrick, Hess launched into what was, in effect, a speech. After over two hours of it, Simon felt he could learn no more and ended the session. As he did so however, Hess asked if he could speak to Simon alone.

The Stellvertreter waited until Kirkpatrick and 'Barnes'

had gone, then spoke fluently in English, which became less and less polished as he got carried away. He accused his guards, the secret service, of maintaining a barrage of noise all night to rob him of sleep. Motorcycles, aircraft, doors – the noises were incessant. And he reiterated his fears of murder. The transcript of this conversation was recorded by the Mytchett bugging system and Simon's calm, matter-of-fact responses are almost a caricature of the stiff-upper-lip Dunkirk spirit: Hess's paranoia was 'childish, idiotic'. His threats to go on hunger strike 'very silly of you', 'perfectly absurd' . . . Indeed they were. As soon as Simon had gone, Hess chomped his way through two plates of cake for tea.

For the rest of the war, and indeed for the rest of his life, Rudolf Hess exhibited an extraordinary range of symptoms suggesting psychosis. He complained of headaches and believed his food was being drugged. And, days after the Simon interviews, he tried to kill himself. Unable to sleep, Hess called the guard for a doctor in the early hours of the morning. As Dr Dicks arrived, sleeping pills in hand, Hess, in uniform and flying boots, dashed past him out of the open cell door and hurled himself over the balcony, bouncing on his leg on the stairs as he went down. In seconds, there was a crash of crockery as a guard dropped his tea-tray and the click of a hammer as his revolver came up to the level. But there was no need for guns. Hess lay moaning on the floor of the hall while Dicks and his staff set about strapping up his apparently broken leg and injecting him with a solution of distilled water Dicks told him was morphine. Although undoubtedly in genuine pain, it was the cutting of his Luftwaffe breeches that upset the Stellvertreter most.

Now, everyone took Hess seriously. The medical regimen was stepped up and two of the three companions assigned to eavesdrop on the man were replaced by psychiatric nurses. Oddly, but perhaps to give him an emotional window on the world, Hess was allowed copies of *The Times*. When news reached Fleet Street that Operation Barbarossa had begun, Hess said to Dicks, 'So, they have started after all' and sat 'with a faraway look in his eyes'.

With hindsight, the German attack on Stalin's Soviet Union was possibly the real turning point of the war – 'the beginning of the end', to reapply Churchill's later quote. At the time, however, the Prime Minister was almost in a minority of one in believing so. Although no accurate figures were available in Britain, Hitler unleashed before dawn on 22 June over three million men, 7,100 heavy guns, 3,300 tanks and 2,770 aircraft. There were weaknesses in the Wehrmacht assault which would become apparent in the coming months and on paper, as always, the Russians looked strong. They had 24,000 tanks and over half a million horses. Their airforce mustered 8,000 planes. But this was the accountant's tally. In reality, less than a third of the tanks were operational. Of the aircraft, well over half were obsolete and in poor repair. If the Panzers and Stukas could strike quickly enough, few had any doubt what the outcome would be. Most ominously of all, Joseph Stalin had ignored the likelihood of this moment for months. On 22 June, he was utterly unprepared for it.

While Hess's broken leg continued to mend throughout the summer of 1941, his mental state appeared to get worse. He knew that the Russians had used various 'truth drugs' to elicit confessions in Stalin's grimly public 'show trials' in the Thirties. He also knew that the Abwehr (the German secret service) used Sodium Thiopental to the same effect. He now appeared to believe that the SIS was applying the same strategy on him. They fitted specially toughened glass to his windows, just in case his suicide bid had been genuine. Then, Beaverbrook came to see him.

William Max Aitken, 1st Baron Beaverbrook, was a Canadian businessman who had entered British politics before the last war. His 'Empire free trade' movement had met with no success in the 1930s, but his newspaper empire was vast. He took over the *Express* in 1918, extending it to a Sunday two years later. His acquisition of the *Evening Standard* in 1923 made him the most powerful man in Fleet Street. It was all the more relevant to Hess's motives for his flight that Beaverbrook had championed the Appeasement cause. He published a series of articles by Basil Liddell-Hart which claimed that the best policy was to make peace with Germany – fast.

As 'Dr Livingstone' (the name on his pass) Beaverbrook went in search of 'Jonathan' at Mytchett on the evening of 9 September. Unlike Simon, Beaverbrook had met Hess before, in Berlin, and they exchanged pleasantries before discussing the war situation *vis-à-vis* Barbarossa. As a former head of aircraft production, Beaverbrook had a natural interest in the hardware of all the participants. In an attempt to learn something, Beaverbrook joked that he was the only friend Hess had in Britain. It did not work. Hess told him nothing.

Summer darkened to winter. Hess waved his hands in the air, talked to walls, carefully wrapped his food in pieces of tissue paper and was 'rather tearful' when he found out about the attack on Pearl Harbor. In the Japanese offensive on the naval base, 3,300 US personnel died and four battleships, three cruisers and three destroyers were lost, along with 188 aircraft. Hitler allied himself with Japan the same day and drove the second strategic nail into the coffin of the Third Reich. His thousand-year state had less than four years to live.

By the spring of 1942, as the Japanese began to push the British back through the jungles of Burma, Hess complained to his captors at Mytchett Place that it was the Jews who were poisoning his food. Since it was standard Nazi policy to blame every evil on the Jews, it seems odd that Colonel J.R. Rees, consultant in psychological medicine to the army, should choose that moment to decide that Hess was deranged. Little of the celebrated paranoia shows through in the Stellvertreter's birthday letter in June to his old friend and mentor, Professor Karl Haushofer:

> Let the waves in thunder roar,
> Life or death may be your lot –
> Whether wrecked or safe to shore,
> Ever stay your own pilot.

It cannot be disputed that I am wrecked. Just as little can it be disputed that I was my own pilot. VVV [Hess's 'in' equivalent of Ha! Ha! Ha!]. In this connection I have nothing to reproach myself about. VVV. At all events I have steered. You certainly know as well as I that the compass we steer by is influenced by forces which, even if we do not understand them, work imperturbably. May they be friendly to you in the coming year![7]

Which then is the *real* Rudolf Hess? The cavalier pilot, launching himself into eternity from the cockpit of his Me 110 and living with Fate, like the philosopher he was? Or the paranoid hysteric, swapping food plates with his captors and whispering to the furniture? Hess knew very well that his letters would be read and censored, but they were his only means of communication with the outside world and through them, at various times, he was able not only to persuade the Haushofers that he was perfectly sane, but even to hint at where he was being held. There is little doubt in my mind that, like Hamlet, Hess was only 'mad Nor' by 'Nor'West' and that a man does not come to be the Stellvertreter without knowing a hawk from a handsaw. It is entirely possible that 'prison psychosis' set in and may help to explain his more bizarre actions, but his ability to snap back into lucidity, as at Nuremberg, makes it clear that his mind had not gone.

Soon it was time to move him on again. Aldershot was not, despite Churchill's wishes to have Hess near to London, the most sensible place to imprison him. Mytchett Place could have been bombed. The proximity of army camps, which were well known to the Luftwaffe, made this eminently likely. So they moved him to south Wales, far enough north of Cardiff and the coal-producing Rhondda valleys to be relatively safe.

Abergavenny is a sleepy border town lying on the meanders of the River Usk at the confluence of the Fenny. Its population in 1942 was about 8,000. On 26 June Hess arrived at the ground floor apartment in Maindiff Court, appropriately perhaps in what had been a lunatic asylum.

By 1 September, the *Daily Mail* had a man on the inside, but whether this was a loose-lipped orderly at Maindiff or a careful leak from Brendan Bracken, Churchill's new Minister of Information, is uncertain. Reporter Guy Ramsey in 'The Story All Britain Has Awaited' spoke of the Maindiff setting 'among gracious trees and bright with flower borders that edge the building'. Hess himself the journalist described as a borderline case before he left Germany, 'hearing voices which do not exist . . .' The myth of Hess's mental decline, reinforced by the distancing propaganda from Berlin, has been partially repeated by every British writer since.

At Maindiff, Hess began to increase the frequency of his letters to his wife, Ilse. He wandered the hills up to Abergavenny in the company of his guards – 'especially nice types'.[8] Lieutenant Walter Fenton, who drove Hess around the countryside, remembered: 'I got to like the old boy very much. I refused to go on leave once because I didn't want to leave him . . . he thought a lot of England and thought it was a great shame we ever came to war.'[9] Hess filled the rest of his time with reading, mostly classic German writers like Goethe, and his correspondence with Wolf-Rudiger – 'Buz' – who was now six. In letters written at this time, the cleverness of his descriptions of his surroundings allowed Karl Haushofer to speculate that Hess's prison was in either Wales or Scotland.

That autumn, his mood swung again. It had been no picnic for the Hess household, his family and followers, since his flight. All arrested for complicity at first, his adjutant Alfred Leitgen was still in custody; and it was clear that Ilse Hess, her son and Rudolf's brother Alfred were an embarrassment to their former Nazi friends (although Ilse's Party financial allowance continued). Martin Bormann, who had replaced Hess as Party boss, took two years even to correspond with Frau Hess.

The Stellvertreter was furious and apparently retreated further into amnesia. By the spring of 1944, he agreed to the use of drugs to unlock his lost memories. Hess was to admit later, at his trial in Nuremberg, that this was a 'tactical' (i.e. faked) memory loss. With a supreme effort of concentration, he clung to consciousness, calling for water, groaning with stomach cramps, mumbling 'I don't know' or staring vacantly around the room. 'It was grand theatre', he confessed to Ilse years later.

Slowly, inexorably, the world that Rudolf Hess knew, loved and had helped to create, was disintegrating. Before dawn on 6 June 1944, in a 'window' of relatively good weather, para-troopers of the 101st Airborne floated like ghosts into the sleeping fields around Pont L'Abbé and St. Mère Église in Normandy. As dawn broke, the greatest armada to leave Britain's shores was sighted by German lookouts from Quineville in the west to Cabourg in the east. One by one, the beaches fell to those wading ashore from their 'ducks', flinging themselves on the barbed wire, as in the last war, clawing their way up the sand. Utah, Omaha, Gold, Juno and Sword – the beaches' codenames passed into legend. By the end of D-Day, the day of deliverance from Nazi oppression, 'bloody' Omaha alone had claimed 2,000 lives. But the gamble of Overlord had paid off and the battle of Normandy was the first body blow to Hitler's invincible Reich.

As the Allies closed in on Germany from east and west, with Mussolini dead and Italy out of the war, an increasingly delusional Hitler hid in the labyrinthine bunker under Berlin's streets, firing off orders to attack to units that had long ago surrendered, lovingly talking of his long-term plans to rebuild the city of Linz once the Wehrmacht threw the enemy back.

On 29 April 1945, the Führer married his mistress, the enigmatic Eva Braun, and the next day she and their dog, Blondi, died of poisoning. After that, apparently, Hitler placed a revolver against his temple and blew his brains out. His numbed staff, some crying, some giggling with the strain of the last months of the beleaguered Reich, carried out the Führer's last orders and poured gasoline over the bodies of Herr and Frau Hitler before setting fire to them.

Hamburg Radio announced to a disbelieving Germany on 1 May that Hitler was dead. Admiral Doenitz, now Führer, vowed to fight on 'to save the German people from destruction by the Bolshevists'. The next day, the hammer and sickle flew over the Reichstag in Berlin. Josef Goebbels, the mercurial, crippled creator of Nazi propaganda poisoned his six children, his wife and himself in the ashes of the city. Martin Bormann, Hess's replacement in the Party hierarchy, disappeared. Dozens of sightings of him were claimed in the years ahead, all over the world, but it is likely that he died in the ruins of Berlin, his body unrecognizable, his passing unlamented.*

All this affected Rudolf Hess badly. At Maindiff he now had access to radio broadcasts as well as papers. On 4 February 1945 he put on his Luftwaffe uniform and sat in a chair. Then he rammed a stolen breadknife twice into his chest. This second suicide attempt seems to have been even

---

* While this book was at the draft stage, the remains of Martin Bormann were found in Berlin, verified by DNA testing.

more half-hearted than the first. Unaccountably, Hess had missed his heart and was well enough three days later to inform his jailers that he intended to starve himself to death. He now came, apparently, to believe that all those looking after him, especially his doctors, had been turned into zombies by a new chemical that produced a glassy expression in the eyes and a limp walk 'with soft knees'. The chemical, Hess had little doubt, was being administered by the Jews.

Nuremberg is the second-largest city in Bavaria and the capital of Franconia. As a key centre of the German railway and canal systems in the twentieth century, Nuremberg was chosen for the astonishing torchlight ceremonies held by the Nazis, flames flickering on the polished rows of helmets, Wagnerian chords crashing over the loud-speakers and all of it proudly filmed by Goebbels. It was here too that the series of vicious anti-Semitic laws were framed and passed. And it was here that what was left of the Nazi elite faced their judgement day in the eleven months that began in November 1945.

As early as October 1943 the United Nations, successor to the hapless League which had presided spinelessly over Nazi aggression in the Thirties, set up a war crimes commission in London. The decision made by the foreign ministers of Britain, the United States and the Union of Soviet Socialist Republics was that when (and in October 1943 that was still, arguably, a hopeful word) Nazi Germany was defeated, those responsible for the atrocities, massacres or executions, should be extradited to the scenes of their crimes and tried by local laws. Major criminals, such as the Nazi high command, were to be tried by a joint court of the Allied governments. This second suicide attempt seems to have

In June 1945, legal experts from these governments met again in London and the result was the four-power agreement of 8 August to establish an international military tribunal for the trial of war criminals whose crimes had no precise geographical location. The proceedings of the court would raise more than eyebrows today because technical rules of evidence were batted aside. The prosecution did not have to prove a fact which was considered common knowledge and the tribunal itself could not be challenged in terms of sentence passed. In other words, there was no right of appeal. Nazis in the dock then, and far more liberal commentators since, have challenged that Nuremberg was little more than the instrument of vengeance all Europe demanded.

At the same time that the plans for the Nuremburg trials were being drawn up, Allied Intelligence officers were being dispatched across Germany in order to seize any relevant Nazi documents that had escaped destruction. The role of Anthony Blunt is often quoted in this context, as he was sent to collect any papers relating to the British Royal Family, withheld from Hess by their relatives. We have also already described how the Americans rifled the Haushofer papers held at the Hartschimmelhof home.

Foreign Office document FO371 reveals the extent of the documents gleaned from Germany in connection with Albrecht Haushofer's role in the Hess affair. It is a remarkable document, prepared by the Research Department of the Foreign Office – German and Austrian Section and was sent by A. R. Walmsley on 1 October 1946 to two other members of the German section of the Foreign Office. Mr Walmsley stated in his introduction that, 'No distribution has been given to this document and none was needed.' Consequently, the file was marked 'Action Completed' on 25 October. In other words, only two other people ever saw the contents of the file at the time of its preparation.

The file contains the Haushofer letters of the summer of 1940 and mention is clearly made of Mrs Roberts and Lisbon. No comment is made by the Research Department as to her identity, presumably because they already knew. It is not clear

218

whether Mr Walmsley was the Robert Walmsley who played a significant role within SO1 at the start of the war, but the lack of questioning does seem to indicate a degree of knowledge that was now being covered up. Mr D. Wilson, one of the Foreign Office recipients, merely stated that, 'No action is necessary on this' and the other wrote, 'I think Haushofer documents have clearly received sufficient attention'.

Also contained within the file is a plea from Carl Burkhardt for the British to issue a denial that he was implicated in the Hess affair. The letter from Burkhardt to Duff Cooper (then Ambassador in Paris) contains the written statement that, 'je ne connais pas M. Haushofer' and 'j'ignore le contendu du memoire Haushofer'.

Clearly, either Haushofer or Burkhardt was lying. Haushofer was dead, so could not reply. Burkhardt was by then President of the International Red Cross, so perhaps he had a position to protect. The British issued no such denial.

Nuremberg was in the American sector of occupied Germany since its 7th Army had taken the city on 20 April, so all security arrangements were organized by the Americans. Headphones, interpreters, solitary confinement, even the row of white-helmeted military policemen who ringed the court were all the responsibility of the United States. On 8 October, Rudolf Hess, in uniform and flying boots, was flown from Maindiff to Nuremberg to take his place alongside twenty-one of his former colleagues to face charges on four counts. The indictment, drawn up at the end of August, specified: 1) conspiracy to commit crimes against peace; 2) commission of crimes against peace, by planning and waging wars of aggression against a number of states; 3) war crimes – murder and ill-treatment in occupied territories, deportation for slave labour, killing of hostages, prisoners of war, plunder and devastation of property; 4) crimes against humanity – murder, extermination, enslavement of civilian populations, political, racial and religious persecution.

The trial took place on the second floor of the Nuremberg courthouse which abutted the Palace of Justice, used to house the forest of documentation necessary to the case. One wall of the court was ripped out to provide space for the gentlemen of the Press and the floor had to be strengthened to take the weight of the unusually large numbers in the room. The two rows of defendants, minus Martin Bormann who was tried *in absentia*, sat behind their counsel. The prosecution benches stood beyond that and the judges faced the defendants.

Hess had brought with him bundles of statements and letters, the rambling jottings of his four years in prison, as well as the 'evidence' of attempts by the British to poison him – food wrapped in tissue paper, dated and signed. For all he had not been a free man during the war years, captivity at Mytchett and even more at Maindiff had actually been relatively pleasant. Captivity at Nuremberg, in time of peace, was not. His cell was thirteen feet by nine with a low iron bedstead and grey army blanket. The table was rickety and the walls plastered white, where the rivulets of rain and damp had not discoloured them. There was a single window high in the wall opposite the door from which at night an electric light shone. A wash basin and lavatory were built into a recess next to the door. It was from the pipe that led to this lavatory that defendant Robert Ley, leader of Hitler's Labour Front, hanged himself on 24 October.

In common with all the defendants, Hess was not allowed personal possessions, nor could he appear in the dock in uniform. His boots, his Luftwaffe tunic and cap, even his carefully wrapped 'poison' specimens were taken away from him. The commandant of the Nuremberg prison was the American Colonel Burton C. Andrus. He was not prepared to tolerate Nazi arrogance: 'When he [Hess] arrived he had some notions. But I pulled him up with a sharp "stand to attention when you speak to me" and he does as he is told now.'[10] There was a great deal of pride to be swallowed, but underneath the

Colonel's bluff exterior was a decent man with a difficult job. He knew that outside Nuremberg's protective walls were millions of people who would have ripped the twenty-one defendants apart with their bare hands.

Hess had only been brought to Nuremberg because of Russian insistence. The cloak of silence that Churchill had thrown over the Stellvertreter's mission in 1941 had led Stalin to his own conclusions. It was universally accepted in Moscow that its purpose had been to cajole Britain into a separate peace so that the Reich could unleash its full force against the Soviet Union. In short, the Russians wanted Hess's head. A more immediate problem however presented itself – was that head fit to stand trial?

Psychiatrists and interrogators, prominent among them Major Douglas Kelley and Colonel John Amen, tried to jog Hess's memory with details of his life. Hess looked alternately blank and worried. How could he defend himself in a trial when he could not even remember where he had been born? Now that Hess was publicly on display and facing a trial literally for his life, the level of psychiatric examination had been stepped up. In the years at Mytchett and Maindiff there had been no need for interrogation of this sort. Hess's questioners were clearly alarmed by his lack of response.

A series of Hess's old friends were now paraded before him. Hermann Goering, in the pale blue tunic of the Luftwaffe, but less like a Christmas tree now that he could not wear his decorations, was first: 'Hess, remember all the way back to 1923 at that time when I was a leader of the SA, that you led one of my SA troops? Do you remember that we made the putsch together in Munich?'

Hess did not.

'Do you remember,' Goering tried a more recent tack, 'that you flew in a plane, you yourself in this war flew to England?'

'No,' answered Hess.

'You used a Messerschmitt plane. Do you remember that you wrote a long letter to the Führer?'

'What about?'

'What you were going to do in England. That you were going to bring about peace?'

Hess could not remember.

Karl Haushofer, Hess's old friend and university professor was next: 'Rudolf, don't you know me any more? We have called each other by our first names for twenty years . . . I saw your family and your child and they are well . . .'[11]

Hess shrugged. He was sorry. He hoped his memory would return one day, but at the moment, it was hopeless. Haushofer, a general in the last war, had seen similar symptoms in shell-shocked soldiers. He wandered away, believing he saw the odd glimmer of recognition in Hess's eyes.

Franz von Papen, Chancellor in 1932 and briefly Hitler's Deputy tried next – to no avail. Then Ernst Bohle, whom Hess had appointed to the Ausland organization in Berlin in 1933, reminded the Stellvertreter that, as a man born in England, he had translated Hess's letter to the Duke of Hamilton. Hess wanted to know who Hamilton was. Bohle was flabbergasted. Even Hess's former secretaries, Ingeborg Sperr and Hildegard Fath, were ignored by him. Fath burst into tears.

When shown film of Nazi propaganda, he said, 'I must have been there, because obviously I was there. But I don't remember.' On film, he recognized Hitler and the same Air Reichsmarshall he could not remember in the flesh.

Almost alone among the defendants, Hess enjoyed the intelligence and *Rorschash* (ink-blot) tests they were all told to undergo. Such tests have been discredited now by the world of psychiatry, and there is gallows humour in Hess's claim to see in the random ink 'two men talking about a crime; blood is on their minds'. Major Kelley concluded that Hess was 'a highly schizoid personality with hysterical and obsessive components'.

During October and November, Hess was examined by a team of ten doctors, three Russian, three American, three British and one French. The upshot of the findings was broadly the same – Hess was suffering from hysterical amnesia triggered first by his failure to win peace with Britain in 1941 and now by his escape into unreality to avoid the brutal consequences of trial and judgement.

David Maxwell-Fyfe, Britain's leading prosecution counsel and later an indifferent Home Secretary under Churchill, gave a masterly explanation in court of the difference between amnesia and insanity. Francis Buddle of the United States Justice Department thought this 'lawyer's bull at first blush' and was far from impressed when his own man, Attorney General Robert H. Jackson, summed up Hess's deception as being 'in the volunteer class with his amnesia'. In short, Hess was sane and malingering. The trial proceeded along those lines, with the American forces' magazine *Stars and Stripes* widely read by the defendants in idle moments in court, its banner headlines blaring in typical American journalese – 'Hess Nuts. Fake Story Fake, Says Nuremberg Psychologist'.

On the first day of the trial Hess read a novel – *Der Loisl*, 'Story of a Girl' – something he was to do on most days in the dock. He sat on the front row with Goering on his right and von Ribbentrop, Hitler's Foreign Minister, on his left. That put him effectively second to Goering in terms of his former status and perhaps his guilt. The only time he recognized the proceedings going on around him at all was to smile and sit up at the mention of Hitler. Then he had stomach cramps and had to leave the court.

Ann and John Tusa in *The Nuremberg Trial* sum up Hess's appearance in court admirably:

> [Hess] was a clown – but a Shakespearean clown. He
> was a grotesque figure, gaunt and with angular projec-
> tions from a baggy, grey tweed suit. Everyone watched

with fascination his constant grimaces and gesticula-
tions, his sudden paroxysms of laughter. His rabbitty
grin expressed no comprehensible delight. When
people laughed at him – and they sometimes did –
they immediately became uneasy. For hours on end,
Hess would show no interest in what was happening
in court; he seemed to have no contact with reality.
Suddenly he would shoot a piercing glance at the visitors in the gallery and smile sardonically and
spectators would feel a chill. At such moments, those
who felt pity for this scarecrow, thin, miserable and
old, those who believed the experts must be wrong
and that Hess was too mad to be on trial, were shaken.
There was a knowingness, a cunning, a shielded
strength in the man . . .

On the second day, he shouted 'Nein' in answer to charges
against him.

His views on the Third Reich and the war as reported on 10
December in *Stars and Stripes* were certainly no more insane
than those of millions of Germans who held similar views. But
it must have been a weird contrast when on the next day, the
American film *The Nazi Plan*, a four-hour compilation of
German newsreel, was shown in court – the swaying, novel-
reading former Stellvertreter looking at himself on the
celluloid of ten years before, standing tall and erect in his SS
black, thundering 'The Party is the Führer and the Führer is
Germany'. Hess's reaction to an earlier film, of concentration
camp bodies being shovelled into mass graves, of the gas
ovens and the human skin lampshades, had been to mutter, 'I
don't believe it.' Goering shut him up.

At the end of the year, Hess refused to attend Christmas
services in the prison chapel in case the world should think
he did it for fear. The hit song of the year that was dawning
was, appropriately, 'Don't Fence Me In'.

Hess changed his defence counsel during the trial. Dr Gunther von Rohrscheidt, whom Hess considered incompetent, was replaced first with Dr Alfred Sauter and then his junior, the tenacious Dr Alfred Seidl. Robert Jackson, the American prosecutor, painted an ironic picture of Hess before giving the lie. The Stellvertreter, he said, looked like 'an innocent, middle-aged man' and likened him to a postman who passed on Hitler's megalomaniac orders unread.

On 31 August, Hess, along with the others, made his last plea. He read his five-page statement at such breakneck speed that he was fighting for breath at the end of it. It was rambling, chaotic – to the extent that Seidl renewed his demand for another medical examination of his client. As for the verdict, Hess was feeling particularly philosophical perhaps when he said to the other defendants, 'From the astrological dates I think a miracle or something will happen.'

The 'miracle' was that the Russians did not get their way. Hess had been Hitler's closest confidant; his signature was on the Nuremberg decrees; he must have known in detail of all Hitler's plans up to and beyond 10 May 1941 – including of course, those that dealt with Operation Barbarossa. On a tribunal vote of 3 to 1, however, Hess was found guilty only on the first two counts, not the last two. As a man innocent of crimes against humanity, the death sentence was not handed down. The French were the most generous, demanding a prison sentence of twenty years. Again by 3 to 1 they were outvoted. Life must mean life.

In the corridor outside, minutes later, a much relieved and repentant Albert Speer said, 'What did you get, Herr Hess?'

'I have no idea,' the Stellvertreter told him, 'Probably the death penalty. I didn't listen.'[12]

What Rudolf Hess got was Spandau. The jail was situated in the British sector of the divided city. Under the Nazis, it was used to hold political dissidents on their way east to the camps. It had a guillotine and scaffold which could cope with the simultaneous execution of nine people.

Hess was one of seven prisoners who now occupied Spandau. On Friday, 18 July 1947, various modifications having been made to the jail, Hess was flown to Berlin's Gatow airport, and then taken under armed escort to the jail. With him were: Karl Doenitz, Grand Admiral and Hitler's successor, sentenced to ten years; Erich Raeder, also Grand Admiral and architect of unrestricted U-boat warfare, who would be released in 1955; Constantin von Neurath, former Foreign Minister, sentenced to fifteen years; Albert Speer, architect and Minister of Armaments in the Third Reich, twenty years; Walter Funk, President of the Reichsbank and Minister for Economic Affairs, life imprisonment; Baldur von Schirach, leader of Hitler Youth, twenty years. They were Spandau's seven, to be known by numbers for some or all of their years in captivity.

Their cells were little better – and of a similar size – to those at Nuremberg. They were given, in deepest irony, the rough blue-grey clothes of concentration camp inmates, and the daily regime was harsh. The seven rose at 6 a.m. and washed in pairs without speaking. Breakfast, such as it was, lasted for fifteen minutes. At 7 a.m., the prisoners made their beds and slopped out their cells. A mindless routine followed – the vast, echoing corridors of the all-but-empty prison were scrubbed and polished, the wilderness of the garden tamed. Hess did little of this. He usually sat in defiance, arms folded, jaw set. As the years went by, the guards bothered him less and less. Even the Russians, to whom Hess was some sort of *bête noire*, left him alone on his garden bench. He recognized his jailers less than he recognized the competence of the Nuremberg court to try him. Lunch was at midday sharp and the chores began again until quarter to five. Dinner was at 7 p.m. and lights out at 10. At first the seven bathed once a week, shaved three times and were turfed out of their cells twice each day for the tiny rooms to be searched.

There was never enough food and all of them lost weight, the plump von Shirach perhaps having the most to lose. Very quickly Hess looked emaciated. The mornings when he lay in bed moaning or when he refused to exercise were followed by solitary confinement – he usually walked into the prison cell without being told. There is no doubt that No. 7 was the most difficult prisoner of all. Even when the regime relaxed in later years, Hess would still be heard groaning or screaming in the early hours and demanding medical aid. According to Albert Speer, he was alternately clown and martyr.

The prison was administered in a three-monthly rota by the four powers and Hess was convinced, with some justification, that the Russian contingent made life as unpleasant for him as possible – shining lights into his cell at night and keeping him awake. His amnesia came and went at random intervals and he always became most morose when news came of the impending release of his fellow prisoners. First to go was von Neurath on health grounds. The Protector of Bohemia and Moravia was eighty-one when they released him in 1954. Next, Raeder, seventy-eight, left Spandau later the same year. In 1955, Doenitz was set free and two years later, Funk. The older men had now gone and Hess was sixty-three by this time. He had already spent sixteen years in various prisons. As early as 1947, his lawyer Seidl had put forward an appeal for his client's release on grounds of ill-health and humanitarianism. Europe was still bleeding too heavily then for that to have any effect and Seidl's second attempt, to the United Nations in 1956, fell on equally deaf ears. Funk's release prompted Seidl to try again – this time to the European Commission for Human Rights at Strasburg; again, nothing.

As the Fifties progressed, Hess seemed to accept his lot with greater equanimity. The death of his mother in 1951 hit him hard. He wrote to Ilse: '. . . the knowledge that she is no longer alive has produced an inconsolable sense of empti-ness; the world has changed.'

It had. Beyond the walls of Spandau to the west it was all rock 'n' roll and the thunder of guitars. Teenage rebellion reached its height while Europe rebuilt itself and dedicated Holocaust survivors like Simon Weisenthal hunted Nazis around the world. The Sixties brought the Bay of Pigs, Checkpoint Charlie and the world to the brink of nuclear destruction. It was the age of protest and flower-power. Everyone, it seemed, by the time Hess was transferred to the British Military Hospital in Berlin with a burst duodenal ulcer, was going to San Francisco.

Hess's family, whom he had stalwartly refused to see for so long, formed their own protest group – the Freedom For Rudolf Hess Association. Its posters described him as 'the man who tried to stop the Second World War' but showed the Stellvertreter in SS uniform and – not the best choice. On Christmas Eve, 1969, the loneliest man in the world met his family again.

'I kiss your hand, Ilse,' Hess said, but he actually saluted her. They had not seen each other for twenty-eight years. 'I'm so happy to have seen them,' Hess told the American prison commandant, Colonel Eugene Bird, 'I'm just sorry I waited so long.'[13]

After his return to Spandau, Hess saw his wife and son regularly. Three year old 'Buz' had grown to be Wolf-Rudiger, a man in his thirties who has never stopped believing in his father and his father's mission. Hartley Shawcross, chief British prosecutor at Nuremberg, added his name to the list of those who believed it was time to release the frail old man.

Somebody else did that, though whether Rudolf Hess died by his own hand or another's is still a matter for debate. The

French President, the American President, the Chairman of the Soviet Union and the Queen of England had all been approached during the Seventies to secure Hess's release. Even Prime Minister Margaret Thatcher tried, but the Iron Lady could not get through the Iron Curtain.

On Monday, 17 August 1987, Rudolf Hess took his last walk in Spandau's garden. It was the American tour of duty and with him was a warder named Jordan. At 2.30 p.m. Jordan raised the alarm and a number of guards, including Hess's male nurse Abdallah Melaouhi, converged on the summerhouse, the little shed where Hess used to spend his afternoons reading. Furniture had been overturned, the carpet was ruched and Hess lay on the floor, on his side, an electrical flex around his neck. Attempts were made to resuscitate him but at 4.10 he was pronounced dead.

The *post mortem* on Hitler's deputy was carried out by Professor J.M. 'Taffy' Cameron in his capacity as consultant in forensic pathology to the British Army. Cameron had already made his name in the celebrated 'Dingo Baby' case which had sent its claims and counter-claims of ritual sacrifice around the world. The marks of bruising on Hess's neck, Cameron concluded after his investigation on 19 August, were consistent with hanging by suspension. His report was so sparse in its findings that the Hess family and their indefatigable lawyer, Dr Seidl, demanded a second opinion. Professors W. Spann and W. Eisenmenger of the University of Munich provided this a few days later. Their findings essentially supported Cameron's, although they found parallel marks like tram lines around the dead man's neck and were less certain about actual suspension.

The evidence at the scene indicated that Hess had wound a lamp flex around his neck and secured the other end to a window catch while sitting in his usual chair. Then he had kicked with his legs, toppling his chair and garroting himself. Very quickly once the facts were known, two

schools of thought emerged. The suicide school argued that
Robert Ley had hanged himself in Nuremberg before the
trial using very similar methods. They pointed to Hess's
innumerable suicide attempts, however half-hearted, and
the fact that loneliness, encroaching senility and Soviet reluctance to release him preyed on his increasingly fragile mind.
The murder school raised the obvious objection that this man
of ninety-three would not have the strength to set up the
mechanics of death. Hess's balance was impaired due to an
earlier stroke and he had difficulty raising his arms and
turning his head. When Ley had succeeded at Nuremberg he
had been a fit man of fifty-five. Most curious of all, to the
murder school, was the suicide note. It was undoubtedly
in Hess's handwriting and was addressed to the prison
directors:

> Written a couple of minutes before my death.
> I thank you, all my loved ones, for all you have done
> for me out of love . . .
>
> Tell Freiburg [Hess's former secretary] that, to my
> immense sorrow, since the Nürnburg Trial I have had
> to act as if I didn't know her. There was nothing else I
> could do, otherwise all attempts to gain freedom
> would have been impossible.
>
> I would have been happy to see her again – I have
> received the pictures of her as of you all.
>
> Your big fellow.[14]

Little of this makes sense, claim the murder school. Hess had
already told Freiburg, via Ilse Hess, how sorry he was for
blanking her – and he had done this in 1969. Neither had he
signed himself *Euer Grosser* (Your big fellow) since the early
Seventies. This, the murder school believe, was a note he had

left for a much earlier attempt. We know that Hess's attempts on his life were frequent, though whether they were genuine or cries for attention and help is now dificult to determine.

The last of 'Hitler's gang' had gone. The need for Spandau was over and the building fell to the wrecking ball and the bulldozers, despite Soviet wishes to keep it as a shrine to the monstrosity that was Nazism. In a supreme and perhaps rather sinister irony, only the prison block was demolished (there is a supermarket on the site) but many of the original garrison buildings, which housed Hess's guard, still stand, a reminder of darker days.

And yet Rudolf Hess is not dead. Because of the dilemma over his passing, the death certificate issued at Spandau was withdrawn and without that, technically, the man still lives. As I write, evidence is coming to light of an extensive neo-Nazi organization permeating the German army. The swastika, the straight-arm salute, the slavish, fanatical devotion to the cause, amongst certain young men in Germany, are back. No, Rudolf Hess is not dead.

CHAPTER 9

The Riddle
Wrapped in the Mystery
Inside the Enigma

And if all the others accepted the lie which the Party
imposed – if all records told the same tale – then the lie
passed into history and became truth. 'Who controls
the past' ran the Party slogan, 'controls the future; who
controls the present controls the past'.

1984
George Orwell

Josef Goebbels simply could not understand it. Quick to dissociate himself from Hess once the flight became universal
knowledge – 'What a buffoon the man next to the Führer was'[1]
– he was nevertheless astonished that Churchill's Government
had not made any capital out of the situation. Had Clement
Attlee or Anthony Eden baled out near Hamburg for instance,
Goebbels' Ministry of Propaganda and Enlightenment would
have had a field day. James Douglas-Hamilton shows a
touching faith in the system back in 1941 – 'It was always the
policy of Churchill to tell the British public the truth'. This line
– and line of thinking – comes from *Motive for a Mission*, first
published in 1971. Perhaps as we approach the millennium we

are ready to be more objective about the man whom some regard as the millennium's greatest Englishman.

On the very night of the Hess flight, for instance, Churchill was quite happy to go along with the official version that twenty-eight enemy aircraft were shot down during the blitz on London. In fact, the tally was only eight and one of these was Hess's Me 110 over Scotland, which technically was not shot down at all. Churchill's motives are of course understandable. An endless stream of bad and depressing news would sap morale, which is precisely what Hitler hoped would happen. But the point remains that the Prime Minister was, to put it mildly, economical with the truth. And in the case of Hess's peace proposals, he seems to have been downright parsimonious.

Why was the silence of the wartime Government so deafening? Why is it still so today? First one must wonder if the proposals that Hess carried reflected badly on Britain's attitude to the Jewish question. Some of today's revisionist historians and the spokesmen for Europe's neo-Nazi organizations question the whole story of the Holocaust. Some see the Jews of Europe as merely one set of wartime casualties among a host of other equally significant dead. Others believe that the bodies found at Auschwitz and Dachau and Treblinka were merely the SS's attempt to cope with deaths resulting from war deprivation and food shortages in 1944–5. Still others claim that the whole thing is a Semitic myth, a gigantic conspiracy similar to the 'Protocols of the Elders of Zion' and the Jewish–Bolshevik machinations that overthrew the last Tsar of Russia. The danger with revisionism of this sort is that the longer governments hide crucial documents in cupboards under the stairs, the more likely are the cranks to gain ground.

Until May 1941, when Hess presented his peace proposals to Ivone Kirkpatrick or Lord Simon or whoever officially took them, Hitler's Jewish policy was based around mass resettlement and ghettoization. But the invasion of Poland had brought a further 3,300,000 Jews into the Reich, and Hitler and Himmler, early in 1941, had begun to consider 'more efficient' means of coping with such numbers. Within weeks of Hess's arrival, the invasion of Russia gave Hitler all the living space – and dying space – he needed. With Barbarossa, the Einsatzgruppen had to cope with a further 2,100,000 Jews in the Soviet Union. It seems that Hess's peace deal talked of allowing Britain a free hand in her Empire in exchange for German freedom in Eastern Europe. If this were the offer in 1941, then such a negotiation would have done nothing to save the Jews. However, during the summer of 1940 the German Foreign Office had been working on the idea of relocating Jews to the Indian Ocean island of Madagascar. British naval power was such that this policy would require British consent, which was only likely if there was a western peace. Was this a term of Hess's peace proposals? Did Hess's incarceration help condemn European Jews to their fate?

Additionally Hess's proposals included elements of the peace plan rumoured to have been circulated by the German legation in Dublin – whereby Hitler agreed to pull out of Poland, or along the lines of those suggested by Borenius to Burkhardt and thence to Hess – then, by rejecting it, Churchill was effectively consigning millions of Jews to death in the camps. We now know that Churchill knew about the Einsatzgruppen as early as the summer of 1941, through documents recently released by the Foreign Office.[2] I believe that it is quite possible that he knew about its likelihood from 11 May 1941 when his underlings first interviewed Rudolf Hess.

The whole question of Poland and the subsequent fate of the Jews is brought into sharp focus by the revelation that General Sikorski, the leader of the Polish Government in exile, flew into RAF Prestwick on the morning of 11 May 1941. Prestwick is no more than 25 miles from either Dungavel House or Eaglesham.

Sikorski had been in America and left New York on 9 May 1941. He landed at Gander in Newfoundland for refuelling and left at 6.35pm on 10 May 1941. Like Hess, once airborne, he had no alternative but to complete his journey and from his log one can see that he took off 45 minutes after Hess left Augsburg in Southern Germany. Were they planning to rendezvous in Scotland?

Sikorski landed at Prestwick at 11.30am on 11 May and spent the rest of the day in meetings with various Polish officials including the Chief of Staff and Cabinet leader. Needless to say, there is no record of a meeting with Hess (who also spent the day at locations in and around Glasgow). In the afternoon, Sikorski flew to another Polish base at Gask in Aberdeenshire.

Was a Sikorski–Hess meeting the reason for the flight? As has already been described, the first interrogation of Hess was carried out by the Polish consul in Glasgow, Roman Battaglia, and papers released by the Foreign Office after this book was first published reveal British annoyance at this fact. Polish aircrew manned RAF Acklington. Is a Sikorski–Hess summit a viable reason to justify Hess making the decision to fly?

It was the German invasion of Poland that brought Britain and France into the war on 3 September 1939. Shortly after the invasion, Sikorski set up a Polish government in exile in Angers, western France, but relocated to London in November 1939. His country's position was dire, being occupied by both German and Russian forces. On 29 September 1939 the German–Soviet Boundary and Friendship Treaty was signed, which effectively divided Poland between the two aggressors: Germany traded the Baltic States in return for Warsaw and the Lublin province. The Polish fate was sealed and the atrocities began. Jews were rounded up and 'ghettoized' if not shot or hanged. Resident Poles were resettled and over one million were deported into the interior of the Soviet Union. In the spring of 1940, some 8,500 Polish officers (including 12 generals) were taken to a wood at Katyn, near Smolensk by Russian soldiers where they were shot in the back of the head and buried.

When the details of the massacre emerged in April 1943, the

Russians were Allies and the resultant German propaganda coup caused a split between Russia and the Polish government in exile. Diplomatic relations were terminated on 26 April 1943 in what was to prove the most serious breakdown of relations between the Allies during the war.

However, that was in the future. In London, in 1940, Sikorski presided over a vast number of exiled Poles, many of whom were to serve with distinction as part of the Allied war effort. Realistically, this was all that he could do. He commented with pride that the Germans could not find a Pole to act as Quisling had done in Norway, and relied upon the fact that exiled Poles, as well as the majority of Poles remaining in Poland, still accepted him as their natural leader.

The relevance of Poland to the Hess affair is simply that if a western peace was to be brokered prior to Barbarossa, a German withdrawal from the occupied territories, or at least some agreement concerning them would have to be a major element of such a treaty. In modern Kosovan terminology, a 'disengagement' would have had to be negotiated, a fact that Hess would have been patently aware of. Consequently, Sikorski would have had to be involved in any negotiations. It has been suggested that Hess may have flown in the knowledge of the Katyn forest massacre, planning to use this information to discredit the Russians, although this seems unfeasible due to the timing of the eventual disclosure in 1943.

Poland was of relevance because it would have to be dealt with if a western peace was to be discussed. Following this line of inquiry, I researched the whereabouts of De Gaulle, on the basis that he too may have been involved. This proved more difficult. The De Gaulle archives are under the control of his son, who does not allow access to the wartime data. However, the British Foreign Office papers at that time suggest that he was in fact on a trip to Brazzaville, in Central Africa, during spring 1941.

Of course, it may have been pure coincidence that Sikorski and Hess were both flying into the same country on the same day:

Sikorski may have been making a routine flight on the night that Hess chose to fly to Scotland. However, given what Hess was undoubtedly trying to achieve, one may understandably question the degree of coincidence. The Sikorski angle is intriguing, especially when seen in this context. The absence of intervention on the East Coast, the order not to attack and the other planes on the 'Durham' map appear to substantiate the view that Hess was being allowed into British airspace. If this is the case, then one is entitled to question the purpose of this 'clearance' by British officials. Was it to allow Hess to attend a meeting with Sikorski and perhaps others? Or, was it merely to entice him into the airspace, that coup itself being enough?

Perhaps a second reason for the silence of the British Government since 1941 is the 'Fourth Reich'. In the spring of 1945 the Soviets had got to Berlin first and the Red Army was now ensconced throughout the eastern European nations it had 'liberated'. Hitler was no longer there to be a bulwark against the westward march of International Communism but it was imperative to the West that Germany should continue to fill that role.

To that end, the de-Nazification programme in post-war Germany was less straightforward than it might have been. With staggering hypocrisy, the Allies vied with each other as to who should obtain the services of key scientists and experts, men like the rocket engineer Werner von Braun, who had served the Nazis so faithfully. In the interests of common humanity – and no doubt, a quiet life after so much death – the full vengeance of the West never fell on Germany. The much-heard cry among Germans in 1945–6 – 'I knew nothing about that' or 'I was only obeying orders' – was believed all too readily. As Hitler had found out, it was incredibly difficult to punish an entire nation. So countless Nazis were allowed to go free. Some fled to South America, where the right-wing regimes of countries like Argentina accepted them quietly. Others, incredibly, slipped off their swastika armbands and carried on their civil existences almost as before. General Wilhelm

Mohnke, the youngest general in the SS, is a classic example. He ordered the murder of eighty British troops trapped in a barn near the French village of Wormhout in May 1940. He burned the barn down, along with its inmates. He personally shot three Canadian prisoners of war in Greece in June 1944 and presided over the executions of forty-nine others. Wherever he went in the Reich, civilians died in large numbers. He was in charge of security in the Bunker in Berlin and supervised the burning of Hitler's body. Yet after the war, despite warrants for his arrest, Mohnke drew a pension of £21,000 and reached managerial level of an agricultural firm before he retired. Today he is eighty-eight, loved by his neighbours as 'Old Willi'; neighbours beat up reporters who try to pry into the old man's past.

There was no shortage of anti-Bolsheviks in post-war Germany who could be relied upon to stand up to Stalin's bullying, but who would lead them? What about the Spandau Seven? Who of them could have led a de-Nazified Fourth Reich after the war?

Karl Doenitz was officially Hitler's successor in the closing weeks of the war. A sailor by calling, he was totally unsuited to politics and complained bitterly in Spandau that it had wrecked his career, while his juniors, mostly devoted Nazis no doubt, had their naval commands again. On his release from prison in September 1956, he was still the haughty Aryan however: 'Don't forget,' he told the remaining inmates on his last day, 'I am still legally entitled to be regarded as Head of the German state.'[3] And he could never forgive Albert Speer for the conscience he showed at Nuremberg – 'It was dishonourable and disloyal to Hitler and to Germany.'[4]

There had been reports in the German press that a 'Doenitz movement' had been set up to re-establish the Admiral as Führer and he had to be smuggled out of Spandau to avoid the huge throng of paparazzi and police. But the 'weekend Führer' was no match for the delicate checks and balances of post-war German politics. He had not the head for it. He wrote an average book about his wartime exploits in the navy and gave a bitter lecture to a German high school in 1963. He remained largely unrepentant of the tens of thousands killed in his unrestricted U-boat warfare.

Erich Raeder was even less likely to lead the Fourth Reich. Like Doenitz, a U-boat man, the Admiral was officially retired in 1943, having crossed Hitler once too often in terms of grand strategy during the war. He left the prison on sticks with the support of his wife. When asked if he had any political ambitions, the old man snarled 'For God's sake, no! Trying to go into politics would just about complete my misfortunes.'

Walther Funk was at first sight totally unsuited to emerge as a new leader in post-war Germany, but in fact his credentials were excellent. A brilliant economist and financier, he had a reputation as a 'liberal Nazi' who might just have shaken off the tarnishing of the Führer's brand. His homosexuality and drunkenness were problems but dozens of successful politicians have hidden vices and enjoyed glittering careers nonetheless. By 14 May 1957 when Funk was released, however, he was a chronic diabetic and had aged very suddenly. Never one of the true Nazi elite, he sloped off to Düsseldorf with his wife and died almost forgotten there three years later.

A better bet by far was Konstantin von Neurath, former Minister and Reich Protector of Bohemia and Moravia. He was largely ornamental in Hitler's Reich, favoured for his aristocratic pedigree. Interestingly, he had never been ruthless enough for Hitler who supplanted him with Heydrich. Von Neurath joined a passive resistance against Hitler early in 1945. Clearly the Allies were not going to allow another Hitler to rise from the ashes of Berlin, but a card-carrying Nazi of impeccable credentials who could be controlled might well be of interest to them. In November 1954, the eighty-one-year-old prisoner was given a sedative prior to being released. Hess thought the release was simply

Communist propaganda, not believing that the Soviet leaders could show genuine compassion.

Von Neurath was given back his gold watch and his daughter walked out of Spandau with him arm in arm. Warm greetings from Konrad Adenauer, the new West German chancellor and Professor Heuss, President of the Federal Republic, spoke of 'martyrdom' and joy that the old man was free. But there was deep suspicion in the new leaders of democratic Germany that in messages of support for the man were hidden messages of support for the mission. Von Neurath died at Enzweihingen on 15 August 1956.

Baldur von Schirach, another of the seven, had been Hitler Youth leader but found himself Gauleiter of Vienna and, as such, implicated in crimes against humanity in his handling of the city's 65,000 Jews. At Nuremberg he railed against the 'millionfold murderer' in a manner which disgusted Goering and von Ribbentrop. By the time of his release, however, prison had broken von Schirach. He was only fifty-nine, but nearly blind and was allowed out of Spandau with Albert Speer on 30 September 1966. He sold his story to *Stern* magazine before publishing his own book on the secret of Hitler's fatal attraction the following year. He lived with his son Klaus in Munich and died aged sixty-seven, having kept fully away from politics for the remainder of his life.

When Albert Speer became a free man, as author Jack Fishman says in *Spandau*, he was 'sixty-one, upright, mentally alert and of steely determination'. His efficiency was terrifying. Switching with incredible mental agility from architect to armourer of the Reich, he was the biggest single employer in Germany and increased armament production eight-fold between 1941 and 1944. This extraordinary feat prolonged the war for two years. Just as von Neurath was welcomed back to freedom, so was Speer. Willy Brandt, then Mayor of West Berlin, sent a bouquet of carnations to the architect's daughter.

More than any other Nazi leader, Speer wrote extensively about the years of the Reich. His definitive account, including notes, runs to 766 pages. He became a celebrity, as seemingly the most repentant of living Nazis. He died in London in September 1981 while taking part in a BBC television documentary on the massive Nazi heist of treasures during the war. Alone of the men released from Spandau, he had kept in touch with Hess.

Rudolf Hess was at once the best and the worst choice to lead a potential Fourth Reich. The best because he had been the Stellvertreter, fully involved in every strategy of Hitler's until May 1941, and closer to the Führer than any of the others. And the worst because of his unreliability and lack of touch with the real world. There is massive documentation on Hess's psychological well-being and all of it rejects insanity. Speer himself summed it up to his biographer Gitta Sereny when he said that, as soon as he knew Hess had told his captors nothing about Barbarossa, he realized that he was indeed sane.[5] What with his suicide attempts, his accusations of poisoning, his rolling on the ground and moaning, Rudolf Hess had done his best to make fools of the Allies. By pinning down scores of guards and running up the gigantic bills necessary to keep Spandau open, in a sense he continued to do that until the day he died.

Hess alone in Spandau had been planning for the Fourth Reich. While others read, gardened or exercised, Hess's plans to emerge as a new Führer took shape in 1947. He planned to take over the Western zones of Germany and drew up lists of prominent Nazis he wanted released from prison. The Stellvertreter's vision of the Fourth Reich was simply the Third Reich without Hitler, and it may have been this 'triumph of the will' to turn the clock back which sealed Hess's fate and kept the gates of Spandau locked on him for ever.

In reality, the Allies were happy with the increasing power of democratically elected Western Germany. With the ballot paper rather than the bully-boys of the SA, West Germany emerged in the post-war years like a phoenix from the ashes, its economy dominating the new community of Europe by the 1970s. Cynics were heard to observe that Hitler had got his wish after all – all Europe was dancing to the tune of the West German Chancellor.

The third possible explanation for the continued silence of the British Government lies in the possible existence of an active peace party who were ready and waiting to stage an anti-Churchill coup with the arrival of the Stellvertreter on British soil. Certainly this is the view of Wolf Hess.

According to Hess's son, the plan was that his father was to fly, not to Dungavel, or Lennoxlove, or Acklington but to Turnhouse, the Duke of Hamilton's airfield. His arrival was to be much publicized and trumpeted in the pro-peace nationals: the *Mail*, the *Express*, *The Times*. He would arrive in London with Hamilton at the head of a peace party of like-minded Lowland Scots aristocracy who would force a peace conference; and the Duke of Kent, brother of the King, was staying at Balmoral that weekend.* Hess probably, and Hitler certainly, had always been impressed and perhaps a little over-awed by British royalty. This would have given the impetus to the sizeable group in the Lords, and those like Halifax in the Cabinet, whose loyalties to Churchill were not unshakeable and who believed his warmongering postures were just plain wrong.

A possible royal connection is fascinating. It is unlikely that the Duke of Windsor had any direct involvement in the Hess case, but from my researches into the aircraft movements of the night of 10–11 May 1941, it has become increasingly obvious that the Duke of Hamilton did not pass all the relevant information on to his son. His involvement with the SIS seems

* The Duke of Kent was also visiting Scottish airfields in the May of 1941. In August 1942, he was killed in circumstances which have never been made clear when his Sunderland flying-boat crashed in Scotland.

greater than James Douglas-Hamilton believes too. Who better to appear to lead a peace party than the most influential royal of them all – the King?

A book being published this year claims that rather than a Sikorski–Hess summit, the Duke of Kent was actually awaiting Hess at Dungavel House. According to co-author Stephen Prior, the Duke was planning to take Hess to England to meet the rest of the Royal family.

Whilst this may seem far-fetched, it is quite possible that this was what Hess was told would happen by the initiators of the ruse. It is certainly not to say that is what would have happened. Prior substantiates his claim by pointing to the two German parachutists captured (and subsequently executed) at Luton Hoo in Bedfordshire on 12 May 1941. He suggests that this was the rendezvous point of the Duke, Hess and the King and Queen and thus explains the presence of the parachutists: their aim was to liquidate Hess, once it became clear that he had been duped, thus stopping him talking permanently. I have now received confirmation from Windsor that the King and Queen were at Windsor Castle on the nights of the 10 and 11 May 1941 (although the whereabouts of Queen Mary is still unknown). It should be remembered that the present Queen spent part of her honeymoon at Luton Hoo, on account of her family's friendship with the Werhner family who owned it.

Although either of these explanations is possible, it is more likely that the Royals were being promised merely as bait rather than being a realistic part of the plan.

My delvings into the Royal Archives confirmed that their majesties slept at Windsor in the spring of 1941 but visited Buckingham Palace during the day. On 9 May, George VI attended a Privy Council meeting. The King kept appointment diaries for this period but the Queen, apparently, did not.

Is it too far-fetched to imagine that Hess had been told, via the SO1 link, that the King himself would be in Scotland to greet him? And does this explain Hamilton's reticence, even in talking to members of his family? Was he actually, patriot as he undoubtedly was, trying to keep the royal family's name out of all involvement with Hess? It is certainly worth considering whether Hess would have flown at all unless he was going to meet someone of sufficient stature to achieve the result he wanted. Undramatic progress could be made diplomatically; Hess sought a dramatic solution.

Churchill would then be ousted and perhaps Lloyd George would be back at No. 10, ready to conclude a peace with the Reich. Another possibility as an alternative to Churchill was Lord Beaverbrook, who had clashed with the Prime Minister and had actually resigned his Cabinet post in late April 1941. His exact whereabouts on 10–11 May are also unclear.

A third potential rival was Robert Gordon Menzies, the Australian Prime Minister. It is clear from his private correspondence and papers of the Australian High Commission in London (recently released), that Menzies was outraged by the high-handed way in which Churchill was determined to win the war at all costs, even at the expense of jettisoning parts of the Empire. Historian David Day believes that however much both Menzies and Churchill sought to paper over the cracks later, the Empire was on the point of disintegration in 1941. In April the series of military reverses that lowered British morale had an equally adverse effect on Menzies. He had seen bombing first hand on his tour of British industrial centres and had noted the stoicism of the people. Even so, he agreed with Basil Liddell-Hart that peace was the only solution if America and Russia were not going to emerge as the only *real* victors of the war.

His stay in England in the spring of 1941 gave rise to the serious suggestion that Menzies be given War Cabinet status. Immensely popular with politicians and people alike, here was a man who also had the intellect and energy of Churchill. By 6 April, he and Beaverbrook were in cahoots, the Australian regarding the Munitions Minister as 'clear headed and forceful' and spending time at his country house at Leatherhead. Neither man had any faith in Churchill's Balkan front as the army continued to lose its hold in Greece and Crete.

On 2 April, a meeting of twenty-three MPs (out of a total of sixty-three possible attendees) had met to discuss an 'alternative to the bitter-end policy so many of the present Government are pursuing'. It was Lloyd George who dominated this group in Parliament. Churchill was unimpressive in trying to explain away British defeats and Hugh Dalton felt a political coup was underway. Beaverbrook and Menzies might well have been its driving force.

The Australian's diary for 14 April, when the British doggedly hung on to Tobruk, read: 'The Cabinet is deplorable – dumb men most of whom disagree with Winston but none of whom dare to say so . . . Winston is a dictator; he cannot be over-ruled and his colleagues fear him. The people have set him up as something little less than God and his power is therefore terrific.'[6] Brutus, Cassius and the others might have written similar comments on Caesar, days before they plunged their knives into him. It was noticeable that when Menzies threw a party at the Dorchester to announce his staying on in London, only Churchill was absent.

It was Menzies' idea to create an inner sanctum of War Cabinet members composed of Churchill's opponents – Beaverbrook, Lloyd George and Sir Stafford Cripps and Herbert Morrison from the Labour benches. Churchill would remain at the helm as a people's figurehead, but he would take no decisions and have little power. Such a War Cabinet would be created under the guise of an Imperial Conference, assuring the Dominions' status.

It was clear too that Churchill was rapidly losing support where it mattered – in the City and in Fleet Street. Oliver Harvey, later Eden's private secretary, wrote, 'At the end of that road lies L.G. [Lloyd George who, abetted by that ass Liddell-Hart would readily be a Pétain to us, with the support of the Press barons and the city magnates.'[7] There was something of a showdown on 21 April when Menzies openly criticized the chiefs of staff and, therefore, Churchill himself. But Churchill was a past master at avoiding sticky situations and changing the subject. He ducked it entirely while *The Times* continued to eulogize Menzies by printing his speeches verbatim.

After lunch with Lloyd George at the end of the month, Menzies was able to focus his criticism of Churchill. He gave directives rather than had discussions, spent too little time on War Cabinet business and too much touring bombed cities. He was a bad organizer, especially when it came to food and transport. Inevitably, the Dominions were being ignored. Churchill had no interest in finance, agriculture or the economy. He loved war and spent hours poring over maps like a Napoleon without Napoleon's brilliance. His foreign policy was deplorable and Germany was always one step ahead. He was surrounded by yes-men like Cadogan, Eden and Anderson. Beaverbrook, the one man who could challenge him, had gone in April.

Menzies was also dining with Lord Sempill, another eccentric peer and member of the Right Club and one this time who had a great deal of sympathy with the Japanese, Australia's main threat in the event of a Pacific war. The *Manchester Guardian* and the *Daily Herald* now backed *The Times* in insisting on Menzies' inclusion in Churchill's inner sanctum. The final meeting in this crucial phase of the war between Churchill and Menzies took place eight days before Hess arrived. Even while it was happening, the *Daily Mail*, the *News Review* and the *New Statesman* all clamoured for the Australian to be made a member of the War Cabinet. *The Times* went further, suggesting him as Churchill's deputy with responsibility for the 'Home Front'. The Canadian Prime Minister, Mackenzie King, heard from Sir Campbell Stuart that Menzies' ambition was to be British Prime Minister, 'and there were perhaps in England some who would be prepared to accept him'.[8]

It was even possible that the Duke of Windsor, more amenable to Hitler than his brother George VI, would be reinstated as king from his villa of virtual exile in Portugal. The timing of this was vital. It all had to be secured before Barbarossa was launched or Germany would once again face the unwinnable war on two fronts.

For Barbarossa to work properly, Hitler had to have his back protected but Germany had lost the Battle of Britain, so an invasion was out of the question. The punishing air raids on major British cities would undermine morale and weaken resolve. At the very least, such punishment would make the olive branch brought by Rudolf Hess seem all the more tempting.

The fly in the ointment, according to Wolf Hess's version, was the Duke of Hamilton, who lost his nerve at the last minute and expressed astonishment that Hess should want to see him. This would explain Hamilton's reticence to interview 'Hauptmann Horn' on the night he landed and his denial that he had ever met the man.

How plausible is this version? The sticking place is the actual motives of the peace party. There is a tendency to assume that, like William Joyce – the 'Lord Haw Haw' hanged for treason at Wandsworth in January 1946 – the peace party were all secret Fascists longing to see the swastika flying over the Palace of Westminster.* Nothing could be further from the truth. Rudolf Hess should have listened to Albrecht Haushofer, who knew his British. There was no peace party worthy of the name, still less an active pro-Nazi fifth column. Once war was declared, most of those who had spoken against it buckled on the sword of patriotism and remained loyal to king and country.

The scale of Wolf Hess's plot is simply impossible. Churchill, for all he had enemies both inside parliament and without, was in an unassailable position by May 1941. Chamberlain's famous

---

* Joyce broadcast from Germany with messages designed to sap British morale. Although most people regarded him as a joke, calling him 'Lord Haw Haw' because of his plummy pseudo-aristocratic delivery on air, he was actually a traitor and hanged as such.

phrase about Hitler missing the bus might well be fitted with more accuracy to Hess. A year earlier, before the Battle of Britain and the blitz had made the British people and its Government defiant and grimly determined to fight to the death, Hess just might conceivably have made some headway. Now, in the spring of 1941 it was just too late. Hamilton's position at Turnhouse might have made it possible to enable Hess to land there, but even this would involve a vast number of outsiders to be in on the plot. Observers from the Royal Observer Corps, radar operators and directors of operations would all have to be briefed – following orders to monitor but not to intercept a lone fighter-bomber somewhere over southern Scotland. This presupposes that the peace party was not only huge, but was able to infiltrate and control vital sections of the country's national defence system.

If Hess had landed safely into the clutches of the peace party rather than a bewildered farmer, a policeman and a slightly hysterical officer of the Home Guard, the first and vital ingredient would be Press involvement. Astonishingly, bearing in mind the official silence, newsreel footage exists of interviews with David McLean and his mother at Floors farm, talking about the polite and highly correct German who had floated into their backyard that night in May 1941. Whether this footage was taken with the co-operation of Brendan Bracken's Ministry of Information or not, its very existence is at variance with Churchill's blanket lack of information on the Hess landing. Only with large-scale press coverage could the peace party publicize Hess's arrival and the only way to guarantee that was to have Fleet Street journalists poised at Lennoxlove or Turnhouse, briefed to expect, on the night of 10 May, an important event. No such briefing and no such gathering took place.

Had it done, then the peace plotters would have tipped their hand and stood as nakedly vulnerable as traitors had the plot misfired. This was political Russian roulette and no sane politician would have risked it. Rab Butler's prime-ministerial ambitions were destroyed forever because he openly suggested that peace negotiations be conducted with Hitler in 1939–40. Churchill promptly moved him from the Foreign Office to Education, where, despite the landmark act of 1944 that bore his name, he mouldered in the chalk and cod-liver oil of postwar schooling, another Prime Minister Who Never Was.

Churchill was already, after a year in office, the hero of the people. This was the People's War and he was their champion. What if he made mistakes and enemies with equal aplomb and duped a desperate nation by having an actor speak his lines over the airwaves? When the bombs fell, there he was, cigar in bulldog mouth, fingers waving victory defiantly. It was his finest hour and the doubtful Lords – Bedford, Brocket, Buccleuch, Londonderry – could offer nothing alongside that.

Hamilton too was not a traitor. Like many international playboys of the Thirties, he counted Germans among his friends; and war in 1939 was not contemplated by many of his class. Such pre-war friendships have been dwelt on by some writers who have seen them in a more sinister light than is warranted. Hamilton, there is no doubt, was a patriot, whose family had given generations of service to king and country. Churchill's Government was anxious to exonerate Hamilton in May 1941 simply because his reputation was blameless. It is a pity they could not be more honest about the real motive for Hess's mission – that the Stellvertreter was a spectacular victim of the black propaganda emanating from Woburn out of SO1.

What *really* happened in the case of Rudolf Hess? I will be the first to admit that because of the reticence of successive British governments to release information, some of what we are left with must be conjecture. But much of it is provable fact. I began this book because of a sense of unease and dissatisfaction with the existing, 'official' story; it left too many questions unanswered.

Let us look at it first from the German point of view. The consensus is that Hitler's territorial ambitions lay in the east. Ever since *Mein Kampf* in 1924, it was obvious that his territorial ambitions centred on the Slavic regions beyond the River Dnieper. Appeasement from Britain and France in the 1930s led him to believe that neither of these countries would seriously resist him; Munich and Chamberlain's lame acceptance of a scrap of paper confirmed that. It seems likely that he was genuinely surprised therefore when his invasion of Poland turned those particular tables on him. The speed and astonishing success of blitzkrieg meant that most of western Europe ceased to be a problem by the end of 1940, but Britain was the exception, the itch he could not scratch. Operation Sealion failed in the skies over southern England and pounding cities into surrender was an untried and ultimately fruitless strategy.

If Hitler was to turn east (and there is evidence that he had planned Barbarossa from mid-1940 or even earlier) then he had to make peace with Britain. This would avoid the dangerous war on two fronts. The problem was that making a separate peace would be construed as weakness or failure (after all, Hitler had sued for peace with no other country to date) and worse, it might alert Stalin's Russia that an invasion was imminent or at least likely. So the sabre-rattling and posturing had to continue in public, whatever furtive peace moves were carried out in private. According to pacifists like the Duke of Bedford, such initiatives arrived regularly in the autumn of 1940, even if those via the Dublin legation proved spurious.

What if Churchill was removable? All the Nazi high command believed the man to be impossible. He was a warmonger, committed to a fight to the death – all his stirring wartime rhetoric was testimony to that. But could there be someone else, a senior politician or even a member of the royal family, who was more of a realist? The Germans believed, like Basil Liddell-Hart, that the war could not be won by the British. By the winter of 1940–41 the Germans were unassailable in Europe. It was therefore in British interests, they believed, to oust Churchill and replace him with an altogether more amenable regime. To that end, I believe, Hitler consulted his Anglophile deputy, his faithful 'Hesserl', who better understood the British psyche and had, in Albrecht Haushofer, a friend with extensive British contacts. Given the delicate nature of this exercise, the approach had to be oblique, the methods highly secret and 'softly-softly'. We know that Hitler mistrusted professional diplomats and preferred to use alternative, rather back-door methods.* The cloak-and-dagger letters and telegrams that winged their way between Hess and Haushofer and the long walks in Bavarian forests are testament to this.

Hess was not the type to make such an extraordinary move off his own bat. I have rejected the commonly held view that he was losing favour – and perhaps his mind – in the months prior to May 1941. That view is a victim of Goebbels' and Dietrich's propaganda after the flight, swallowed whole by the German and British public at the time and ever since. The Stellvertreter was in full command of his faculties on 10 May – no one who was not could have undertaken such a difficult solo flight and so coolly given nothing away on Barbarossa. But he was also deeply, even pathologically, loyal to Hitler and his regime. He could never denounce either, as von Schirach and Speer would do at Nuremberg. On a day-to-day basis, Hess was perfectly capable of the administrative complexities demanded by his positions as Party leader and head of the Ausland

---

* This was confirmed by Dr Geoffrey Waddington of the University of Leeds in the Channel Four *Reputations* programme dedicated to Ribbentrop, broadcast in July 1998.

Organization. But a subject as vital and sensitive as a peace with Britain would need Hitler's approval – and that, I believe, is precisely what Hess got.

Who else in the Nazi hierarchy knew of the gamble is impossible to say, but by 10 May Goering certainly knew and others probably soon after. To someone like Speer, who was not part of the chosen inner group around Hitler in 1941 (when it came to delicate political matters), the Führer's play-acting at the Berghof in response to Hess's flight seemed genuine enough.

From the British point of view, 1940 was a desperate year indeed. But I do not believe remotely that the Hess lure was Churchill's brainchild. It would not have occurred to him. It has all the hallmarks of a group of brilliant, maverick insiders, men who knew the German psyche almost as well as their own. They were fighting a black war that seems absurd as it is still only partially understood. Their brief, especially in the Woburn-based SO1, was to use words as a weapon and seemingly pointless ruses were dreamed up in pursuance of that. While still at Electra House, they came out with ideas to suggest that all Poles were lice-infested and that German farmers should have no contact with them. They planned to spread rumours that SS men were sleeping with Wehrmacht wives while their men were away, in order to improve Aryan stock. We still have examples of the Heinrich Himmler stamp, designed to make Germans believe that there was open rivalry in the Führer's camp. One wonders whether they could they plan all this and *not* invite Rudolf Hess to Britain. Even if the plan was eventually discovered, whilst there was the prospect of peace time was being bought and lives were being saved. The British had little to lose as long as the plan remained secret – and it certainly has.

Underneath the schoolboy pranks and the pseudo-German radio broadcasts was a deadly seriousness. And, by sheer luck, vital links were already there. Walter Stewart Roberts, whatever his role in SO1, was the nephew of Mary Violet. She was a personal friend of the Haushofers, who in turn were confidantes of Rudolf Hess, the man close to Hitler. It may have been Peter Fleming's curious novel *Flying Visit* that gave somebody the idea and that somebody could have been his brother Ian Fleming, Sefton Delmer, Leonard Ingrams or any combination of the dazzling minds at SO1.

The first contact was made by Mrs Roberts with the Haushofers. The letter was either written at the behest of someone at SO1 or forged by someone like Ellic Howe, urging some kind of reconciliation, wishing perhaps that the war could be over. When Rudolf Hess talked to his friend Albrecht Haushofer about what connections he might make in Britain in pursuance of the Führer's peace, Haushofer inevitably mentioned 'the old lady'. Unimportant politically, without influence or party, Violet Roberts was the vital, all-important link that would lure Hess.

The rest was a matter of careful postage, using the expertise of Thomas Cook who ran the Lisbon agency in wartime and whose secretarial staff serviced SO1. Hess needed evidence of a genuine peace party, if his flight to this country was to happen at all, still less have a slim chance of success. Haushofer came up with the names of the Hamiltons; old Sir Ian, the Germanophile General of the Great War; and the aviationist Duke, who had moved in Hess's circle at the Olympics in 1936. Other names must have been mentioned too – perhaps the pacifist lords like Bedford, Brocket, Buccleuch and Londonderry; perhaps the realists like Basil Liddell-Hart and the doubters of Churchill like Beaverbrook and Menzies. Who was listed and how this information was relayed to Hess we do not know. The 'paper trail' quite properly demanded by historians is not there.

However, in the recently released Soviet file No. 38856 on the wartime heads of Czech military Intelligence, Colonel Frantisek Moravec reveals that he told the wartime head of Russian Intelligence (NKVD) in London that he had seen the letters purporting to come from Hamilton, by which Hess

was lured to Britain. This information was deemed so significant that it was the subject of a special report to Stalin. Who
knows what paper trails may still lie in the Kremlin archives?

Somehow – and perhaps time and the passing of a Freedom
of Information Act will reveal this – Hess was given enough
concrete evidence of a welcome to persuade him to go. The final
details may have been supplied via go-betweens with an international reputation, men who still, even in wartime, were able
to travel in Europe. Carl Burkhardt of the International Red
Cross may have been one; Tancred Borenius, the international
art expert another. To hook Hess – and Hitler – permanently, it
is likely that a figurehead for the peace party needed to be
provided. Was this Lloyd George, whom Hitler had met in the
Thirties and knew to be a grudging admirer? Was it the King,
whose elder brother had been so impressed by Hitler's Third
Reich only four years before? Whatever the constitutional position in Britain and the actual political importance of George V1,
if the King declared publicly for peace in 1940–41, even
Churchill's sabre-rattling might cease.

Why did Churchill make no capital out of Hess's arrival?
Josef Goebbels could not understand it; neither, from different
perspectives, could Stalin and Roosevelt. Sefton Delmer, who
was in at the beginning, could only fume in exasperation. But
Churchill's road was a lonely one. As Prime Minister and the
arch-opponent of Hitler in the West, his hands were effectively
tied by the complexities of international politics. On the one
hand was the need to handle the Soviet Union with kid
gloves. Churchill could not know the exact date of Barbarossa,
but it was common knowledge in Intelligence circles in the
West that such a mission was imminent. If Hess was
welcomed with open arms, fêted publicly or even given the
high-ranking prisoner-of-war status of, for example, Field
Marshal Gerd von Runstedt in 1945, then this would convey
absolutely the wrong message to Stalin. As it was, the Soviet
dictator believed that Hess was lured over by British

Intelligence as the precursor to an Anglo-German peace deal. If Churchill had gone to lengths to reassure the Russians, he would have had to be careful with the Americans.

As vital as it was for Russia to turn against Germany (the inevitable result of Barbarossa) it was also essential for Churchill's war effort to bring America in, beyond existing lend-lease provision agreed in March 1941. America's stance was a little ambivalent. Despite its occupation of Danish-owned Greenland on 10 April to guarantee Danish colonial rights there, there was a powerful isolationist lobby in Congress and elsewhere. If Churchill had made a big deal of Hess's arrival, then the increasingly pugnacious Roosevelt might also have been given the wrong message, and assumed that Churchill was weakening, to the extent of doing a deal with Hitler.

Hess knew the flight was a gamble. He had the blessing, I believe, of the Führer, but his sense of loyalty to Hitler would not let him admit this to the world. So unlikely was it to succeed that he left the famous letter – 'simply say I was mad' – which would let Hitler off the hook. He went to Augsburg and took off in the specially tailored plane Messerschmitt had provided for him. Whether following the *knickbein* system or not, he misjudged his approach. Aiming for Lennoxlove or Acklington, where he had been told a peace party was waiting for him, he overshot them in the darkness. Out of fuel and out of time, he baled out over Eaglesham Moor.

On capture, he demanded to see the man whose name was uppermost in his mind, perhaps because he had been told the Duke of Hamilton, another flyer, would be responsible for keeping interceptors away from him. Hess hoped for a welcoming committee of key politicians, people with enough influence to alter public opinion so dramatically that the tide would turn against Churchill and an Anglo–German peace could become a reality. For him personally, this would have been the ultimate triumph of his life. If, as many commentators have assumed, he felt that his relationship with Hitler was deteriorating, then here indeed was his chance to restore it. At some point, perhaps over Eaglesham Moor, or at Floors Farm, or in the barracks at Maryhill, Hess must have realized that the dream had died. There was no welcoming committee, no peace party. Even Hamilton, whose name he had been given as a go-between, was unmoved; clearly the RAF officer did not speak the language of Appeasement. This above all else, is the key to Hess's eccentric behaviour in captivity. For the rest of his life, he lived, not just with a sense of failure, but with the knowledge that he had been duped.

The final reason for the cover-up in the case of Rudolf Hess is that it shows an altogether less positive picture of the British at war. If it could be proved that Churchill was actively seeking genuine peace proposals, via Borenius, Burkhardt, the Haushofers, Hess or whoever, while adopting at the same time a gung-ho stance of defiance, then his bulldog reputation would have disintegrated. And Winston Churchill was a man who put great store by such things. Clive Ponting in *1940, Myth and Reality* sums it up nicely: 'British peace efforts in the period 1939–40 [and, he might have added, 1941] remain a highly sensitive subject for British governments, even though all the participants are now dead. Persistent diplomatic efforts to reach peace with Germany are not part of the mythology of 1940 . . .' More than the reputation of just one man, these possibilities affect our perception of the integrity of the wartime generation. Those of us who have grown up since have done so in the comforting glow that our fathers and grandfathers (and mothers and grandmothers) were heroes. But what if a small group of them were secretly negotiating with the enemy? It would not only add to our uncertainties about the conduct of the war, but could, even now, shock a nation.

Who we are today is inextricable from who our fathers were yesterday. What if, after all, they were not what we have been told to believe?

There is one positive element in all of this. The riddle of Rudolf Hess is that he was set up, to use the modern vernacular. That he wanted to believe there is no doubt. Loyal to Hitler, perfectly placed with his friendships and his contacts, an able flyer, he and he alone had the temperament and the credentials to broker a peace. It was his misfortune – and Germany's – that he fell for the black propaganda of men cleverer than he.

And it is our misfortune that these men – Leonard Ingrams, Sefton Delmer, Dallas Brooks, Ian Fleming and Walter Roberts – have carried their secrets to their graves. And we should not be surprised that if a miracle happened – if a Freedom of Information Act was passed tomorrow or a bomb should blow wide open the closed cabinets and locked cupboards of Whitehall so that their contents fluttered into public view – we would still know nothing more about the case of Rudolf Hess. As John Costello wrote in a letter to the *Financial Times* after his book, *Ten Days that Saved the West*, received a critical mauling:

> There can be no absolutes, or monopoly of wisdom, in the relatively new field of Intelligence history. Reviewers who plough the same furrow ought not to be so hasty to dismiss the work of rivals by branding them as conspiracists simply because they have succeeded in uncovering fresh evidence

In the case of the black propagandists of SO1, the rest will always be silence. As Sefton Delmer said in *Black Boomerang*: 'I know there will be a great temptation for Psychological Warriors to come forward and take a bow. They will want to tell the world of the great things they have done. We "black" men . . . must resist that temptation . . . Propaganda is something one keeps quiet about.'

Notes

Introduction

1. Hugh Thomas was on the army medical team at Spandau where Hess was finally imprisoned. His theories are discussed in Chapter 2.
2. Letter from Hess to Hitler delivered by hand at Berchtesgaden 11 May 1941.
3. Quoted in Peter Padfield, *Hess: Flight For the Führer*.
4. *Ibid*.
5. At the end of the war, Churchill actually prevented the Duke of Hamilton (who is central to the Hess story) from going to the United States because he feared that the Americans would probe too deeply into the case. As Churchill wrote to the Secretary of State for Air, 'It is not in the public interest that the whole of this affair should be stirred at the present moment. I desire therefore that the Duke should not, repeat not, undertake this task.'
6. Padfield, *op.cit*.
7. It was the historian Peter Padfield who established this likelihood in *Hess: Flight For the Führer*.
8. F.H. Hinsley, *British Intelligence in the Second World War*.
9. Commander Crabb disappeared in 1956 on the occasion of a state visit – the first by a Communist Russian leader – by Nikita Khrushchev. A headless and handless body, believed to be that of navy frogman Crabb, was found near Chichester harbour fourteen months later, a long way in

miles and time from the *Ordzhonikidze*, moored in Portsmouth harbour, back in April of the previous year. The official Government line was that Crabb had been testing 'certain equipment' when he disappeared. This was the height of the Cold War and talks between East and West spoke at best of peaceful co-existence. Rumours were rife that Crabb had been held prisoner by the Russian navy and even that he was a double agent. No satisfactory answer has ever been forthcoming from the British Government but clearly the implication was that Crabb was carrying out underwater espionage in Portsmouth harbour.

10. Conflicting evidence in accounts of the car crash in which Diana died – of the proximity of paparazzi on motor bikes, of a mysterious (and so far untraced) white Fiat car and blinding flashes in the tunnel – have given rise to theories that the crash was deliberately staged, possibly by British Intelligence, to end a liaison between the mother of a future king and a Muslim. At once extraordinarily and predictably, MI5 released a statement eleven months after the crash, saying, 'We do not kill people.'

11. Jeffrey M. Bale, quoted in Peter Hounam and Derek McAdam, *Who Killed Diana?*

12. Quoted in James Douglas-Hamilton, *The Truth About Rudolf Hess*.

13. Political Warfare Executive Files (Public Record Office F0 898).

Chapter 1

1. Winston Churchill, *The Second World War*.

2. Alone of the European powers at the outbreak of the war, Britain possessed a complete and highly developed radar system of proven reliability. By 1938 the aircraft detection range was 150 miles and by 1941 two 'chains' of coastal

radar stations were in operation. It was undoubtedly this invention that gave Britain the edge in the decisive Battle of Britain in the summer of 1940.

3. Letter from Hess to his son Wolf, quoted in Peter Padfield, *Hess: Flight For the Führer.*

4. Letter from Hess to Frau Ilse Hess, quoted in Padfield, *op.cit.*

5. Quoted in James Douglas-Hamilton, *The Truth About Rudolf Hess.*

6. In reading this book at the draft stage, an expert historian gave a number of possible reasons for this response. Churchill 'may not have heard or understood properly', he surmises, 'or he might have overdone the brandy (a common enough occurrence)' but he is absolutely correct when he says, 'all one can safely infer from this . . . is that he had already been told.' Indeed he had!

7. The Junkers 87 divebomber was a vital weapon in blitzkrieg and spearheaded the ground attack pincer-movement of the Wehrmacht that was the key to the tactic's success. Its nickname was the Stuka. The German Panzer (literally 'tiger', but meaning 'armoured') divisions had a fearsome and deserved reputation that was not damaged until Bernard Montgomery's defeat of Erwin Rommel's Afrika Korps at El Alamein in October 1942.

Chapter 2

1. James Douglas-Hamilton, *The Truth About Rudolf Hess.*

2. Peter Padfield, *Hess: The Flight For the Führer.*

3. Padfield, *op. cit.*

4. James Murphy, *Who Sent Rudolf Hess?*

The image of the 'terrible rain' is common to much poetry of both world wars. With grass and trees destroyed by shells, tanks, trench warfare and incessant marching, the ground became quickly waterlogged. The milk-faced boys contrast sharply with the 'hard-boiled' veterans, so beautifully portrayed in Erich Maria Remarque's *All Quiet on the Western Front*.

Defenders of Hess – and those who see his flight to Scotland as a humanitarian mission – cannot fail to empathize with this poem and the prose images of the Konigsburg speech. Is it too fanciful to wonder, at least in passing, that on 10 May 1941 Hess's rhetorical question 'Can humanity not be spared all this in future?' was not uppermost in his mind?

5. Hugh Thomas, *The Murder of Rudolf Hess*.
6. Padfield, *op. cit.*
7. Robert Payne, *The Life and Death of Adolf Hitler*.
8. Padfield, *op. cit.*
9. August Kubizek, *The Young Hitler I Knew*.
10. Adolf Hitler, *Mein Kampf*.
11. Payne, *op. cit.*
12. *Ibid.*
13. *Ibid.*
14. *Ibid.*
15. *New York Times Current History*, November 1923.
16. Egon Larsen, Bachman and Turner, *Weimar Eyewitness*.

Chapter 3

1. Robert Payne, *The Life and Death of Adolf Hitler*.
2. James Douglas-Hamilton, *The Truth About Rudolf Hess*.
3. James Murphy, *Who Sent Rudolf Hess?*
4. Payne, *op. cit.*
5. Kurt Ludecke, *I Knew Hitler*.
6. Payne, *op. cit.*
7. Murphy, *op. cit.*
8. Rosenberg Diaries, 30 June 1934.
9. Peter Padfield, *Hess: His Flight For the Führer*.

10. Days after Hitler came to power, in March 1933, a decree was passed forbidding Jews to ask for compensation in the event of their property being damaged. By April no Jew could work in the civil service. In June, a law was passed forbidding young married couples to spend their state loans in Jewish shops. Jewish doctors could treat Jewish patients only.

    The first Nuremberg Law was announced by Goering in September 1935, as part of the drive to 'protect German blood and honour' which was already being served by sterilization 'to prevent hereditary illness'. It established two categories for the Reich's population: those of 'pure German blood' were citizens, while the impure were merely subjects of the state. These measures were carefully designed so as not to appear specifically directed at Jews (and indeed other ethnic groups and 'undesirables' suffered also, although the vast majority of those affected were of course Jewish). The next decree forbade the two groups to cohabit or marry. Another law ordered abortion where either partner suffered from a hereditary disease.

    Over the next few years there followed a succession of decrees, more specifically aimed at Jews, but introduced with little publicity: Jews were excluded from all professions and had to provide information on their finances; Jews were excluded from German schools and higher education, and were not allowed to own most sorts of business; Jews were banned from the performing arts. As of October 1936 all Jewish passports had to be stamped with the letter 'J' and two years later Jews were forced to add the name 'Israel', or 'Sara' if female, to their signature if their names were not typically Hebraic. They were forbidden to attend theatres or cinemas. At the outbreak of war an 8 pm curfew was imposed 'to prevent Jews from using the blackout to molest Aryan women'.

11. *New York Times*, 11 November 1938.

12. Albert Speer, Hitler's architect and later Munitions Minister, refers thus to these searchlight beams that shone 25,000 feet into the night sky. Neville Henderson, the British Ambassador in Berlin, called the rallies 'cathedrals of ice'. Horst Vessel was a Nazi Party member killed in a sordid fight over the services of a prostitute. In the 'stirring' song written about him – still available to neo-Nazis today – he became a folk hero-martyr who died for his political beliefs.

13. Payne, *op. cit.*

14. The most powerful ship afloat was launched four years after the Anglo-German naval agreement. She displaced 56,000 tons, carried eight 15-inch, twelve 5.9-inch and sixteen 4.1-inch guns. Her armour plate was formidable and on 24 May 1941, two weeks after Hess baled out over Scotland, she sank Britain's foremost battleship, the *Hood*, and damaged another, the *Prince of Wales*. With her propeller hit by a lucky shot from a Gloster Gladiator, her speed was slowed sufficiently to allow other British warships to catch her. She was sunk by the cruiser *Dorsetshire* on 27 May.

15. Harold Nicholson, *Diaries and Letters 1930–39*.

16. Payne, *op. cit.*

17. *Ibid*.

18. *Ibid*.

19. *Ibid*.

20. BBC broadcast, 3 September 1939.

Chapter 4

1. Quoted in *Chronicle of the Twentieth Century*, Longman.

2. *Ibid*.

3. Speech made by the Marquess of Tavistock at Kingsley Hall, London, 3 April 1940.

4. Quoted in *Chronicle of the Twentieth Century*, Longman.

5. G. Ward Price, *I Know These Dictators*.

6. *Ibid*.

7. *Ibid.*
8. *Ibid.*
9. The Condor Legion was the name given to the German military and airforce units which arrived in Cadiz in July 1936 to aid Francisco Franco's Fascists in their civil war against the Communists. Their destruction of the town of Guernica was the first example of saturation bombing the world had ever seen.
10. Ward Price, *op. cit.*
11. *Ibid.*
12. Letter from Hitler to Lord Rothermere, May 1935.
13. Ward Price, *op. cit.*
14. Quoted in *Chronicle of the Twentieth Century*.
15. *Ibid.*
16. Douglas-Hamilton, *op. cit.*
17. *Ibid.*
18. William Shirer, *The Rise and Fall of the Third Reich*.
19. Duke of Bedford, Pacifist Literature.
20. *Ibid.*
21. This tantalizing telegram is referred to in Peter Allen's *The Crown and the Swastika*. It was sent to Berlin on 28 July 1940 and was addressed to Albrecht Haushofer, Hess's friend whose role was crucial in the whole affair:

    Just a note to keep you informed. Our friend 'Tomo' [Hess] met with 'C' and 'Willi' this morning. Seven point plan was discussed in detail. Meeting again on 29.7. Urgent you contact the old lady as soon as possible. S.'

This telegram, while fascinating, is almost certainly a forgery. It will be discussed further in Chapter Six.

Chapter 5

1. One of the most bizarre examples of potential 'turning' has recently come to light with the opening of certain Special

Operations Executive files in Whitehall. The idea was mooted in 1944 to hypnotize Hess and send him back to Germany to assassinate Himmler, head of the SS. Maverick and improbable suggestions such as this, at which traditional historians raise dubious eyebrows, are very relevant to the sort of thinking in the corridors of power in 1941.

2. Richard Deacon and Nigel West, *Spy!*
3. M.R.D. Foot and J.M. Langley, *MI9*.
4. Donald McCormick, *The Master Book of Spies*.
5. Ellic Howe, *The Black Game*.
6. Kurt Ludecke, *I Knew Hitler*.
7. *Ibid.*
8. Howe, *op. cit.*
9. *Ibid.*

Chapter 6

1. Duke of Bedford, Pacifist Literature.
2. Bedford Papers.
3. *Hansard*, March 1940. (Courtesy of News International)
4. *Hansard*, May 1940. (Courtesy of News International)
5. Liddell-Hart Papers.
6. Sefton Delmer, *The Black Boomerang*.
7. *Ibid.*
8. Public Record Office, FO 898/181.
9. Robert G.I. Waite, *The Psychopathic God – Adolf Hitler*.
10. Donald McCormick, *The Master Book of Spies*.
11. Berlin Radio Broadcast, May 1941.
12. Peter Padfield, *Hess: Flight For the Führer*.
13. Nicholas Campion, *Liberty* Magazine (New York), 12 July 1941.
14. Delmer, *op. cit.*
15. McCormick, *op. cit.*
16. Delmer, *op. cit.*

17. *Ibid.*
18. *Ibid.*
19. Ellic Howe, *The Black Game.*
20. Article on Richard Ingrams, *Daily Mail*, 29 July 1995.
21. *Ibid.*
22. Rudyard Kipling, 'Bobs', 1898.
23. Rudyard Kipling, 'The Master Gunner', 1914.
24. James Douglas-Hamilton, *The Truth About Rudolf Hess.*
25. *Ibid.*
26. British Intelligence Papers, Public Record Office. This report, reproduced here in full, was sent with a letter to C.A.C.J. Hendricks by Lord Thomas of Swinton, Chairman of the Security Executive, 1940–2.
27. Douglas-Hamilton, *op. cit.*
28. *Ibid.*
29. Haushofer Papers.
30. A complete list of these undercover addresses has now been published: C. Entwhistle, *Undercover Addresses of World War II.*
31. This of course was also the month that a telegram was sent to Albrecht Haushofer – see note 31, Chapter 5. 'The old lady' referred to here, whom Haushofer was to contact urgently in connection with a seven-point plan, is clearly Mrs Roberts. But in 1982, when Peter Allen wrote *The Cross and the Swastika*, her real identity had not been established. The telegram was sent by 'S' and this, according to Peter Allen, was Walter Schellenberg, the brilliant German agent who had engineered the Venlo fiasco. According to this thesis, Schellenberg's intention was to win the Duke of Windsor over to the Nazi cause while the Duke was staying in Lisbon. 'Willi' in the telegram refers to the Duke and 'C' is Reinhard Heydrich, Himmler's second in command in the SS and a friend of Hess's. What is odd about this telegram is that an outsider like Schellenberg should use the nickname 'Tomo' for Hess, when this seems to be a 'nickname' of the Haushofers. Michael Bloch's *Operation*

Willi, which followed Allen's book, poured cold water on many of the latter's theories and refers to the book as 'amusing'. We will probably never get to the bottom of this mysterious telegram, but it certainly, if genuine, points to the on-going correspondence between the Haushofers, Hess and Mrs Roberts during the first year of the war. The references quoted by Allen (who is now dead) are not recognised by either the Bundes Archiv, or the Amtwartiges Amt. Much time has been spent trying to locate the telegram.

32. Haushofer Papers.
33. *Ibid*.
34. *Ibid*.
35. *Ibid*.
36. *Ibid*.
37. Quoted in James Douglas-Hamilton, *op. cit.*
38. Quoted in Peter Padfield, *Himmler, Reichsführer SS*.
39. Montagu Norman Diaries, Bank of England, London.
40. Von Hassell Diaries.

Chapter 7

1. James Leasor, *The Uninvited Envoy*.
2. The letters to Wolf Hess from his father concerning the flight are discussed in the most recent edition of Peter Padfield's *Hess: Flight For the Führer* and essentially reiterate the accepted flight pattern. We have no way of knowing of course under what circumstances Hess wrote those letters. They would certainly have been censored, but were they also written to someone's dictation?
3. Meteorological Office.
4. Letter from Hess to Hitler, 10 May 1941, quoted in Peter Padfield, *Hess: Flight For the Führer*.
5. David Low, Beaverbrook Newspapers.
6. Berlin Radio.

7. Padfield, *op. cit.*
8. Von Hassell Diaries.
9. Padfield, *op. cit.*

Chapter 8

1. James Douglas-Hamilton, *The Truth About Rudolf Hess.*
2. Douglas-Hamilton, *op. cit.*
3. Cadogan Papers.
4. Peter Padfield, *Hess: Flight For the Führer.*
5. *Ibid.*
6. *Ibid.*
7. Letter from Hess to Karl Haushofer, June 1942.
8. Padfield, *op. cit.*
9. Jack Fishman, *Spandau.*
10. Fishman, *op. cit.*
11. Eugene Bird, *Hess in Spandau.*
12. Padfield, *op. cit.*
13. Bird, *op. cit.*
14. Padfield, *op. cit.*

Chapter 9

1. Quoted in Peter Padfield, *Hess: Flight For the Führer.*
2. These papers, again contradicting the views of numerous traditionalist historians, were made available for the first time in 1997.
3. Jack Fishman, *Spandau.*
4. *Ibid.*
5. In her book, *Albert Speer: His Battle With the Truth.*
6. David Day, *Menzies and Churchill at War.*
7. *Ibid.*
8. *Ibid.*

Appendix 1: The Roberts Family Tree

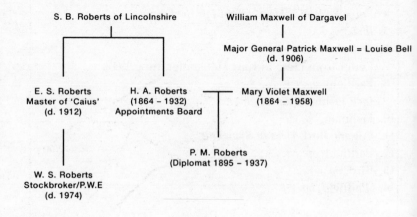

S. B. Roberts of Lincolnshire

William Maxwell of Dargavel

Major General Patrick Maxwell = Louise Bell
(d. 1906)

E. S. Roberts
Master of 'Caius'
(d. 1912)

H. A. Roberts
(1864 – 1932)
Appointments Board

Mary Violet Maxwell
(1864 – 1958)

P. M. Roberts
(Diplomat 1895 – 1937)

W. S. Roberts
Stockbroker/P.W.E
(d. 1974)

Appendix 2: SO1 Operations in the Woburn Area – 1939/1945

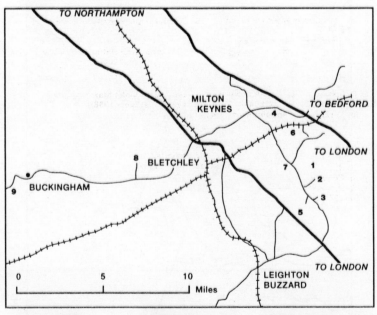

1. **WOBURN ABBEY** –
   Stables & Hall, The Centre
   of Operations to 1942
2. **PARIS HOUSE** – Quarters
   for Head of SO1
3. **MILTON BRYAN** – Centre
   of Operations from 1943

4. **WAVENDON TOWER** – Short
   Wave transmitter
5. **POTSGROVE** – Short Wave
   transmitter
6. **THE ROOKERY, APSLEY
   GUISE** – Delmer's Office and
   Quarters

7. **WOBURN VILLAGE** – Various
   staff quarters
8. **WHADDON** – Original centre
   at Whaddon Hall
9. **GAWCOTT** – Short Wave
   transmitter

Appendix 3: The Flight Plan

A. The '1947' Flight Map

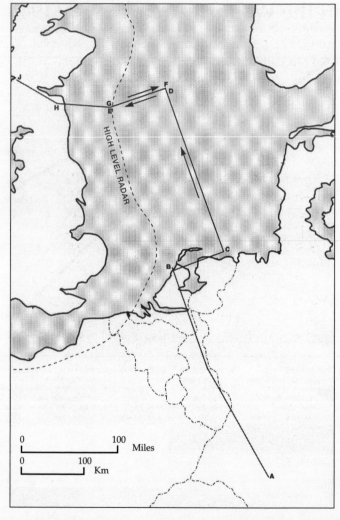

Appendix 3: The Flight Plan

This is the version which appeared in John Rees's book, *The Case of Rudolf Hess*. There is no evidence that it came from Hess at all. The copy currently on display in Lennoxlove House covers only the flight pattern over Scotland and is simply a school atlas map, not an aeronautical flight plan.

We are entitled to ask where is Hess's original, which would have covered the North Sea crossing and Germany too? Has this not surfaced because it would demonstrate Hess's means of navigation – the *knickbein*, which in turn proves that the Luftwaffe colluded in the flight and his destination, which was not Hamilton's house at Dungavel.

Analysis of the 1947 Flight Plan

Route	Mileage	Time Taken (*mins*)	MPH
A–B	400	103	233
B–C	100	30	200
C–D	250	54	277
D–E	80	20	240
E–F	80	20	240
F–G	80	20	240
G–H	100	28	214
H–J	140	49	170
Total	1,230	324	227 (average)

B. The Alternative Flight Map

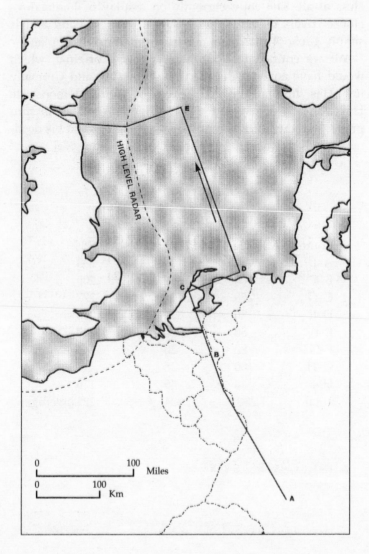

There has long been speculation that Hess did not make the Scotland trip in one haul, but landed somewhere in Germany to refuel. This version describes that alternative which makes no difference to the manoeuvres over the North Sea. Even allowing for this, Hess would still have reached Scotland by 23.09.

Analysis of the Alternative Flight Plan

Route	Mileage	Time Taken (*mins*)	mph
A–B	300	76	238
Lands/refuel		30	
B–C	100	30	200
C–D	100	30	200
D–E	250	54	277
E–F	320	104	184
Total	1,070	324	219
			(average)

C. The New Flight Plan

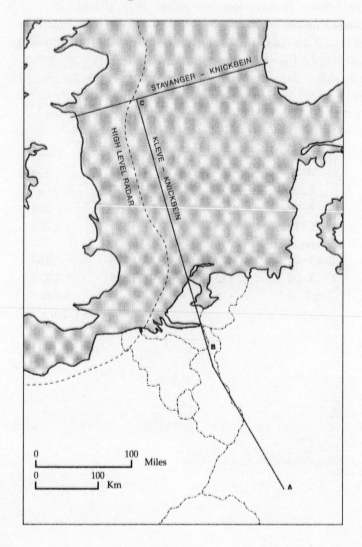

Appendix 3: The Flight Plan

Common sense dictates that this was actually what Hess did. Refuelling in North Germany, he picked up the Kleve *knickbein* as he crossed the Dutch coast and flew along it, north-north-east over the sea. Where the Kleve *knickbein* intersected that from Stavanger in Norway, he banked left just out of radar range to take him over the Lowlands. This would put him on track for either Lennoxlove or Turnhouse, but if he missed it and flew solely by landmarks dimly visible at the coast, he may have been making for Acklington. The estimated landing time is 22.00 in Britain.

Analysis of the Actual Flight Plan

Route	Mileage	Time Taken (mins)	mph
A–B	300	76	238
Lands/refuel		30	
B–C	420	114	220
C–D	130	35	220
Total	850	255	226
			(average)

Appendix 4: Operational R.A.F.
Bases – 10.5.1941

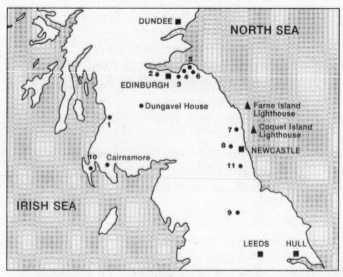

1. R.A.F. AYR
2. R.A.F. TURNHOUSE
3. R.A.F. MACMERRY
4. R.A.F. LENNOXLOVE
   (HADDINGTON)
5. R.A.F. DREM
6. R.A.F. EAST FORTUNE
7. R.A.F. ACKLINGTON
8. R.A.F. OUSTON
9. R.A.F. CATTERICK
10. R.A.F. WEST FREUGH
11. DURHAM R.O.C. CENTRE

278

Selected Bibliography

Allen, P., *The Crown and the Swastika* (Robert Hale, 1983)

Barker, D., *Adolf Galland* (Windrow & Greene, 1996)

Baumbach, W., *Broken Swastika* (Hale, 1949)

Bedford, *A Silver Plated Spoon* (Cassell, 1959)

Bird, Eugene, *Rudolf Hess in Spandau* (Sphere Books, 1976)

Birkenhead, *Halifax* (Hamish Hamilton, 1965)

Bloch, Michael, *Operation Willi* (Weidenfeld & Nicolson, 1984)

Boyle, A., *The Climate of Treason* (Hutchinson, 1979)

Brettingham, L., *Beam Benders* (Midland, 1997)

Byrne, Richard, *Prisons & Punishments of London* (Grafton, 1992)

Cave Brown, Anthony, *The Secret Servant* (Sphere Books, 1988)

Channon, Sir Henry, *Diaries* (Phoenix, 1996)

Costello, John, *Ten Days That Saved the West* (Bantam, 1991)

Day, David, *Menzies & Churchill at War* (OUP, 1993)

Deacon, Richard, *British Secret Service* (Grafton, 1991)

Deacon, Richard, and West, Nigel, *Spy!* (BBC, 1980)

Delmer, Sefton, *Black Boomerang* (Secker & Warburg, 1962)

Douglas-Hamilton, James, *Motive For a Mission* (Macmillan, 1971)

   The Truth About Rudolf Hess (Mainstream, 1993)

Entwhistle, C., *Undercover Addresses of World War II* (Chavril, 1992)

Ferguson, Niall (ed.), *Virtual History* (Picador, 1997)

Fishman, Jack, *Spandau* (Grafton, 1986)

Fleming, Peter, *The Flying Visit* (Cape, 1940)
   Invasion, 1940 (Rupert Hart-Davies, 1957)

Foot, M.R.D., and Langley. J.M., *MI9* (Book Club Associates, 1979)

Gilbert, Martin, *Churchill – A Life* (Minerva, 1991)

Goebbels, Joseph, *Diaries* (Hamish Hamilton, 1948)

Griffiths, R., *Fellow Travellers of the Right* (Constable, 1980)

Hess, Wolf, *My Father, Rudolf Hess* (WH Allen, 1986)

Hinsley and Stripp, *Code Breakers* (OUP, 1993)

Hitler, Adolf, *Mein Kampf* (Paternoster Library, 1936)

Hoare, S., *Ambassador on Special Mission* (Collins, 1946)

Hounam, Peter and Macadam, Derek, *Who Killed Diana?* (Vision, 1998)

Howe, Ellic, *The Black Game* (Queen Anne, 1982)

Irving, D., *Hess: The Missing Years* (London, 1989)

Jones, R.V., *Most Secret War* (Coronet, 1990)

Kaspar, *Teach Yourself Air Navigation* (English University Press, 1942)

Keegan, John, *Churchill's Generals* (Warner, 1991)

Kilzer, L., *Churchill's Deception* (Simon & Schuster, 1994)

Kirkpatrick, Ivone, *The Inner Circle* (Macmillan, 1959)

Lamb, R., *Churchill as War Leader* (Bloomsbury, 1991)

Landau, R., *The Nazi Holocaust* (IB Tauris, 1992)

Langer, W., *The Mind of Adolf Hitler* (Secker & Warburg, 1973)

Leasor, J., *Rudolf Hess: The Uninvited Envoy* (George Allen & Unwin, 1962)

Low, David, *Autobiography* (Michael Joseph, 1956)

Ludecke, Kurt G.W., *I Knew Hitler* (Jarrolds, 1938)

Lycett, Andrew, *Ian Fleming* (Weidenfeld & Nicolson, 1995)

McCormick, Donald, *The Master Book of Spies* (Hodder Causton, 1973)
   The Life of Ian Fleming (Owen, 1993)

Masterman, J.C., *The Double-Cross System* (History Book Club, 1972)

Meyer, S.L., Rutherford, W., ed. Walther, Herbert, *Hitler* (Bison, 1978)

Myerscough, *Air Navigation Simply Explained* (Pitmans)

Padfield, Peter, *Hess: Flight For the Führer* (Weidenfeld & Nicolson, 1991)

Himmler, Reichsführer SS (Papermac, 1991)

Payne, Robert, *The Life & Death of Adolf Hitler* (Corgi, 1973)

Pearson, J., *The Life of Ian Fleming* (Companion Book Club, 1966)

Ponting, Clive, *1940, Myth & Reality* (Cardinal, 1990)

Price, A., *The Luftwaffe Data Book* (Greenhill, 1997)

Pye, M., *The King Over the Water* (Hutchinson, 1981)

Quarrie, Bruce, *Hitler: The Victory That Nearly Was* (David & Charles, 1988)

Rees, J.R., *The Case of Rudolf Hess* (Heinemann, 1947)

Rutherford, Ward, *Hitler's Propaganda Machine* (Bison, 1978)

Schmidt, R., *Rudolf Hess: Botengang eires Toren* (Econ, 1997)

Sereny, Gitta, *Albert Speer: His Battle With the Truth* (Macmillan, 1995)

Seth, Ronald, *The Truth Benders* (Frewin, 1969)

Shirer, W.L., *The Rise and Fall of the Third Reich* (Mandarin, 1960)

Speer, Albert, *Inside the Third Reich* (Sphere Books, 1971)

Sylvester, A.J., *Life With Lloyd George* (Macmillan, 1975)

Thomas, H., *The Murder of Rudolf Hess* (Hodder & Stoughton, 1979)

Thomson, M., *The Life & Times of Winston Churchill* (Odhams, 1946)

Tusa, Ann and Tusa, John, *The Nuremberg Trial* (Macmillan, 1983)

van Capelle, Dr Henk, van de Borenkamp, Dr Peter, *Hitler's Henchmen* (Bison, 1990)

von Hassell, Ulrich, *Diaries* (Hamish Hamilton, 1948)

Waite, Robert G.L., *The Psychopathic God: Adolf Hitler* (Basic Books, 1976)

Ward Price, G., *I Know These Dictators* ('Right' Book Club, 1937)

Weitz, J., *Hitler's Diplomat* (Weidenfeld & Nicolson, 1992)

West, Nigel, *MI6* (Weidenfeld & Nicolson, 1983)

Winterbotham, Frederick, *Secret & Personal* (William Kimber, 1969)

Wood, D., *Attack Warning Red* (Macdonald & Janes, 1976)

Wistrich, Robert, *Who's Who in Nazi Germany* (Weidenfeld & Nicolson, 1982)

Anon, *Celebrities of the Army* (London, 1902)

Anon, *The Black Book* (Imperial War Museum, 1989)
   Bf 110 Flugzeug – Handbuch (1942)
   Dictionary of National Biography
   Encyclopedia Britannica

Fellowes, Blacker, Etherton and Clydesdale, *First Over Everest* (Bodley Head, 1933)

Anon, *Action Stations Seven – A Guide to Scottish Airfields* (Stephens, 1983)

Sources

Collections

England and Wales:
Avon Papers, Birmingham University
Beaverbrook Papers, House of Lords, London
Butler Papers, Trinity College, Cambridge
Cambridge City Library, Local Studies Section
Cambridge University Library, Appointments Board Records
Churchill Papers, Cambridge, Churchill College
Companies House, Cardiff, Archive Section
Dalton Papers, London School of Economics, London
Devon and Cornwall Police, Exeter
Durham Record Office
Eton College Archives, Windsor
Gonville & Caius College, Cambridge
Hamilton Papers, King's College, London
Imperial War Museum, London
Lloyd George Papers, House of Lords, London
Lockhart Papers, House of Lords, London
Meteorological Office, Hatfield
National Monument Records, Swindon, Rokeby Collection
Norman Diaries, Bank of England
Northampton Borough Library, General Enquiries
Oriental and Indian Collection, London, Roberts family
    genealogy
Portuguese Consulate, London

Probate Registry, York, Roberts family history
Public Record Office, London:
  Air 27/1706, Air 27/624, Air 27/2079, Air 27/624, Air 27/2093, Air 27/969, Air 28/861, Air 28/219, Air 28/220, Air 28/624, Air 28/511, Air 28/235, Air 29/684, Air 29/683, Air 29/764, Air 40/195
RAF Museum, Hendon
Register of Archives, London, Durham Map
Stock Exchange, London, Roberts family history
Tatler Archives, London Hamilton family history
Who's Who, London

Scotland:
East Kilbride Library
Museum of Flight, East Fortune
National Monuments Office, Edinburgh
Probate Office, Edinburgh

Germany:
Amtwartiges Amt, Bonn
Archiv Militar, Freiburg
Bundesarchiv, Koblenz
Haushofer Papers, Hartschimmelhof, Bavaria & Bundesarchiv, Koblenz (also National Archives, Washington, USA)

Portugal:
Camara Municipal de Cascais
Espirito Sanctos Foundation, Duke of Windsor
Lisbon City Library

Switzerland:
Burkhardt Papers, University of Basel
International Red Cross, Geneva

Interviews

J. Costello, historian, London 1994

R. Griffiths, historian, London 1994

W.R. Hess, son of Rudolf Hess, Munich 1996

A. Page, conscientious objector, Kettering 1994–5

W. Kean, writer and Anglo-Deutsch Club Founder, Ober Ramstadt 1995–8

Michael Ryan, broadcaster, Rothwell 1994

A. Smith, author, Northampton

A. Schroder-Haushofer, niece of Albrecht Haushofer, Munich 1996

A. Stewart-Roberts, nephew of Mary Violet Roberts, London 1993

R. Wilborn, friend and Devil's Advocate, many and various meetings, all enjoyable.

Index

Index

Index